—

Inside Out

—

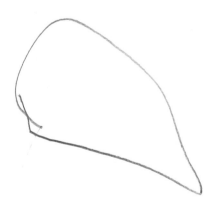

Inside Out
Strategies for Teaching Writing

THIRD EDITION

DAN KIRBY
DAWN LATTA KIRBY
TOM LINER

HEINEMANN
Portsmouth, NH

Heinemann

361 Hanover Street
Portsmouth, NH 03801–3912
www.heinemann.com

Offices and agents throughout the world

Library of Congress Cataloging-in-Publication Data
Kirby, Dan.
    Inside out : strategies for teaching writing / Dan Kirby, Dawn Latta Kirby, Tom Liner.—3rd ed.
    p. cm.
    Includes bibliographical references.
    ISBN 0-325-00588-5 (alk. paper)
    1. English language—Composition and exercises—Study and teaching (Secondary).
    2. Report writing—Study and teaching (Secondary).   I. Kirby, Dawn Latta.   II. Liner, Tom.
    III. Title.
LB1631.K53 2003
808′.042′0712—dc21   2003012426

Editor: Lisa Luedeke
Production editor: Elizabeth Valway
Cover design: Linda Knowles
Compositor: House of Equations, Inc.
Manufacturing: Steve Bernier

Printed in the United States of America on acid-free paper

12 11 10 09 08 VP   7 8 9 10

Contents

Contents

Preface

Do I need to say it? School teaching continues to grow more challenging, more frustrating, and more dangerous in recent years. Our classes are more likely to be larger and more linguistically diverse. Politicians and legislators are more critical of our work, and they continue to pass legislative roadblocks to our success in the name of accountability. High-stakes testing threatens to trivialize what and how we teach. Teachers have learned through school violence that their classrooms are no longer safe havens into which they can retreat to escape the dangers of the streets. Dawn and I live here in Denver, not far from the horror of Columbine, and we are reminded almost daily of the courage and commitment that teaching in the twenty-first century requires.

Parker Palmer has written eloquently about a teacher's temptation to lose heart in the midst of so challenging a vocation. He says, "Unlike many professions, teaching is always done at the dangerous intersection of personal and public life" (1998, 39). That's not an intersection for the faint of heart or for those who are unsure of their calling. The temptation to lose our passion for teaching and to withdraw and distance ourselves from our subject and our students is always present. We know, however, that teaching English, and teaching writing in particular, cannot be done at a distance with antiseptic methodologies. To teach literacy well, we must interact personally with our students, helping them to make sense of their lives through reading and writing.

Such work is tiring. Exhausting. Draining. As only real teachers seem to know, teaching requires enormous amounts of physical and emotional energy. As I said in *Mind Matters*, "Teaching is a disposable art; it can deplete your enthusiasm for experimentation, dull your mind, and erode your sense of self" (1991, 48). To maintain a long tenure as a teacher requires that you engage in constant self-renewal and monitor carefully your passion quotient.

As my wife, Dawn Latta Kirby, Tom, and I have worked to rethink and re-write this third edition of *Inside Out*, we have found it to be renewing work. Through this process of revision, we have reconsidered our beliefs about teaching and learning, deepened our faith in the value of teaching writing up close and personal, and found new energy and enthusiasm for our work. This reexamination of *Inside Out* has also restored my personal confidence that such a book can bring hope and encouragement to teachers of English wherever they interact with students, at whatever stages of their career they find themselves.

The word *hope* seems to be showing up more where English teaching is concerned these days. Peter Elbow entitled his new book, *Everyone Can Write: Essays Toward a Hopeful Theory of Writing* (2000), and Barry Lopez offered in his recent book, *About This Life* (1998), that he wants his work to contribute to a "literature of hope." *Inside Out* has had a history of sustaining and challenging novice and experienced teachers. We want this new edition to renew your passion for teaching and to rekindle your hope that teaching makes a difference in the lives of your students.

Twenty-five years ago or so, the first edition of *Inside Out* was born out of notes that a young professor and a young high-school teacher wrote to each other as they thought about how to explain to themselves what this teaching of writing was all about. Tom and I surprised ourselves and the rest of academia by writing a book that teachers found to be entertaining and helpful. In the second edition, Tom and I invited another remarkable high-school teacher to join us in the revision process. Ruth Vinz's contributions to that edition were substantial and helped bring a much needed ring of authenticity to that text.

Thanks to the urgings and support of Lisa Luedeke at Heinemann, the friendly competition and support of my colleague Bill Strong in the College of Education at Utah State University, and especially the tireless, insightful work of Dawn Latta Kirby, this new, third edition is born. Dawn and I have worked to modernize the third edition and to render its ideas and suggestions in more contemporary language. Earlier editions did have a decidedly seventies ring to them. But we have done more than add a few Botox injections around the eyes of the Blue Book (the second edition). We have tried to rethink our fundamental assumptions about literacy and learning to write, keeping those we still believe and altering those we have reconsidered. In writing this third edition, we were challenged by the words of Annie Dillard who said a writer's problem is always, "What to put in and what to leave out" (1998, 143).

We have kept stuff on the journal and of course we have retained (and updated) Tom's poetry chapter. We have rewritten the first two chapters and completely overhauled the Expository Writing chapter, giving it a new title and a new focus. We have added ideas about using the computer, portfolios as tools for writing instruction, and working with writing and young adult literature, to name a few of the fresh concepts in this edition. And, Karen Hartman, the director of the Colorado Writing Project, has produced a fresh chapter on resources for the book (Chapter 16).

We still talk about *the writing class* and *the literature class* for the sake of convenience even though we know most of you teach in more integrated literature and writing curricula. And we hope our tone is still irreverent and a bit skeptical of the conventional wisdom where teaching and learning are concerned. We still take a few cheap shots at the five-paragraph theme even though we know you gave that up after you gave your heart to *the process*. I guess you'll also recognize our continued dislike of any corporate-strength writing pedagogies that the curriculum director or the governor or the president suggests should be done to all kids. We remain unconvinced that one-size-fits-all instructional strategies have much impact on growth in writing. Six-trait scoring and its generic prescriptions come to mind.

We hope that you will hear in our writings the voices of teachers who have continued to experiment and alter their teaching strategies to meet the needs of students. We hope you will notice that we spend more time coaching students with their writing as we teach, and less time in full-frontal teaching. Most of all, we hope that you will come to share our belief that learning to write is not just for the few or the gifted.

I asked Tom if he had any wisdom for the new preface and he said, "Be sure to thank the folks who have bought and read *Inside Out* in the past." That's vintage Tom. He remains our humble, insightful, and caring friend.

I attended and spoke at the Colorado Language Arts Society Regional Spring Conference a few weeks ago. Late in the afternoon, I drifted into a social hour graciously sponsored by a publisher. The day had left me feeling a bit dated, and I couldn't help noticing that most of my teacher friends looked a bit like I felt—gray and fraying at the edges. Within minutes, a dozen or so young people arrived, all sporting piercings and somewhat suggestive clothing. They moved through that crowd of tired looking teachers, bringing noise and energy wherever they went. "Who is that group?" I inquired, thinking it might be party crashers or high-school theater refugees. "That's a bunch of new high-school teachers," came the reply. A wave of relief and genuine celebration swept over me.

There is a new generation of English teachers spoiling not only to replace us, but also to bring new life and energy and insight to the teaching of English. One of the young teachers separated himself from the others and came up to me. "You're Dan Kirby," he said. "You were my teacher. No, I never sat in your classroom, but you've been my teacher because I've read *Inside Out* and use it constantly."

Aside from just making me feel good, that comment reminds me why we continue to revise this book. It's for the new, vibrant teachers looking for ideas. It's for seasoned—and perhaps slightly tired—teachers wanting to enliven and update writing instruction in their classes. It's for the preservice teachers learning what this business of teaching writing is all about. The fact that this book continues to speak to those and other audiences delights and humbles us. And one day, maybe we—you and I—will talk about writing together at a conference, telling stories, sharing ideas, enjoying our craft, and finding new energy together.

—Dan Kirby

Works Cited

DILLARD, ANNIE. 1998. "To Fashion a Text." In *Inventing the Truth: The Art and Craft of Memoir*, edited by William Zinsser. Boston: Houghton Mifflin.

ELBOW, PETER. 2000. *Everyone Can Write: Essays Toward a Hopeful Theory of Writing*. New York: Oxford University Press.

KIRBY, DAN, AND CAROL KUYKENDALL. 1991. *Mind Matters: Teaching for Thinking*. Portsmouth, NH: Boynton/Cook.

LOPEZ, BARRY. 1998. *About This Life: Journeys on the Threshold of Memory*. New York: Alfred A. Knopf.

PALMER, PARKER. 1998. *The Courage to Teach: Exploring the Inner Landscape of a Teacher's Life*. San Francisco: Jossey-Bass.

Coming out of Jacks River, near dark

the trail goes out, turning down
shadows opening into shadows
the last sun going from the leaf-fire
up the dancing ridges the day gathering
at my back like a song remembered in quiet
the river gathering the sky into itself, sharp and cold
talking in the rocks at the crossing, pulling
across my thighs, laughing and strong
silver running into black

I feel something waiting
in shadows at the next turning
leaves move, wind whispers, the long rod trembles
the bright fly hooked into the handle, light
as the dipper's wing, a dance over water
the trembling touch remembers the flash and fight
of the bright strong fish
sharp light in the long pools below the sun-warm rocks
where the kingfisher's laugh teases the sight upriver

but something is waiting beyond the shadows
granite and tree, leaf and water singing
like promises down from the high gorges
and mountains bunching in the narrow sky
and I must hurry, carrying the river with me

the weight of the water and the feel of the light rod
the speed and grace of the fish I hunted
touching each like a bright blessing
before turning this light back into the cold
alive and alone

something is saved back
from the day's prayer of water-light
and mountain whispers, the river turns
the trail moves ahead of me into tree and
this darkness rising to meet me
at the turning

Tom Liner
(in *Clay and Pine*, 1988)

1

Thoughts on Becoming an Effective Teacher of Writing

As a young teacher, I yearned for the day when I would know my craft so well, be so competent, so experienced, and so powerful, that I could walk into any classroom without feeling afraid. But now, in my late fifties, I know that day will never come. I will always have fears, but I need not become my fears—for there are other places in my inner landscape from which I can speak and act.

—PARKER PALMER, *The Courage to Teach*

You may be reading this book in a methods class in preparation for entering the teaching profession. You may be a novice teacher thumbing the chapters on a quiet Sunday afternoon, desperate for something to do tomorrow. You may be a crafty veteran of the classroom wars looking for encouragement or for the Life Map activity that Tom talks about in Chapter 4 that always works with your students. Whatever your purpose in reading this book, we are willing to bet that you long to feel more confident and comfortable as a teacher of writing. Maybe you've taken some composition methods courses or earned your masters at the university. Maybe you've been in a National Writing Project program and felt the pain and joy of becoming a writer. Maybe you've read a number of books on how to teach writing. Maybe you've given your heart to the writing process and your classes are going much better now. Let's hope so. But we work with many teachers in many schools, and we still see lots of teachers who remain frustrated—at least at times—about the teaching of writing.

What is it about teaching writing that is so incredibly challenging and frustrating? Maybe at its core, the teaching of writing demands that those who would succeed at it be thoroughly convinced that teaching writing is even possible. As we said in earlier editions of this book, the temptation for teachers who have tried and failed to see improvement in their students' writing is to conclude that writing just isn't for everyone. Maybe knowing how to write well is a genetic thing—it's in the DNA or it isn't. Maybe some people have been selected by God to be writers. Those creative accidents of the deity just show up in fourth-period class, all bright and articulate, and they whip out amazing texts while asking little of us as coaches. Maybe the rest of our students, the ones who show little interest in writing and only marginal growth as writers, should just be given grammar exercises and vocabulary worksheets and condemned to functional literacy. But maybe not.

As we say numerous times throughout this book, we believe that all kids have unique and worthwhile thoughts and language in their heads. We believe that all young people, however impaired and reluctant, can learn to negotiate the difficult process of bringing that inner language to the page. We believe it is possible for teachers to learn to act as effective coaches of their students' meaning-making processes by encouraging and cajoling and questioning and nurturing the efforts of these students, however halting they might be initially.

In addition to their doubts about whether the ability to write can actually be taught and learned, many teachers tell us they have a sinking feeling that the school classroom is a poor venue for teaching the complexities of writing. For one thing, there are too damn many kids in there. You can't coach and interact with all 150 or more of your students every day, especially when some of them struggle with English because it's not their native language or they've been absent for twenty-two days so far this semester. For another thing, the curriculum is a bloated, unwieldy hodge-podge of stuff to teach, much of which the kids don't even care about learning. Besides that, "they" always interrupt your class for testing and assemblies and "Please excuse the tennis team today at 1:40." What's more, your kids are evaluated by state tests and the school scores are published in the local paper for public scrutiny.

Teaching writing takes time: time for practice and time to share writing, time to complete assignments and time to respond to and evaluate all of that writing. "Lack of time to teach writing is the problem," you say. We agree with you. The kids are tough, the curriculum is demanding, and the conventional fifty-minute class is not particularly amenable to the teaching of writing. You're frustration is justified. You're off the hook. Relax and teach *Julius Caesar* for eight weeks.

But wait. Is it possible that you're missing the joy of seeing kids discover their own voices? Is it possible that you have coaching skills and writing talent that you haven't fully explored and developed? Maybe you could find some new strategies for getting kids going as writers and keeping them going. Maybe you could find some revision and editing strategies that students could and would use. Maybe you could transform your class into some kind of community of writers. What if you gave this business of teaching writing a chance? That's where this book wants to take you. We want to help you avoid the mistakes that many teachers before you made as they tried and failed to teach writing well. More importantly, we want to build your confidence and entice you to take risks in your classes.

Maybe it's important for you to know that we are still working on our skills as writing coaches even as we author this text. We confess that, after years of teaching writing and English, we still have to confront our doubts and uncertainties about our teaching abilities on a daily basis. We still experiment, alter strategies, devise new materials, and learn as we teach. Don Murray, whose name you will hear mentioned in this text many times, has been one of our gurus; he is an incredibly successful teacher of writing. One of the singularly most helpful things Don ever said was, "I am apprenticed to two crafts I can never master: writing and teaching" (1989). So, we write this book as teachers who continue to learn to coach writing, as teachers who continue to read, experiment, and grow; and we think that's a good thing because we think that ceasing to learn is personal and professional death.

Becoming a successful teacher of writing is a journey. As Parker Palmer points out in the opening quotation, it's a journey that never ends. We want you to join us in slouching our way toward proficiency as writing teachers. Parts of this book should serve as cheerleading and encouragement as you try to become a strong teacher of writing. Most of this book is an attempt to share our successes in teaching (and some of our failures so you can avoid them), the philosophy and beliefs that guide us as teachers, and the strategies that we have used to work with *all* of the kids who show up in classes every day to learn whatever it is that we have to teach them.

When Dan and Tom wrote the first edition of this book in 1981, they felt the need to argue for a developmental view of writing growth. At that time, writing instruction was often insensitive to the ways in which young people learned language. Teaching writing was primarily correcting writing. Assignments were owned by the teachers. Student work seldom measured up. The teaching of composition was largely a plantation-like enterprise with students at the bottom of pecking order. Dan and Tom were possessed by some kind of crusader mentality (maybe by other things as well) to advance the premise that written language could be learned similar to the ways in which children learn oral language. They admonished writing teachers to put away their red pens and support and respond to students' writing in much the same way in which parents respond to a young child's first efforts with speech. They pointed out that when a young child asked for "Wa-wa," the parent didn't say, "I'm sorry, there will be no *water* [enunciating clearly and emphatically] given to children in this house until they learn to say *that* word correctly." Dan and Tom called for an acceptance of writers' approximations of language and for moving away from a deficit model that emphasized what kids couldn't do. They suggested that what young writers needed most was freedom to render experience into words in whatever ways they could muster and adults who would offer strong support and encouragement for those efforts.

So much has happened in the teaching of writing since the early 80s when this book was first published. Thanks to an impressive body of continuing research on language development and writing, a growing acceptance of a constructivist learning theory, the success of the National Writing Project, a growing body of outstanding texts for teachers on writing methods, and the institutionalization of writing-process pedagogy, that original argument about adopting a developmental stance toward teaching writing seems superfluous, dated. We say hurrah for enlightenment!

If you're a soon-to-be teacher or a novice, you have probably missed out on four decades of composition wars. If you have never read the "Orange Book" or the "Blue Book" (as fans of *Inside Out* refer to the first and second editions) or the works of Jim Moffet, Ken Macrorie, Anne Berthoff, Don Murray, Donald Graves, Janet Emig, Peter Elbow, James Britton, Nancy Martin, or other pioneers, we hope that you might have opportunity to visit the writings of those scholars who remain so influential in contemporary thinking about teaching writing. Knowing the roots and origins of what you're doing every day in your classes can ground you as a teacher, giving you ammunition for the critics and helping you expand your ideas for instruction.

So, in the age of enlightenment, what does it take to create a positive environment for the teaching of writing? What are the essentials? What are our basic beliefs and values about how to create growth in our classrooms?

Belief 1: Writing Is Social and Is Best Taught in a Collaborative and Communal Setting

This belief is shamelessly constructivist. For many years the act of writing was characterized as a mysterious, solitary, even lonely enterprise. The myth was that semi-drunken writers worked alone in clean, well-lighted places. In the 70s, when writers began to come out of the closet and confess that indeed they needed to share their writing with others and that they thrived on response and feedback, the paradigm began to shift. A decade or so later, constructivist learning theorists began to insist that all learning was both personal *and* social. Those theorists pointed out that learners and writers needed to construct personal versions of the world around them, but then they also needed to submit those unique versions to peers for response, negotiation, and confirmation. Viola! Writing response groups became both a sound instrument for learning and growth and acceptable composition pedagogy.

The hard truth for many teachers was that living this belief meant altering conventional and even comfortable classroom structures to provide greater opportunities for students to work together, share their writing, and support and coach each other's work. Many high-school teachers tell us that modifying the classroom to allow for more collaboration remains problematic. They find themselves spending more time on crowd control and playing the group cop. Elementary- and middle-school cultures seem more supportive of flexible instructional structures. Centers and flexible groupings and collaborative effort are more often the norm there. High-school folks report that their students tend to misuse opportunities to work in smaller groups. Chapter 8 should give you more ideas on how to maximize student-to-student learning. Workshops, literature circles, and studios can serve as models for classroom organizations that facilitate the kinds of interactions that are necessary to maximize growth in writing. Learning to manage and feel comfortable in more interactive structures takes time and some resolve, but the payoff in student growth is worth the pain of change; and the constructivists are right.

Belief 2: Coached Practice Is Essential

Writing is complex, high-level human behavior. It cannot be crowded into hurry-up quarter courses or left to one grade level or relegated to one day a week. Proficiency in writing requires consistent practice. But just letting them write, mere practice, isn't the answer. If students are to grow as writers through practice, that practice must be coached. Someone who knows something about writing must interact before, during, and after the practice.

As novice teachers of writing, we were often intimidated by poorly written student texts. Our first reaction to some of the really bad papers we received was, "There's something wrong with this paper, but I don't know exactly what it is." It all seemed pretty lame. So we hid behind written comments on their papers and correction marks like *Awk* and *Frag* and *Needs work*. We didn't know how to help kids improve those texts, and we lacked a vocabulary to talk about writing with our students. Fortunately, there were mentors for us. As Karen points out in Chapter 16 on Resources, there were a host of angels and saints whose workshops and writings informed our practice and encouraged us to persevere until we could improve as writing teachers. We learned from the likes of Don Murray and Ken Macrorie that we didn't have to be an expert writer to interact with student work. We learned from Peter Elbow that our students' writing could improve if we got better at enticing them to work together as collaborative writers. We learned to ask leading questions of the writer. We learned to point to places in the piece of writing where we were confused or where we wondered if elaboration might be appropriate. We learned how to ask writers what they planned to do next with the piece.

In short, we learned that time for writing and talking and sharing were more important than lectures and advice-giving and marking their papers. We came to understand that practice was not just asking kids to work quietly at their desks, but was rather a rich interactive process.

Belief 3: Begin Working with Fluency First

That formulaic, freshman composition style of teaching writing in which we worked almost exclusively on forms—the expository essay, the comparison and contrast essay, the persuasive essay—has mercifully been altered by process pedagogy that fosters the use of writing workshops in many middle- and high-school English classes. But we still see lots of emphasis on the structure of the essay as promoted by mundane assessment instruments and formula pedagogy with steps and color-coded paragraphs. These shortcuts and trivial exercises teach students little about writing. We still see lots of too-tense teachers of writing who are preoccupied with correctness and the "we-don't-write-like-we-talk" syndrome. Such preoccupation with format and correctness often pushes teachers to hammer away at the feeble attempts of their students to approximate the demands of form, even when the students have neither read that sort of piece nor written it before.

Putting fluency first means *easing* into new, unfamiliar forms. It means offering students many opportunities to read examples of the forms they will eventually write. It might mean deconstructing a form to understand its elements and how they work together within the piece. It means devoting a good deal of time to the *early* stages

5

of writing a piece, namely idea-finding, drafting, and experimenting. Oversimplified formulas don't encourage experimentation; instead, they stress getting the *form* right. When developing writers are required to focus on forms, they learn to plug lifeless words and mundane ideas into the formula; they don't learn to create unique expressions and to figure out the form in which the writing might work best.

In writing, all of us probably expect too much too soon. In contrast to the ideas of the late 1800s, we now know that children are not, developmentally, miniature adults; similarly, we also now know that inexperienced writers don't write as do adults, nor should they be expected to do so. Their thinking, sentence patterns, and vocabulary all need time and practice to develop. We shouldn't expect young writers to have all of the elements of form mastered from the beginning.

We suggest that when you begin teaching writing to a new group of students, you declare a moratorium on concerns about rigidly defined forms and structures of writing. Emphasize fluency. Use expressive and reflective forms of writing that offer maximum opportunity for your students to get a feel for producing text without the pressure to meet all of the constraints of a well-defined form. Encourage them to write about themselves and their own experiences first and to value and interact with those pieces of writing. Developing writers need time to experiment with their ideas and words and the connections between the two. Practice in rendering the tangled web of their emotions and imaginations into written language will help writers learn to express their ideas clearly, precisely, and fluently. Let them write and let the forms emerge.

Don't rely on finished pieces as the only evidence of students' abilities to write. Trust that not every piece of writing must go through the full-blown processes of prewriting, drafting, and revising. Provide writing experiences in the classroom that help students build a repertoire of strategies they can use *in progress*. Students will discover their own strategies as they work. They'll find ways to get writing generated, drafted, revised, and edited that we've not considered before. The truth is that we'll borrow their ideas to help other writers if we are keen-eyed and responsive to what they show us.

Belief 4: In Writing, the Whole Is More Than the Sum of Parts

Schools have always been pretty good at teaching parts and not so good at helping students see the big picture and create wholes. Part-to-whole, word-to-sentence, that deductive mindset seems so logical: Begin with the word, next the sentence, then the paragraph; then, when students get *real good*, they get to write a whole five-paragraph theme. Wow! Master the parts, get those labels straight; memorize those ten transitional words to plug relentlessly into every accordion paragraph. It all adds up.

Except that it doesn't. Unfortunately, in writing, the whole is far more than the sum of parts. By fragmenting instruction and drilling on one part or one structure at a time, we kill motivation and destroy the very processes we're trying to develop.

Our thinking has changed a bit since Dan and Tom wrote the first edition of this book. Then, Dan and Tom proposed a developmental sequence moving students from simple to complex forms, from personal to objective subject matter. They offered examples from simple poems to extended analogy, or from simple short stories emphasizing a straight narrative line to highly involved stories using more varied narrative techniques. In the past two decades, however, we have seen genres blur and lose their clear boundaries. We have seen the emergence of narrative technique in all forms of writing. Now, we read memoirs by Terry Tempest Williams or Janisse Ray that record both their deeply personal and reflective interactions with nature and also attend to factual, scientific, and historical details of the natural world. We see short stories by Bobbie Ann Mason or Rick Bass that are as complex and artfully tuned as any novel. We consume the stunning essays of Annie Dillard and Barbara Kingsolver and are amazed at their ability to weave simple and complex forms together with personal and objective ideas to create highly readable and interesting texts. Newly emerging forms such as literary memoir, and even novels in poetic form, convince us that there is more to writing than our traditional emphasis on argumentation, formatted poems, or complex short stories. Even the simplest of poems requires control of language and vision. Intensity and vividness may be more difficult in a short piece than it will be in a fleshier piece of extended analogy. It's all very individual. Each piece has its own challenges. We don't look at a student's one-page story or two-stanza poem with disdain. Length doesn't equate with effort.

We've studied the components of good writing extensively, and have worked at coaching writing for many years. We consider ourselves writers who have a sense of good writing when we see it. Writers fashion subjects in individual ways. We assist student writers by designing occasions that help them rehearse their skills and techniques through a variety of writing experiences. We coach them by providing a third eye or ear. We avoid writing exercises taken out of an authentic context, and we make careful judgments about when and how to intervene in students' writing processes.

It is unrealistic to expect students to drill on the parts of the language or the parts of a composition for years—especially when such instruction occurs out of the context of real language and real writing—in anticipation of some far-off future when they can begin to use the parts to explore the options of discourse.

At eight years old, Dan's older daughter, Mindy, bugged him about taking guitar lessons. He, of course, preferred a less frivolous instrument like the piano or the cello. She took guitar lessons. Dan remembers how excited Mindy was after her first lesson. She couldn't wait to share "her song." She strummed those two monotonous chords and sang her song. She smiled. She was pleased with her song. That pride in producing a *whole* composition of her own was her motivation to continue and practice. Had her guitar teacher given her a quiz over the parts of the guitar? Had he told her to learn the names of the strings or to practice a chord until she got it right? No. One strums a guitar to produce a song. The song's the thing, no matter how simple. So must it be with writing. The piece is the thing—and we must learn to help young writers produce an authentic piece every time they write. There is technical knowledge to be learned, but writing is first to be read and communicated. No approach to writing that forgets the joy of singing your own song will work with novice writers.

Belief 5: Assessment Must Support Growth

Let's be honest here. We have assessed writing too early, too often, and in contexts that are too artificial to be informative about how real writing occurs. Some of our grading has been punitive, some of it shamelessly crowd control. Many of our assessments tell us little about the writing skills our students do or don't possess. Grading, assessment, and testing practices are, in many cases, an anathema to the very kinds of teaching strategies that we know work best with developing writers. Most teachers believe that not every piece of writing has to be fully processed and completely finished and graded. Most teachers lament that students pay only passing attention to the careful marking of their papers. Most teachers hold little credence in students' scores on mandated assessments of writing. Most teachers know that standards-driven assessments of writing are often one-shot samples of a student's writing at a particular moment in time with very few assurances that such a sample represents the student's best work. And yet most teachers continue to spend an inordinate amount of time alone with student papers, meticulously marking them. What's even worse, the preparation and class time that teachers must expend on mind-numbing state-mandated tests consume their energies and rob them of more valuable time that could (and should) be spent coaching and responding to student writing.

What's to be done about this dilemma? Is there a twelve-step program around for compulsive graders? Will politicians and ideologues give up their wrong-headed notions about accountability and testing? Will pigs ever fly?

Rather than succumbing to teaching to tests that foster a stilted, stylized, five-paragraph theme or accordion paragraph-kind of prose, we have found that following a curriculum that stresses authentic writing in a range of forms and for a variety of purposes and audiences leads to improved student performances in writing. Real language used in real ways for authentic purposes that matter to the writer promote writing that matters, that others want to read and discuss, and that students value enough to work on and revise. Incidentally, such writing practice raises students' scores on standardized and high-stakes tests as well. When writing and the written word live inside a classroom as part of the intellectual conversation each day, writing and thinking flourish, as will test scores. When we as teachers grade fewer papers and take seriously our responsibility to coach writing that is meaningful to students and demonstrate effective strategies for improving content, appearance, and structures, students and their learning benefit.

Belief 6: Growth in Writing Takes Time

Even in this age of instructional enlightenment, the chronicle of many children's experiences with writing in the schools remains a fitful series of stops and starts. Too often, writing instruction is a patchwork of writing short stories this week, short essays next week, and critiques the week after that, and of delving into literature with no writing at all for the following six weeks. In other words, writing instruction too often consists of a sporadic pattern of quantum leaps and long silences. In too many schools and school districts, we continue to fail to provide enough consistent instruction and practice to reap the rewards of better writers and writings. As we have seen in the schools where we work, just because it's in the curriculum guide doesn't mean it gets taught. And just because it gets taught doesn't mean it's taught well.

Recently, Dan met with the writing committee of a middle school with a reputation as a strong school. The committee was a volunteer group of the school's most enthusiastic and knowledgeable teachers of writing. The meeting was ostensibly to shape goals and plans for the coming year since students were to be tested for the first time on a state-mandated assessment in the spring. As teachers talked about what kinds of writing they required of their students, it became apparent that most were following their own version of the district's framework for writing instruction. Indeed, several teachers were even unaware of the existence of such a district document. Others confessed that the pressure to raise reading scores had been so intense that they had given up time for writing altogether. The teachers were a bit embarrassed to realize that none of them were teaching writing in consistent and thoughtful ways.

For writing instruction to produce good writers, it must not only be well-articulated in curriculum guides, textbooks, and in-service workshops, but it must also be practiced by a community of professional teachers who interact with each other to build proficiency over time.

From Belief to Action

How do the beliefs that we have shared become realized as classroom practice? How do teachers translate values and ideals into reflective and successful practice? What do we need to tell ourselves in order to implement our beliefs? First, we need to clarify and examine our beliefs. A good deal of research on teachers' classroom practice has documented that most teachers make instructional decisions based on tacit belief structures. That is, they act from unexamined beliefs some of which are conflicting and inconsistent. We have found it helpful periodically, perhaps before each new school year or as we begin preparing to teach a new class, to reexamine and restate our beliefs about how kids learn best in that context. We actually explore those beliefs in writing, considering whether we still believe them. Once we're satisfied that we have a solid set of belief statements, we construct a set of ideal teacher practices that are consistent with those beliefs. We challenge ourselves with these practice statements. They serve as ideals, aims, and goals to which we aspire. Because teaching is complex intellectual activity in which we sometimes lose our way, these practice statements serve as mile markers, as directional lights, and as boundaries. They are concrete, specific, and personal. They serve as reminders to keep us from falling into the trap of blaming others for our failings and shortcomings.

Dan calls his lists of ideal practices "Notes to Myself as a Writing Teacher." He considers and reformulates these notes each time he begins a new writing class. The following are the notes he wrote this past summer as he prepared to teach a writing workshop class.

1. My primary role as a teacher of writing is not to make assignments or correct papers but to "coach practice."
2. As a teacher, I am a reader and a writer, modeling the life of a literate person.
3. I lower my standards for works in progress and have higher standards for finished products.
4. I rely on students to help each other, teaching them how to work together to support each other's writing practice, so that they become a community of thinkers, responders, and writers.
5. I create time for extensive writing practice: many shorter writings and few large completed works.
6. Reading supports writing in my class. I use multiple short excerpts as examples to illustrate what professional writers do.
7. I offer students a wide variety of literature to illustrate multiple perspectives of culture, language, age, and gender.
8. I use genre-based writing strategies to teach students how to read and write new forms.
9. I teach writing as a craft that can be learned, offering students a repertoire of revising, crafting, and editing strategies.
10. I hold regular conferences with my students to engage them in discussions about their work, listening to their ideas and concerns to better direct my coaching efforts.
11. My assessment and evaluation strategies value both process and product. My students help develop the rubrics we use to evaluate completed products.

It has taken Dan thirty-seven years of teaching to believe and seek to implement these statements. We don't suggest that you take his list and walk into your class and try to implement these beliefs all at once. These are the values that Dan holds for his class. We want your reading of *Inside Out* and other significant sources to help you begin a journey to your own statements of belief. We encourage you to read this book with a pen and a notebook in hand or to use your computer to construct an electronic notebook. Before you read further, construct a set of your personal belief statements about teaching writing. Be prepared to amend and revise those beliefs as you interact with this text. Begin to keep lists of teaching practices and specific activities you want to think about and consider using in your classes. See what you like in this book and what you think will work for your students. Think, create, reflect. That, after all, is what teaching is all about.

Works Cited

PALMER, PARKER. 1998. *The Courage to Teach: Exploring the Inner Landscape of a Teacher's Life.* San Francisco: Jossey-Bass.

MURRAY, DON. 1989. *Expecting the Unexpected: Teaching Myself—and Others—to Read and Write.* Portsmouth, NH: Boynton/Cook.

2

Notes on Writing Processes

*For writing is discovery. The language that never leaves our head is like
colorful yarn, endlessly spun out multicolored threads dropping into a
void, momentarily compacted, entangled, fascinating, elusive.
. . . Indeed, writing is largely a process of choosing among alternatives
from the images and thoughts of the endless flow, and this choosing is a
matter of making up one's mind, and this making up one's mind
becomes in effect the making up of one's self.*

—JAMES E. MILLER, JR., *Word, Self, Reality*

We still love the picture that James Miller paints of inner language as colorful yarn
that may be spun into multicolored threads of written language. When we concep-
tualized the first edition of this book, we believed strongly in the remarkable richness and diversity of inner language that flows in the heads of all of us. We still believe
that. We still believe that teaching writing involves helping our students attend to,
collect, and select from that inner flow, and then to spin that language onto the page
as text. Miller's description of language as a ceaseless flow inside each of us still makes
sense. When we write, we dip into that flow and pull out ideas and words to put down
on the page. We begin to impose order as we write one word after the other on the
page, but there is a feeling of anxiousness, sometimes almost panic, as we try to capture
meaning from the stream of language. We are afraid something will slip by, that we'll
miss that special word or phrase we need to get it said right. Every writer knows that
feeling.

Some critics of our faith in inner language have suggested that Miller's metaphor
oversimplifies the teaching of writing. Some have said it romanticizes the complex
workings of the brain. We know that writing is more than spinning yarn, and sometimes our students' heads seem empty, devoid of language and ideas. Sometimes what
comes out of our students' heads looks more like overcooked spaghetti than colorful
yarn. We often have to jumpstart the student writer's processes for generating ideas
by offering heuristic devices or questions or brainstorming tools and tricks. We know
that teaching writing is more than just freewriting and brainstorming. But we remain

adamant about the importance of believing in students' inner language and in nurturing and coaching their efforts to render it as text.

Consider how most of us write. We want the reader to understand and accept our feelings and reasons and postulations. We may write half of the first sentence of a paragraph, stop, scratch it out, and write that half-sentence again, slightly differently this time. The rest of that sentence was there a second ago; now it has evaporated. Something else flashes into our minds, and we finish the sentence. There are long "silences," one of the important parts of this business of writing, while we watch the interior flow of language and wait for just the right word or phrase to surface. We back up to the paragraph before this one, and change a word here and there. We jump ahead, anticipating where we want to go next. Other thoughts intrude, and we re-read what we've written to get started again.

This recursive process is something of what writing is like even when it's going well. For those of us who write often, these things, and more—usually happening so fast and so naturally that we're long since used to it—are all part of the *feeling* of writing as it is going on.

Cary, a talented high-school senior, describes his process this way.

> I guess the best analogy to the way I write is that it's like a man beginning a maze. He tries his best to memorize every turn and path, and then runs ahead at full speed, running as hard as he can until he makes a mistake and runs into a wall. Then he gets up, checks his bearings, and starts again from this point.[1]

That's a good image, and one with the feel of truth about it. Before you write, you're anxious, worried about getting something down. Even a writer as good as Elie Wiesel says, "Writing is painful pleasure and the most difficult part is to begin. . . . Ultimately to write is an act of faith" (1995). You try to plan what to say in your head. You worry and worry. You walk around the room. You stare out the window, waiting for inspiration and that flash of insight that will take this onerous task out of your hands and put it in the hands of the gods where it belongs. You stall on your computer by reading your emails. You sharpen your pencils and line them up in a neat row on your desk. And you worry some more. You search your mind, gone suddenly blank, for a hook to get into the writing—a word or phrase or sentence to start the piece of writing—anything to get it rolling. You sharpen the pencils again.[2] (You don't even write with a pencil, do you?) And you finally catch a hook, take a deep breath, and begin. You rush as hard as you can through that first part until something doesn't work. You hit that blank wall about which Cary talks. But you'll begin again soon and drive through that first draft. And like the man in the maze, you really don't know exactly where you're going until it appears in front of you on the page.

One of the important aspects of these actions of composing that we're describing is the chaos of that inner flow from which the writer draws words and ideas for the page and with which all writers must struggle. The immature writer needs to know that this feeling of chaos is natural, that even the best writers experience it, and that it's really one of the gifts of a human being who is writing. For in that chaos is variety, the kaleidoscopic flux of life itself from which the writer can capture words and ideas, phrases and concepts that are beautiful and well-suited to the writing task.

Processes

Let's be sure that our meaning of *process* is clear. When we teach writing as a process, we are trying to align our instruction with what "real" writers do when they write. In other words, we attempt to teach writing in more natural and less artificial ways. Frankly, as Peter Elbow suggests, that often means getting out of the way of student writers to let them write. Our job as writing teachers is not to put our students through academic exercises. It is to make writing a part of their lives, just as it is a part of ours.

The idea that writers follow a fairly consistent process as they produce text is well-established in the consciousness of most teachers of English and Language Arts. This general understanding has led to composition texts and state and district curricular frameworks that are reasonably consistent and uniform both in their conceptualization of the writing process and in the terminology they use to describe and talk about it. That's the good news. The less than good news is that *process* really means *processes* and that writers tend to invent their own ways of working. Few English professionals, textbooks, and curricular frameworks acknowledge the idiosyncratic nature of writers at work and the need for individual writers to customize the process to meet their own needs and preferences.

So here is our first caution: Avoid the temptation to conceive of the writing process as a prescription or as a singular immutable construct and worse yet to present it to your students that way. We know you have that poster in your classroom that has *the steps* of *the writing process*. We don't think that's a sin as long as you make sure kids understand that it's an exemplar, a "for example," and that you don't generally beat them up about the steps and turn *process* into a verb in your classroom. Don't structure lockstep, iron-clad procedures that all student writers must follow. Dawn confirmed in her early research that writers follow unique, even idiosyncratic processes in order to produce assigned texts (Latta Kirby 1985). She observed tenth-grade writers who began by writing a draft, not by jotting or brainstorming. Sometimes form and structure intrude into writing so that they take precedence in the writer's mind over shaping content, at least for a while. Writing processes are untidy for most writers, even for those who rely on the automatic neatness imposed on a written product that results from composing on a computer. The uniqueness of individual writers' processes reminds us that requiring all students to do a web or cluster before they begin a draft is only slightly different from requiring that all writers turn in a full-blown outline before they proceed to writing the draft. In reality, writers use many different processes depending on their moods, the rhetorical situation, the type of writing, and a host of additional factors.

Books and teachers teach the writing process in steps as though it were a singular phenomenon because it's easier and simpler to do so. We often do that as well. But we need to keep reminding ourselves that writing processes themselves are recursive, and writing does not follow neat, separate steps. Most student texts do begin somewhere and end somewhere else, usually but not always with a finished product of some kind. We agree with the writing process assumption that our students' writing is usually better when talking, drafting, revising, reading aloud, and editing are part of the writing experiences that students have; but as students step ahead in the process, they may also need to step back.

We think that a teacher's primary responsibility where process is concerned is to introduce students to a variety of ways of beginning, drafting, revising, and completing their work. More specifically, we need to help student writers wrestle their ideas onto the page and then teach them writerly strategies that will help them shape and refine those ideas into effective texts. Essentially, what process pedagogy should provide for students is an ever-expanding repertoire of strategies for enhancing their own ways of producing text.

How do you learn to appreciate and accommodate student differences where writing processes are concerned? We suggest that when you first begin your writing class, you talk to your students about what they do when they write. Talk about the hard parts of writing. Ask them about their writing processes. What do they do to get going? How do they revise? How do they know when a piece is finished? When you give them that first opportunity to write in class, write with them and then talk about the writing together, sharing with one another your feelings about the writing and about what you do as you write. Have them do some freewriting. Ask them to think about writing and talk to you about it on the page as though they were talking aloud to you. Pass out a short questionnaire on writing (see Chapter 3 for a sample), or have them write a short narrative about their past experiences, good and bad, with writing, and go over the responses with the kids as a way to get them talking about writing. Watch them writing every chance you get. Make some time each week for at least thirty minutes of in-class writing so that you can coach them while they're at work. We know you will observe differences in how students write, but we think you will notice important similarities as well. Use those observations to help you design and select instructional strategies that support and extend the ways in which your writers work.

Our Model of Writing

From observing and talking with our students and from reading research and methods texts, our approach for teaching writing to *all* students emerges. It is not a lockstep, drills-and-skills, part-to-whole method, but rather a processes approach that builds on the intuitive language resources common to all human beings. We believe that, simply stated, writers' processes move along a continuum from fluency to control and precision. Or as Tom describes it to his students: getting started, getting it down, getting it right, and checking it out. Here's that model:

Fluency ↔ Control ↔ Precision

and

Getting Started ↔ Getting It Down ↔ Getting It Right ↔ Checking It Out

In our model, fluency is the first consideration. It is the basis for all that follows. Jotting, writing, drafting, brainstorming, and revising will all help writers develop fluency. Fluency isn't a step in *the* writing process. It's a state of written language development during which writers become comfortable with written expression and able to develop and express thoughts with relative ease. Because fluency is so basic to successful writing, your first priority must be to get students writing and keep them writing. Our mantra is, "You can't teach writing if you can't get writing out of your students." You can teach *about* writing, but you can't teach writing. Without that daily practice in a humane and accepting atmosphere, writing is drudgery for most students and grows very little.

Fluency

We have found confirmation about the importance of building fluency first from other teachers, particularly those in the arts. Harold Shubert was an art teacher and a good one in a northeast Georgia high school. Students of differing abilities were drawn to his classes from all over the school. The first thing he did with them was to get them *fluent* in art, whether the medium was drawing or painting or working in clay. They messed around a lot, experimented with their own expressions, checked out options, and got a *feel* for the medium. Harold encouraged and praised the good things he saw— and there was always something good eventually. Then he and the kids got down to work on the forms that felt right for them. They practiced with those forms and began to elaborate on them. By midwinter, the halls of the school were crowded with paintings and drawings and beautiful creations by the art students—fluency, control, and precision in the art class.

We believe that fluency brings control in even the hardest and most frustrating cases, but you have to be patient. John was diagnosed as an a learning disabled (LD) and dyslexic kid who was in classes with Tom for three years. Reading and writing were epic struggles for him. He and Tom worked together on his journal. He wrote very slowly, and all the laws of logic and education decreed that John would not develop fluency. But one spring, while he was writing daily about skiing and motorcycles and sex and things in which he really was interested and about which he really wanted to write, something happened in John's journal. The words began to come. Tom watched them growing daily with wonder and excitement. John was as excited as Tom was. John had never been much of a speller. John improved his spelling and began to form sophisticated sentences and write paragraphs with some organization and

16

rhythm and movement. He was learning to write by writing a lot and by writing about things that he wanted to express on paper. At the end of that class, John still had a long way to go, but he could write, if slowly and painfully, and he *knew* that his writing was improving and that he could keep on improving.

Control

After fluency comes control in our model. Some of the controls in written language come almost immediately when the native speaker learns to write. He writes from left to right across the page. The patterns of his sentences are already formed in the subject-verb-object order. His spelling may be rudimentary, his syntax may be inchoate, his capitalization may be scattered, his words may be simple and unsophisticated, his punctuation may simply not be there—but you can *understand* what he's saying because you share a common language with him. And that language works in predictable and patterned ways. A large part of this control comes from an intuitive carryover from oral language, but it goes beyond that in writing. When the student writer reaches the point at which she can put words down on paper easily, at which she has found her *voice* and uses it, she will be able to control her writing to a large degree.

Many of us are now experiencing a somewhat different phenomenon as we encounter nonnative speakers for whom English may be a second or third language. Vocabulary, syntax, and lack of cultural knowledge can make their initial attempts at getting language on the page look almost hopeless. We know that some of these students are not really skilled in any language, so the task of making writers out of them seems impossible. We remain cockeyed optimists, however. We believe that helping them talk their way into writing and lowering the bar of our expectations for written texts can give fluency a chance to grow.

By the time students enter your high-school English class, a lot of what they need to do is to practice their writing skills and techniques and processes over and over again. If we coach that practice effectively and don't discourage them entirely with our red pen, the controls will come.

We're not saying that all you have to do is get the student fluent in a particular form and he'll suddenly begin to turn out perfect papers. Nor are we saying that you can't help him in many ways to control his writing-in-process with minilessons and exercises. We are not saying that writing comes easily for most kids. We are saying that, just as in learning speech, control follows and is closely linked with fluency. *Getting it right* comes from *getting it down*.

Precision

As students become fluent and acquire more control over their written texts, many of them will set higher standards for their writing. They will refuse to be satisfied with just any old word or sentence pattern. They will spend more time revising and crafting texts. In short, they will demand precision in their finished pieces. Precision in writing means choosing the precisely right words, using organization effectively, connecting with an audience, proofreading, and otherwise producing quality writing. We talk extensively in Chapter 9 about the features of good writing. Writers who are beginning to be effective with most of those features are beginning to develop the precision in their writing that is the hallmark of quality. As our students develop confidence and a sense of their own authorial power, our coaching strategies will change with them, giving us opportunities to demonstrate new and more complex text strategies.

Teaching Writing

Because we're convinced that writing is learned in a relatively consistent pattern with recognizable stages, we believe that writing is understandable. Writing is wonderfully complex, beautifully intricate, sublimely and frustratingly human—but it's not a magic something that rises from dark depths within us, unknowable and unknown. We know what it is and how it works, and that means we can *teach* it.

What Do Writers Need?

If writing processes are not lockstep and may not look at all like that poster on your wall, how can you design writing instruction that is consistent, flexible, and process-based and that meets the diverse needs of the students in your classroom? Maybe a good way to get a handle on the issues of process is to think about the common ground that all writers share. Of course, writers' needs depend on how proficient they are as writers, but most writers work best when the following conditions and resources are available.

IDEAS AND POSSIBILITIES If the writing process movement has contributed significantly to the improvement of writing instruction in schools, it is because of its primary emphasis on idea-finding. For long years, teaching writing consisted of assigning topics, insisting on an outline, and prescribing a due date for the assignment. Teachers spent very little time helping students find and develop ideas. Now, however, brainstorming, listing, clustering, webbing, zero drafts, freewriting, journals, writers' notebooks, and more are all part of the writing process legacy for ways of engaging writers in the work of exploring and trying on ideas before they commit to a topic and a draft. The term *prewriting* was originally associated with this first step in the writing process model, and the term remains popular even though it sets apart idea-finding from drafting when, in reality, writers are bouncing back and forth between idea generation and drafting. In order to avoid this inaccuracy of the term *prewriting*, Tom and Dan coined the phrase *getting it started* to describe the preliminary stage of writing.

Equally as important as teaching students to use a variety of strategies for generating text-worthy ideas is the need to create opportunities for them to share and test those fledgling ideas with peers and potential readers. The interaction between idea-finding and talk is a strong one, and we need to learn to manage some of the chaos and tension that is inevitably present as students spend time generating and exploring ideas for writing together.

EXCERPTS AND EXAMPLES Every bit as important as the time for idea-finding is the opportunity for students to read and examine excerpts and examples of the kinds of texts they are to compose. When Dan teaches memoir, he and his students read and examine as many as thirty cuttings from contemporary memoirs. This close reading work gives students a sense of the options of form and layout that the genre may provide. Memoirs, for instance, may include prefaces, maps, photographs, chapters, sections, letters, poems, and epilogs. Reading these excerpts aloud will also give students a feel for the language, voices, and syntax that successful writers employ in the genre. Reading and idea-finding are compatible processes that feed and enhance each other. We really can't conceive of initiating a writing process instructional model that does not include both reading and writing.

CONSTRAINTS AND FREEDOMS We are firm believers that student writers need and want certain boundaries and constraints in a writing process environment. In the first edition of this book, Dan and Tom found themselves in conflict with a school of thought that eschewed the notion that teachers should suggest topics for students' writing. The logic was that when teachers were too active in students' choice of topics, the writing really became the teacher's rather than the student's. We understood that concern, but we were high-school teachers and we knew that students enjoyed both the freedom to find text-worthy ideas and some sense of what options and expectations the teacher had for such texts. The conflict is perhaps moot at this point with most contemporary writing theorists now suggesting that teachers be much more active in creating boundaries and constraints for student texts. Even an early guru of student freedom in the classroom such as Don Graves now says that "We've learned that, right from the start, teachers need to teach *more*" (1994).

We have adopted as our metaphor for the writing time in our classrooms the Game Preserve, a metaphor developed by Dan. The preserve is bounded not so much to keep the animals in as to keep the poachers out. We set limits for our writers: "Yes, you have to write a memoir; no, it can't be a fictitious story." But we also offer freedoms: "Sure, you can stick some of your poetry in there if it fits, and yes, you can make up stuff if it's true to the piece." In a game preserve the animals are allowed to be animals. The game officer doesn't drive around in the Land Rover to demand that the elephants be more elephant-like. The game officer checks to see that there's water in the water hole and adequate food supply for all. The teacher in a writing process style class moves around to offer assistance and support, to clarify expectations, and to listen to students' efforts.

RITUALS AND ROUTINES Because writing is work, we have always insisted that our classrooms maintain a work-like atmosphere when students are writing. To maximize the efficiency of writing time in your classroom, we think it is important to establish an agreed upon set of routines and rituals with your students. These agreements can be quite specific to your needs as a teacher and their needs as writers. "Students working on exploring a topic do this. . . ." "Writers working with a partner do this. . . ." "Response groups use these guidelines. . . ." The successful teacher marks the intellectual boundaries for inquiry and initiates a set of expectations or classroom values that establish rituals and celebrate work. We like Tom Sergiovanni's term *covenants* for the mutual promises that students and teachers make to each other (1996). We think the writing classroom goes much better with agreed upon roles and rules.

COACHING Donald Schön has said, "Students cannot be *taught* what they need to know, but they can be *coached*" (1987). Schön elaborates upon his idea by suggesting that the most effective coaching of student learning happens *while* they are working or "doing." Most writers need some encouragement and feedback while they are struggling to construct a text. Good coaching is not advice-giving, however, nor is it telling writers what they should do with their drafts. Effective coaches are, first, good listeners who work both to understand what the writer is trying to say and to discern what specific difficulties the writer is having in saying it. Good coaches ask questions and explore possibilities with the writer, as we discuss in more detail later. (See Chapter 8 for more ideas on how to respond to student writing.)

A COMMUNITY OF WRITERS Because learning to write is both a solitary and a social process, writers need opportunities to work alone and to engage in public sharing of their work. As Parker Palmer says, "The growth of any craft depends on shared practice and honest dialogue among the people who do it" (1998). For that reason, we provide plenty of time for solitary writing in our classes, but we also have students read their drafts to us and to peers and to others they trust. We celebrate finished pieces with displays and readings. We talk together about how to do this thing called writing. We become a community of thinkers and learners and writers who work and share and celebrate together.

Teaching Writing Processes: One Way to Begin

This stepwise writing activity is a good starting place for introducing writing process pedagogy to your students because it makes the "skeleton" more visible than some other kinds of writing. Dan taught it to Tom, and perhaps Donald Graves is the source of the idea. It is one of those assignments, like freewriting, that has become a classic. Usually just called The Anatomy, although it goes by various names, you will find versions of it in classrooms all over the country, and especially among the National Writing Project folks. Tom uses it a lot with his own writing, and he's taught it to students from third grade to retirement age. Like freewriting, Tom has never known this structure to fail, a strong claim for any writing assignment. But you must do it *with* your student writers.

Step 1: Remembering and Sharing

Talking is an important part of starting this writing, as it is with most good writings. Ask your students to jot down in a word or phrase three to five memories about which they want to learn more by writing about them. Demonstrate this step before they finish their lists by jotting three of your own ideas on the board or the overhead. Ask them to pick memories they can locate in a particular place on a particular day, an incident or a moment. Doing so seems to keep the writing away from vague and meaningless sentiments.

Talk about your memories with them briefly. Choose the one about which you want to write, discussing your choice with them. Let your students help you choose the writing. Sometimes Tom takes the advice of his students; sometimes he has a strong writer's preference of his own. Either way, the discussion gives you and your students a chance to talk about how writers decide what they will write.

Step 2: Selecting a Memory

Now it's their turn. Ask them to share their list with a partner, just as you have done with them. Warn them not to talk it to death or they won't want to write about it. Give them a ten-minute time limit. Then fudge on it if you need to do so. Their job is to pick the one on which they want to work. Talking has lots of benefits for writers, so we frequently use talking as a precursor to writing.

Step 3: Jotting or Other Prewriting on Paper

At this point, Tom demonstrates jot listing, clustering, or webbing for the writing he has chosen, and then he has students choose their own way of getting some ideas down on the page. You may know other prewriting strategies for initial brainstorming like "turkey tracking" or cataloging, and you may prefer to use one of them. The point of all such techniques is to help students get details down on paper so that when they start writing, they won't run out of steam and their writing will be alive.

Jot listing is the easiest technique with which to start. It is simply brainstorming words and phrases in no particular order to use in the writing. The first time we do this kind of writing together, Tom asks them to jot list in categories, such as seeing, hearing, smell, or touch, to focus on sensory details.

Push your students to get down as many details as possible. Often the quantity of details on the jot list predicts the quality of the writing.

Try to get through this part before the end of the first class period.

Step 4: Getting It Down

This is the "zero" draft, the discovery draft. Encourage students to write fast, to freewrite. As Dan says, write around the hard parts. Push students to write through and finish the first draft. If a student gets stuck, tell him to go back to his jot list. With this kind of writing, however, not many students get stuck.

Step 5: Sharing

This step involves students in reading to a partner or a response group. It is not for them to receive criticism. Mainly, it is to let the writer *hear* her piece for the first time. It is a different kind of reading. Tom calls it "reading with a pencil," and he models how he stops and fixes things or makes notes as he reads his piece. If you're in a high-tech place, the document camera is perfect for allowing students to see the writer at work. This reading is not meant to be a polished performance. We are reading aloud to hear the piece—really *hear* what has been written. The reading may be halting and tentative. Tom stops often to add or strike out words and to make substitutions. He asks questions of his listeners as he reads. "Does that part sound right?" and "Did that sentence work?"

Tom requires the reader to tell her listeners what help she wants with the piece before she reads it to them. That sets the tone for the listeners as well as the writer.

Step 6: Reworking

There are papers that never go beyond the zero draft for one reason or another. We generally push students to revise, and typically they resist. Word processing on the computer is a big help in encouraging students to revise because fixing writing is so much easier on the computer. We make distinctions between two types of reworking—revision and editing. Revision deals with substantial aspects of the writing, what works and what doesn't, and editing deals with fixing the errors. The actual experience defies neat divisions, but it helps us organize our thinking and our teaching. At some point as students are reworking their papers, we also hold another conference with them to discuss revising and editing suggestions and ideas.

Step 7: Publishing and Celebrating

Some pieces will be reworked through several drafts, depending on the student's working style and the writing itself. Sometimes a student considers a paper to be finished, but we may ask for more work on such a paper when we see problems in it. Nonetheless, there has to be a deadline for any kind of writing. That's just how it works. Then there is another conference about publishing options, and we help the student to select and follow through with some form of publishing his paper. (See Chapter 15 for ideas on publishing and celebrating students' writings.) One form of publishing that we like is the *read-around* so we can show off and enjoy our writings together. For a read-around, each student selects an excerpt from his piece of writing to read to the class. We applaud and celebrate the writer's achievement by making specific comments about the good stuff we heard in the writing.

Once students have followed this "anatomy," we tell them that these are the processes of writing that they'll use for almost all of the writing that they do in our classes. They've just finished a piece of writing on a topic they chose. They've just heard applause and praise. The writing class is off to a fine beginning.

Notes

1. Cary Quinn was a student at Gainesville High School, Gainesville, GA.

2. The reference to pencil sharpening is from an interview with Ernest Hemingway by George Plimpton (1984) in *Writers at Work: The Paris Review Interviews* (2nd series). New York: Knopf.

Works Cited

GRAVES, DONALD. 1994. *A Fresh Look at Writing.* Portsmouth, NH: Heinemann.

KIRBY, DAWN LATTA. (formerly, Bruton). 1985. *Toward a Definition of Written Fluency.* Unpublished doctoral dissertation, University of Georgia.

MILLER, JAMES E. JR. 1972. *Word, Self, Reality: The Rhetoric of the Imagination.* New York: Dodd, Mead.

PALMER, PARKER. 1998. *The Courage to Teach.* San Francisco: Jossey Bass.

SCHÖN, DONALD. 1987. *Educating the Reflective Practitioner.* San Francisco: Jossey Bass.

SERGIOVANNI, THOMAS. 1996. *Leadership for the Schoolhouse.* San Francisco: Jossey Bass.

WIESEL, ELIE. 1995. *All Rivers Run to the Sea.* New York: Schocken Books.

3

The Classroom Environment

A learning space must be hospitable—inviting as well as open, safe and trustworthy, as well as free. . . . [It] must have features that help students deal with the dangers of an educational expedition: places to rest, places to find nourishment, even places to seek shelter when one feels overexposed.

—PARKER PALMER, *The Courage to Teach*

The thought of taking or teaching a composition class does not always inspire students or teachers. There are many negative feelings and nagging fears to overcome when you initiate composing into your classroom. The first few days and weeks are critical. Some attention to the physical setting—the way the room looks—and some attention to the psychological setting—the way the room feels—can change the composition class into a *writing class*—a place where students feel like working and enter with expectations and a "What are we going to do today?" feeling.

The Way the Room Looks

We don't want to spend too much time talking about how to decorate your room. Interior decorating is, after all, a personal matter. Tables versus desks, carpets, and workshop designs have all been described better by others elsewhere. The important point to make about decor is that there should be some obvious indications that you believe that the physical environment is important, and these touches need to be present even in a rather sterile classroom setting that leaves little to your personal tastes or preferences. Maybe you're stuck with a windowless room with brown carpet and the same desks that two generations of students have occupied. There are still things that you can do. The fact that you've done *something* with your room is a signal to students that you care about the writing environment. The opposite is also unfortunately true, so take the pledge. You will do *something* with that room to make it a warmer, less sterile place.

Remember one thing: The focal point of any good writing class is the display of student products. Elementary teachers do a good job of showing student work. Smiles and gold stars are everywhere. Teachers of young children don't go to this trouble because they're softheaded. They know that displaying student work builds pride and enthusiasm and dramatically enhances motivation.

Rule 1 for Writing Environment

Make a Place in Your Class for Student Products
- Let students know that writing is the primary business of your writing class by making written products the *center* of attention. Have a poets' corner, a graffiti board, a gallery of finished pieces. Display (framed, laminated, or glued on colored mats) some of your favorite pictures, and encourage students to post creative responses around them. Use three-dimensional displays and mobiles. Use the ceiling, walls, and floors.
- Encourage students to display drafts and unfinished pieces of writing by designating a Works in Progress area.
- Have a Quotable Quotes display with typed excerpts from student journals (with author's permission, of course).
- Take pictures of your students while they're writing, and have a photographer enlarge them, or do so yourself with your computer scanner or with the user-friendly equipment found in most photo developing shops. Post them around the room.
- Post some of your own writing, as well as the writing of other teachers and adults in the school community. (Maybe the custodian is a secret poet . . . ask him.)
- Post pictures and short biographical sketches of the authors of the displayed products.

Rule 2

Arrange the Room in a Way That Is Comfortable to You
The number one priority in room arrangement is that it be a place where you feel comfortable. If you feel good about your room, chances are the students will too.

Dan prefers a division of the classroom into specific work areas to give student writers a functional place to be during the various businesses of writing. When there's enough space in the classroom, he designates a writing area, a responding area, a resource area, a revising area, and an escape area. He uses a circle or semicircle for group reading and evaluation of student papers. He moves around among the areas, providing help and counsel where he's most needed. Students know what behaviors are appropriate in each area, and he can provide gentle reminders if he sees students doing something inappropriate.

Many teachers and some students need quieter, more structured-looking environments. Some physical spaces in which we teach just don't adapt easily to rearrangement. Do what you can with the space that you have. Don't apologize. Arrange the classroom your way.

Tom's classroom often has desks in rows and looks surprisingly conventional—except for the mass of books, posters, and student products. He says he just feels better with rows. He frequently breaks up the rows, asking students to turn desks toward each other. Dawn prefers concentric semicircles or clusters of desks and frequently re-arranges the furniture to accommodate the task at hand. Her students become skilled furniture movers. We all agree on one thing completely: We need music in the writing class. We keep a small stereo system, complete with CD and cassette tape players, in the room with a large library of different kinds of music. (We lock up the stereo and the CDs in a storage cabinet at night.) The music comes on at the drop of a hat: background music for workdays or foreground music as stimulus for a variety of creative responses. Students can also contribute music to the class play list. We've never been able to teach writing without music—it makes us feel better.

The Way the Room Feels

Far more important to the successful teaching of writing than the way your room looks is the psychological climate—the way it feels.

A good writing class must feel like a safe place. Writing is scary business; sweaty palms are the order of the day. Good writing teachers work hard at reducing fear in the writing class. If you expect students to experiment, to try things out, then you'll have to convince them that they are safe and won't be shot down in flames.

Offer support and plenty of pats on the back. Ask questions that show you are genuinely interested in what they have to say. Encourage students to externalize their feelings; extend empathy when the going gets rough. Tell them about times you've had difficulty getting ideas to work on paper. Show them examples of the way you struggle through drafts by showing them the actual marked-up and crossed-out drafts of some piece of writing on which you are working—maybe even your own version of the assignment you've asked students to do. Hold frequent idea-sharing sessions in which you encourage students to talk about their work. Dawn calls these sessions *press conferences* in which students present their writing ideas or problems and listen as fellow students respond with helpful ideas. Dan calls such conversations *writerly talk*, and he holds such sessions each week in his class. To foster the reflective atmosphere essential to the writing classroom, offer extended periods of class time for students to find, draft, share, and refine ideas. You'll foster a classroom community of writers if students know you care about each writer's progress.

A Writing Preserve

We teach our students to treat our classroom as a refuge, a haven for experimenting and trying out words. We don't tolerate cheap shots, and we tell them so. We post a large *No Hunting* sign on the door because writing and learning occur best in a supportive, protective environment. As we'll discuss throughout this book, having a supportive environment doesn't mean that we adopt a Pollyanna attitude toward writing or that everything that everyone writes is praised or that we don't criticize one another's work. *No Hunting* simply means "No cheap shots." The writing class must not become a hacksaw operation where people criticize each other's failures. If a piece of writing is bad, then we tell students that it "didn't work." It either needs to be reworked or filed. If it needs reworking, then specific, constructive suggestions are helpful to the author. Offer suggestions such as, "How about throwing out that first paragraph and beginning here?" or "I want to know why this character felt he was a failure." Suggestions offered in the spirit of coaching a writer to rework a piece so that it becomes a better piece of writing serve to improve the piece of writing and to keep the writer's ego intact.

If the piece has no potential at all, then simply suggest that the writer file it in her Writer's Notebook (which we discuss in detail in Chapter 5) and begin again. Beginning again is often the best remedy for an ineffective piece of writing. Note that "file it" does not mean fold, spindle, or mutilate. The piece that didn't work goes into the student's Writer's Notebook as evidence of the student's overall work and effort to write. In the Writer's Notebook, the piece is an artifact that is available for review by both you and the writer; the piece may even be resurrected later.

It's so easy to get out the hacksaw. "That piece didn't do a thing for me," or "I won't read this piece until you learn how to spell" are comments that cut deep. None of us would feel heartened by such a response to our own writing. Not only are young writers likely to be discouraged by such comments, but they may also hear indictments of personal—not just academic—failure in such cutting remarks. Students often find it difficult to separate comments about their writings from comments about them as people. Remind yourself often that students are most vulnerable when they submit a piece of genuine writing. Proceed with caution; put away the hacksaw.

Beginnings

Feelings of competition, grade-grubbing (the "Is this going to be graded?" syndrome), apathy, and even outright hostility are all factors that work against you in the writing class. We believe teachers must meet these attitudes head-on with some serious anxiety-reducing, group-building activities.

The first days in any writing class are critical. Because you want students to write often, because you want them to write honestly and openly, because you want them to share their work and respond to one another's work, and because you want them to accept criticism and work on revising their writing, you have many new attitudes and behaviors to develop in your students. If you want them to function as an audience for one another's writing and to become careful critics of their own and others' writings, then attending to the psychological climate of the class is essential. The following starter activities will help you get to know your students and help them get to know one another.

A few words of advice about these starter activities: Don't try to do all of them. You'll overwhelm the students and take the focus away from the purpose of such activities, which is to improve the climate for writing. In fact, we suggest strongly that you ask students to react to the selected activity *in writing* either in a journal or a short feelings paper. Writing their responses reminds them that the central business of this class is getting words down on paper.

A good many composition teachers may scoff at these starter activities or label them as the games teachers play to entertain students. Many composition teachers take their work very seriously and think such games belong in drama classes or creative writing classes. On the contrary, we have found them to be well received by students. Taking time for relating to one another as real people, time to have some fun, and the experience of writing from sources of personal knowledge all increase students' potential for learning and for writing in an individual, authentic voice. When used with follow-up writing activities, they cause the class to come together as a unit. These activities do not lessen the seriousness of the writing class or turn the teacher into an entertainer; rather, they pave the way for more authentic interactions among students and for more genuine writing throughout the school year.

The First Writing

Right after we take the roll on the first day, we ask students to do a ten-minute freewrite on their feelings about and experiences with writing. Freewriting is an excellent way to begin a writing class. We ask students to write without stopping about themselves as writers. We suggest they give us a little past history of their experiences with writing. How do they feel when they write? Have they ever written anything they're proud of? Have they had any disasters with writing? Here are some typical student responses:

Writing. Actually writing is not that important to me—I prefer verbal expressions. All of my writing career I have received good grades on content and rather poor grades on grammar. This improved only somewhat last year after Trad. Gram. and Theme Writing. I get my ideas from my experiences and what I've read. I love to read. My major problem with writing is subject matter—how unoriginal. Anyway— in my journal, I just write down what I'm thinking about—very seldom do I get out and create something. I don't have time and like I said, I'd rather talk or read than write. Even now I've got writer's cramp.

—*Laura*[1]

I have had bad experiences with writing since the first days of school. The main problem has been that I was assigned to write and *had* to write on the teacher's topic in the teacher's style. I love to write. I dream of someday writing a book that will be the most profound literary work ever; Nobel Prize in Literature and all that.

—*Todd*[1]

28

The worst time for me to write is now in a class with other people around. My favorite time to write is lying in bed on a cool night with a glass of hot rum tea. That's when I can really grind it out. I like writing about pleasant memories like the beach, girls, drinking, summer vacations. I've always had the feeling that I've had to keep my writing secret, except for a couple of girls I have dated, because until now writing and music and art have been looked down upon by fellow "athletes." Until now I've been afraid of verbal sensitivity in my life but now I have more of a don't give a damn attitude about everything.

—*Tommy*[1]

These excerpts are honest and full of information for the teacher of writing. Use them to talk openly with your students about some of the problems and frustrations of writing. Engage them in lively conversation about the whole process. Talking about writing should reduce some of the tension in the writing class. Dawn follows up the freewriting and discussion with a more finished product on the students' individual perspectives on themselves as writers. Display these finished products or excerpts from them in the room, accompanied by each writer's picture. These displays are great tools for Parent Night or Open House at your school when parents want to see what their students are doing in your class.

Names

Names are important. Spend some time each day for the first week or so helping students learn one another's names. Don't leave this name-learning process to chance; writing classes go better with names.

We go around the room a time or two with the old name chain: Say your name and the names of those before you and then use the "who are your neighbors" game in which you point to a student and ask her to name the person on either side of her. There's nothing new here, but students tell us, "This is the first class in which I've known the names of everyone in the room." When students know each other's names, they feel more like a community and take more interest in responding personally and authentically to each other's work. If you're not the name-game type, ask students to make themselves name cards to stand on their desks. Ask students to call one another by name. Writers' names are important. Work at it.

Lives

No less important than names are the students themselves. Who are they? Where do they come from? What do they do well? Motivating students to participate in your class will be easier if you can get them to invest something of themselves in the class at the beginning. Self-disclosure—sharing something about themselves—is a subtle and important way to do so.

One note of caution: Move slowly with this self-disclosure business. Remember that this is a writing class, not psychoanalysis. Your purpose in opening kids up a bit is to soften them so that they are less fearful of sharing their writings and more open to constructive criticism. Remember also to share some tidbits of your own reading and movie preferences, school stories of yourself as a young student, or funny life stories with your students. Not only are you modeling what you want students to do, but when everyone in the writing classroom, including you, is open and responsive, community- and confidence-building increase.

The least threatening of these activities is probably a simple writer's questionnaire that asks students questions about how they spend their time, where they live, their favorite music, the latest book they have read, their favorite movies and television shows, and so on. See Figure 3–1 for an example.

Be sure to tell your students the purpose of such questionnaires: to know them and their interests better.

Sentence Completion Survey

Another low-threat activity is the sentence completion survey (see Figure 3–2 on page 32). This activity lets the students set the level of openness. If they feel safe in your class, they may be very honest. If they are still uncertain about the class, they can provide superficial answers.

The follow-up on the sentence completion activity is teacher response. Read the sentences carefully and write personal comments and observations on them. Select some of the most honest, humorous, or serious completions and share them with the class. Be careful to protect the identity of the writer.

These three activities acquaint you with your students' attitudes toward writing, their interests, fears, and hopes. You can help students overcome writing problems, aid them in finding writing topics that interest them, and monitor their attitudes toward writing now that you know something about the way they feel.

Invitations for Peer Dialogue

We need to get to know our students in the writing class. They need to get to know each other. The next series of activities will open the dialogue among student writers.

Lie Game

Our friend Ken Kantor says he invented the Lie Game. Ask students in your class (if you have a large class, select fifteen volunteers) to think of something that has or might have happened to them in the past—for example, "My father was an Olympic swimmer," or "I broke my nose in fourth grade," or "We have ten aquariums in our house and 100 guppies." Give them a minute or so to think about something.

Ask the students to take out a sheet of paper and number from one to however many students are participating in the Lie Game. There is one basic rule in this game: Whatever they tell about themselves must be wholly true or wholly false. No half-truths are allowed.

Writer's Questionnaire

NAME _____

What do you like to be called? _____

_____

How do you like to spend your weekends? _____

_____

Do you have a job? _____ Where? _____

_____

What kind of music do you like? _____

_____

Who's your favorite singer or group? _____

_____

What shows do you watch on TV? _____

_____

Do you write poems or stories on your own? _____

_____

When was the last time you wrote something you really liked, and what was it?

_____

_____

Figure 3–1. *Writer's Questionnaire*

May be copied for classroom use. © 2004 by Dan Kirby, Dawn Latta Kirby, and Tom Liner from *Inside Out, Third Edition.* Heinemann: Portsmouth, NH.

Sentence Completion

Instructions: Complete the following sentences. Write as much as you wish on each one. Your answers will be kept confidential unless you wish to share them.

1. I'm not happy _____ .

2. Sometimes I wish I were _____ .

3. I'm pretty good at _____ .

4. My friends think I'm _____ .

5. Writing assignments are _____ .

6. When I get home from school I _____ .

7. I'm afraid of _____ .

8. School is _____ .

9. The most important thing to me is _____ .

10. I have hopes _____ .

Figure 3–2. *Sentence Completion*

Begin the game by telling something about your past. Tell a good lie: "I was on a high school basketball team that went to the state tournament," or "Right after college, I spent a couple of years hanging out in Hollywood, trying to make it as an actor." Whatever you tell them, make it a good one. Your lie or truth will be a model.

After you have made your statement, ask them to mark True or False beside number one. Continue around the room. Keep it moving. Ham it up a bit. When all players have made their statements, ask the person who made the statement to give the correct answer. How good was each student at lying or at detecting a lie? What surprising facts did you learn about each other?

The purpose for the Lie Game is rather obvious. First, it's a talking activity. Second, it's a composing activity. Third, it's a self-disclosure activity and a good way to get the writing class moving.

Secret Telling

Use this activity early in the class. Pair students with someone they don't know well. The pair is to tell each other three secrets:

Secret 1—something you don't care if everyone knows
Secret 2—something only your friends know
Secret 3—something nobody knows

To follow up this activity, ask the students to write a short piece about the other person without revealing any secrets.

Role-Taking Interview

Another good way to get classes started is to pair students and ask them to interview each other for five minutes. They are to learn as many specific details and facts about the other person as they can. At the end of the five minutes, ask each student in turn to introduce himself as though he were the person interviewed. He is to take the other person's name and speak in the first person.

Interview Poem

For the Interview Poem you need five good questions for students to ask one another. Brainstorm with your class or write the questions yourself. Brainstorming typically gets questions such as, "What do you do on Saturday afternoons?" "What's your sign?" "What do you love most?" and an assortment of sex and drug questions. Use your own judgment. Students interview each other and then write a poem about the other person.

Discussions with students who have tried these activities reveal that most of them feel they talk more openly with class members because of the sharing:

I told Sarah a couple of really important things about a certain person in my life and what I want in the future. I worked with Jeff on the interview poem. I found out his father died last year and he is still really bitter about that. I tried to write the poem about him to show that I was sensitive to his hurt and anger. I especially liked a couple of the lines he wrote about me. "Jennifer skitters her way through ideas, lining them up like lures for me to chew on." I feel comfortable with both Sarah and Jeff now.

—Jennifer[2]

Creating Visual Portraits

We try to plan at least one activity that involves students in creating a visual portrait of themselves. This is an attempt to satisfy our natural impulse toward image-making as well as promote the use of visuals and visualization in the writing class. Here are four of our favorites.

Coat of Arms Game

You may have seen this activity before; it's been around awhile. It works in a writing class for the same reasons the Lie Game works: It lets students share some of themselves in a nonthreatening way. All you need for this activity is a facsimile of a shield and some specific instructions.

Tell your students not to worry about artistic results. Do this activity with them. As follow-up, students may share, in small groups, the drawings on their coats of arms,

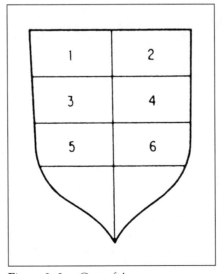

Figure 3–3. *Coat of Arms*

explaining the significance of the symbols; or you can post the coats of arms and hold a gallery walk.

1. Draw two things you do well.
2. Draw the place where you feel most at home.
3. And so on.

As a *variation*, other value questions may be used. For example:

1. What is something about which you would never budge?
2. What is something you're striving to be or become?
3. What one thing do you want to accomplish by the time you're 65?
4. Draw three things you're good at.
5. What is a personal motto you live by? (We allow words for this response.)

With younger students you can use silhouettes instead of shields.

Activities such as this one work well in a composition class because they involve the students in talking about themselves and their own experiences. Personal experiences are the beginning writer's best resources. Talking before writing is priming the pump. The disclosures your students make during these activities also reveal information about them that a skillful teacher can use to motivate them further. You may learn which student is an artist, who loves motorcycles, reads widely, lives on a farm, is a musician in a band, or who works in a mortuary. The good composition teacher stores these nuggets and uses them at appropriate times to suggest topics, draw out students, cast them in the role of expert, or simply engage them in spirited conversation.

Remember, the purpose of those self-disclosure activities is not to pry into students' lives, to embarrass them, or to single them out. In general, the more you know about your students and the more they know about one another, the more a climate of openness and safety prevails. These are precisely the conditions that foster maximum growth in a writing class where students work closely with the teacher and with one another.

Secret Box

Make a hit on the shoe store for shoe boxes or ask students to bring them from home. Armed with scissors, glue, and a stack of magazines, ask the students to decorate their boxes with pictures, words, or advertisements that tell something about themselves. "Ah, ha," you say, "a variation on the personal collage." Exactly. The outside of the box should illustrate the outside of the student's interests, hobbies, talents, and so forth. The secrets go *inside* the box. Ask each student to put three artifacts in the box that reveal something about her inside self. Pair the students up and ask them to explain the outside to each other. They should reveal the secrets inside only if they feel comfortable with their partner.

Road of Life

This activity is a variation on the Life Map activity found in Chapter 4. For this activity all you need are paper and pens, or markers. Ask the students to make a map of their lives from birth to present. Tell them to illustrate the hills and valleys, the thrills and conflicts. Give them time to share the maps with at least three classmates. Collect the maps and decorate your walls.

Behind the Mask

Use butcher paper to cut out a huge mask, or give students construction paper to make their own masks. Supply them with a stack of newspapers and magazines and ask them to cut out and paste words and letters on the mask to form a message from behind the mask.

Creating Metaphors of Self

We have a natural inclination to compare one thing with another. In the final two activities, students create metaphors of self in words or through a shape that represents them. In both activities, students exchange ideas and information about themselves with their peers.

Impressions Word Game

Use this activity several weeks into the course after the students have become comfortable with one another. This activity brings students together. They talk among themselves, share humorous perceptions of one another, and learn something about themselves. In the process, they practice creative uses of language and vivid detail. Prepare a grid something like the one in Figure 3–4.

Divide the class into groups of five students, give each student a copy of the grid, and ask them to write in the names of each person in the group. Now they're ready to go. Ask them to fill in the blanks. A few suggestions:

1. If your students have not worked in groups much, structure the activity carefully.
2. Make up the groups any way you wish, although random groups are probably best for this activity.
3. Tell students to be as *specific* as possible: If it's a car, what kind? What color? Any unusual things about it, like a dented fender or bumper sticker?

Impressions Word Game

Names of Group Members	Three Words	A Car (Be specific.)	A TV Personality	A Food
1.				
2.				
3.				
4.				
5.				

Figure 3–4. *Impressions Word Game*

4. During the sharing phase, be sure that all students receive some feedback quickly.
5. Be sure the atmosphere is positive.

For follow-up, ask the students to respond to the activity by writing in their journals what they learned about themselves.

Wire Sculpture

We got this idea from our friend Hugh Agee. All you need for this activity are pieces of floral wire about 18 inches long. Before you give each student a wire, spend some time talking about symbols and logos. We are all familiar with logos such as those of the Red Cross, the Olympic games, McDonald's golden arches, and others. Ask the students to begin thinking about a logo for themselves. Ask what symbol would best represent them. Pass out the wires and ask the students to shape the wire so that it becomes a logo for them. Sometimes we use one of the following ideas:

1. The students shape the wire so that it makes a statement or represents an idea about something important to them.
2. The students shape the wire so that it becomes a *life line* that graphically depicts important events in their lives.
3. The students shape the wire so that it characterizes someone they have known for a long time.

As follow-up, have students pass the finished creations around the class and discuss the following:

1. Discuss what the shape says about its creator.
2. Have the creator discuss his wire to explain its significance.
3. Have each creator explain his creation to at least three other class members. (Free movement around the class is required for this activity.)
4. Have each creator write a short paragraph discussing the significance of his creation. Mount the wires on construction paper and tape the written paragraph to the back of the paper. Set up a display of the sculptures and invite students to browse.

Variations of this activity can be done with straws, clay, paper, or paper clips. Manipulating a wire and then talking about the creation allows the student enough psychological distance to be more open and honest about himself.

Students have exercised a wide variety of imaginative ways to generate the subject of self. They've written, talked, made visual representations, and made metaphoric leaps. They've practiced many of the strategies they'll use to generate writing. Through these exercises, your students have functioned as audience for another's writings and ramblings and visual representations as well. This is a classroom in which you have already encouraged a community of sharing, listening, and advising.

Beyond the Classroom

After you've done everything to make your classroom a pleasant place in which to write, it will still be a classroom. Leaving that classroom—changing the environment completely—can produce dramatic and positive effects on student writings. Look around the school to see what interesting places are available. The cafeteria before and after lunch period, the gymnasium, the parking lot, the area under the large tree on the school's front lawn, the cemetery down the street, the shopping center around the corner—all may provide interesting environments for writing. Because any such deviations from standard operating procedures must be carefully defended to administrators, let us give this changing of the environment a name and make a few suggestions.

Walking Compositions

Defend leaving the classroom by saying that classrooms are often sterile places in which to teach writing. Students' powers of observation have been dulled. Good writers must see and hear and feel their environments directly. You are taking your writers outside the classroom to develop fluency, increase motivation, and sharpen their powers of observation. You, too, will be outside the classroom, circulating among students, reminding them of why they are out and about, encouraging them, and helping them to observe, note, jot, and write.

Give students the opportunity to practice the Walking Composition on a regular basis. We like to do so once a week to establish the routine, but select a time interval that works for your situation. When students have only occasional experience with the Walking Composition, they begin to think that it's just fun and games or what you have them do when you aren't prepared to teach. Establishing routine and structure lets both the students and the administrators know that the activity is meaningful.

Give each student an instruction sheet something like the one in Figure 3–5. We suggest that you use the following list of procedures to be sure you have structured the activity carefully:

1. Make the necessary arrangements with administrators. (They already think you're weird. This activity will not surprise them.)
2. Have a preplanned, written itinerary for the tour. We usually have three such tours and ask students to choose their favorite. Give specific directions.
3. Ask students to go alone, and make them swear in blood they won't smoke in the parking lot.
4. Tell students to be a sensory sponge, a CIA agent, a careful observer. Have them make notes in four columns: what they hear, see, feel, and smell.
5. Set time limits for their return. Synchronize watches. Send watchless students to an area with a large clock, or send them with a partner who wears a watch.
6. Follow up the activity with in-class sharing of observations and journal writings or short descriptive papers. The activity is excellent for short descriptive pieces because students must select from their list only those details that fit the mood and purpose of the paper they subsequently decide to write. Note also that many district- and state-level tests require students to write focused papers full of specific detail. Such requirements on lists of state standards or on state tests may be one more validation of this activity that will interest your administrators.
7. Use the short descriptive papers as the starting scene for a short piece of fiction. Ask students to imagine what might have taken place during their walk that didn't or what might happen there at ten o'clock tonight.

Walking Composition Instruction Sheet

Grab your Writer's Notebook and a pen or pencil. You are about to take a trip. As you walk, please observe the following guidelines.

1. Go alone (or be alone in yourself). Talk as little as possible.

2. You are a *sensory sponge*. Soak up and record sensations and observations.

3. Look for the small, important *details*.

4. Record your observations in four columns: things you see, hear, feel, and smell.

5. Be considerate of your neighbors.

6. We'll return to our classroom in fifteen minutes. Then, you'll select observations from your notes for a *place/feeling description* or a *sensory poem* or a *written meditation*.

Choose one of the following itineraries:

Tour A: Go to the gym. Walk around the gym floor, sit in the bleachers, and visit the locker room. Return to our classroom ready to write.

Tour B: Enter the cafeteria. Sit down and pretend to be studying. Change seats at least twice to view different areas of the room. Return to our classroom ready to write.

Tour C: Leave the building toward the parking lot. Turn right and proceed to the grassy knoll with the large trees. Stand under a tree. Wait, observe, and listen. Return to our classroom ready to write.

Figure 3–5. *Walking Composition Instruction Sheet*

Alternatives to Leaving the Classroom

Remember, there are many ways of walking out of the classroom doors if you are not comfortable with the tour. Assign the Walking Composition for homework when students can go outside of the classroom on their own time and turf. Prepare your assignment sheet the same as you would for an in-school activity. List tour options that are more extensive and lengthy outings, such as going to the mall or to the local hardware store, taking a short trip on the light rail, sitting in the city park at lunchtime on a Saturday, or whatever locale is sure to yield sights, sounds, and impressions. Or, "go outside" with music, film, invited speakers, or fine pieces of writing. Most of the subjects for student writing come from outside the classroom from their experiential, intellectual, and emotional lives. The classroom cannot provide the content to keep the writer enriched, but it can provide the stimuli. We can trigger memories and encourage student writers to sensitize themselves to the world around them.

Final Thoughts on the Writing Environment

Creating a unique environment for the teaching of writing is absolutely essential. The writing portion of your class should feel different from the other activities that occur within the normal routines of your class. The writing portion of your class must be perceived as safe, as a time to experiment, and as a time when encouragement can be expected; but it must also be perceived as a time when everyone may be prodded a bit and asked to rework and revise, and above all as a section of class during which everyone writes and writes and writes.

Such an environment does not occur by chance or by the "I don't know what to do during fifth period; I think I'll have them write something" method. A writing class must be carefully and yet tentatively planned.

Notes

1. Laura Jacobs, Todd Williams, and Tommy D'Angelo were all students at Cedar Shoals High School in Athens, GA.

2. Jennifer Kelly was a student at Boise High School, Boise, ID.

Work Cited

Palmer, Parker. 1998. *The Courage to Teach: Exploring the Inner Landscape of a Teacher's Life*. San Francisco: Jossey-Bass.

4

Getting It Down

When you first start writing—and I think it's true for a lot of beginning writers—you're scared to death that if you don't get that sentence right that minute it's never going to show up again. And it isn't. But it doesn't matter—another one will, and it'll probably be better. And I don't mind writing badly for a couple of days because I know I can fix it—and fix it again and again and again, and it will be better.

—Toni Morrison, "The Site of Memory"

Personal Writing

Many of our student writers seem inordinately worried about getting it right before they get it down. As a result, they write in a halting, overly cautious, and tentative manner. We believe an initial emphasis on fluency can help students to write with more ease and comfort, putting off concerns about correctness until they have writing worth fixing. Personal writing is the natural place for students to begin to develop fluency by rendering experiences into words on paper. We suggest that you begin your support for growth in fluency by providing students with lots of opportunities to write about what they know and feel. Encourage them to express themselves in their own words.

When you teach the new student writer or the immature writer, you begin with only two real attainable objectives: to build a feeling of confidence in students that they *can* write, and to help the student find a voice in writing. Building confidence is your first job. As tender as the ego of the beginning writer is, there is little wonder that most of our students dislike and fear the experience of writing. Better said, they dislike writing—often intensely—because they are afraid of writing. To a large degree, our first job with most of our students is to teach them that they don't have to be afraid of writing, a task not really as difficult as it may first appear. Thankfully, a little success goes a long way.

Tom remembers two of his teachers who made him feel successful. Mrs. Crutchfield (Yes, that's *Mrs. Crutchfield*, not Ms. They called her *Missez Crutchfield*, of course.) was a stern eighth-grade English teacher at Fort Hill Junior High School. She was a demanding lady who brooked no nonsense from the thirty students who squirmed in their seats and assaulted paper with pencil more or less regularly. But Tom thinks he was a little in love with her for all that; all the boys in that overcrowded and restless room were. Otherwise, he remembers her as a not particularly inspiring teacher, although she was thorough and precise. Tom asserts that he certainly was not an inspired student of the English language. He thoroughly hated facing that blank sheet of paper each week, and he thought that was a perfectly natural way to be. *All* of the students hated writing, just the way God intended and their teachers expected.

That was until one spring afternoon when Tom wrote a paper for her and, for some reason, got carried away with it and wrote far longer than the usual page called for. Tom remembers that it was something about werewolves, a favorite subject of his at that time. It must have been awfully juvenile drivel, but Mrs. Crutchfield praised it loudly and lavishly, perhaps more for the work Tom put in the piece (finally!) than for its artistic merit. Tom blushed, he beamed, he basked in the glory of her approval. He began to think that maybe writing this stuff wasn't so bad after all.

Her praise sustained Tom for the next two years until he met Mr. Cone, a young man who smiled owlishly behind his glasses at another overcrowded classroom, this time filled to the walls with high-school sophomores. He was a demanding teacher also, and a writer of no small merit himself. When students pleased him, he sometimes read to them from his writing. The students liked that. It was a special treat.

"You're a good writer, Tom," he suddenly said one afternoon. It was in the early fall this time, and he was talking about some theme Tom had sweated over in class. Tom doesn't even remember what the paper was about, but he was hooked. Tom says he's been trying to please people with his writing ever since.

Since then, Tom has seen students of his who appear to have no real desire or talent for writing blossom into fairly competent, hardworking young writers. It's obvious that writing has become important to them because their teacher found good things in what they wrote and told them so. Tom built their confidence just as his teachers had once done for him.

Your second task as a teacher of fledgling writers is to help them find their individual voices when they write. When we deny students their unique, individual voices in their writing and even in much of their speaking, we cut off much of their authentic ways of knowing themselves and the world; we cut off their authentic self-expression. Look at Miller's classic explanation of voice:

> The human voice is the bearer of the human spirit. To still it would be, in effect, to still humanity. . . . [I]t is through language that the individual creates and knows his reality, and it is the human voice that projects that reality into the void. Perhaps our most precious possession and human legacy is the individual voice, but it is up to us to cultivate that voice and to make it heard in what we say and what we write. (1972)

There is a lot of talk in rhetoric texts about *style*, but the writer's style *is* the writer's voice. It is the way writers talk in writing. It is the sense of a unique, individual, recognizable person in the writing. Voice is the writer's hallmark. The immature writers in your class need to write enough in an unthreatening situation to become comfortable with written language so that they can get a feeling for their own voice when they write. In order to do so, they need to practice using their voices on the page, and they need to practice a lot. They need to do a lot of fooling around with written language; they need to play with writing. They need to write *every day*, and they need to try a lot of different techniques and tones and styles when they write. And in the early stages they need your almost unqualified support and encouragement of what they write.

Developing the expressive voice is an essential beginning for immature writers. The idea that only impersonal writing is serious and important, and therefore worth teaching, is nonsense. As Miller argues:

> So many people have been indoctrinated with the view that good writing is primarily "correct" writing, and that the best writing is "objective" and "impersonal" (and therefore devoid of the first-person singular), that there is abroad in the country an "ideal" prose that is so correct, objective, and impersonal that it is almost unreadable. This prose pours out of government offices, universities, businesses; has become a kind of establishment prose; and might be described as prose in the gray flannel suit. It is faceless and voiceless prose: the sound that arises from it is monotonous and boring. (1972)

On the other hand, writing that is readable and interesting is expressive. As Miller and Tchudi (1978) point out in *Writing in Reality*, "The one constant that runs through all good writing is the writer's voice, the distinctive accent transferred from the depths of the self to the blank sheet of paper."

And what does that voice sound like? There is no one answer. Each writer's voice on paper is as distinctive as a speaking voice. But there is always a moment of recognition when you hear that personal and genuine voice coming through someone's writing, as in this freewriting by a student who describes a friend of his from Pearidge, Georgia.

Phagan

Mike Phagen—Mike, Meiguel, Pierre, he's got all kinds of nicknames. Everybody in Pearidge, Georgia, has a nickname or they aren't a real Pearidger. There isn't any set rules for becoming a select member of the Pearidge community—you just have to be accepted by the whole group and not break the Pearidge code. It wasn't written but it was understood. Now, Mikey is what I would call the Prince of Pearidge. People look up to him. People listen when he says anything about anything. In a way he is a legend. He was a dope addict—acid, THC, barbs, reefer—just one of the boys, more or less. Mikey took a liking to me because he saw I had a little common sense—back then a little was a lot cause every other Pearidger had none. Mikey—well—he's not too bright sometimes—like in the bars and discos. I'm talking about with the women. I still laugh when I remember some of his stupid funny lines he uses, especially when he didn't even need to talk at all to get what he was after.

—Richard[1]

Too often we demand that students write about subjects about which they care little (and sometimes know less), and we forbid them to use their own natural voices. Then, we immediately search out every mistake, large and small, that they make writing within these narrow restrictions. And we worry that our students don't seem to have anything interesting to say, and that they despise writing.

We offer some alternatives in this chapter to the "How I Spent My Summer Vacation" kind of writing, and alternatives to the slightly more humane but rarely more successful "Tell Me About Yourself in an Essay" assignment. Expressive writing is not merely writing about personal experience. Because a writing topic has *I* or *me* in it does not mean you will get personal writing. If writing in your class is always governed by topics you pick, you will be disappointed in the results.

Sometimes, students need a concrete prompt to get them going with personal writing. One technique that works well is to use a snapshot. The instructions to students are simple: "Bring in a photograph that is important to you. It will be posted in the room for a few weeks, so don't bring in one that will embarrass you or that is so precious your mother will kill you if something happens to it. No boyfriends or girlfriends, please."

Tom brought in an old snapshot of his father just out of boot camp at Parris Island before World War II. His colleague, JoAnn Lane, brought one of herself in a cowgirl outfit when she was about seven years old. They and their students had an uproarious good time sharing their snapshots. Then, they wrote about the photographs. After the pieces were drafted, edited, and proofread, they put the pictures and writings together up on the walls. For days afterward, it was difficult for Tom and JoAnn to get their students in their seats and away from reading the walls.

Jonathan was a tall redheaded baseball player with an earring and a quick sense of humor. Tom expected him to come in, late, with a photo of himself at some athletic event. He bought in a snapshot of his half-brother, on time. His resulting personal writing was surprising, pleasing, touching, and full of his personal voice.

Brothers

Chad is my brother. Even though we have a different mother but the same father, I still consider him as a real brother instead of a step-brother.

He was born on July 7 on a Wednesday morning. He lived in South Bend, Indiana, with his true mother for most of his childhood. When he was sixteen he moved to Albany with his true father and his step-mother who is my real mother and father.

He is currently married at the age of nineteen to a very nice young lady named Dreama. Dreama and Chad have one daughter named Jordan Nichole. She is almost one year old.

My most vivid memories with Chad occurred when he first moved in with us. I think I wanted to be just like him when he got here. Seeing how he did not know his way around town, I went everywhere with him. I didn't mind being his chauffeur because he was cool, and he had a license.

We probably spent the whole summer together. We had a lot of fun until school started. When school started, I think that was when we started hanging around other people. He started making a lot of friends, most of them girls, and he usually didn't have time for us to go cruising, or he just plain out didn't want to go.

My bother and I are starting to become more "in touch" with one another, but I don't think it will ever be like when he first moved here to be with his father, his step-mother, and his little brother.

—*Jonathan*[2]

The experience of authoring a work is powerful; it builds self-esteem and self-efficacy. When students have authored a work in their own voices, when they have seen readers nod their heads in agreement and in recognition of shared experiences, and when they have received praise for their efforts, they feel as if they "know stuff" that others want to hear and that others will like. They feel like an authority, at least of their own experiences and expressions. That's a powerful and self-enhancing feeling. That is part of the power of writing authentically about subjects that only you, the writer, know best. Initially in the writing class, our job is to help students write in their own voices about their own areas of authority—their own experiences, feelings, and perceptions. We begin small with tasks easily finished, like a freewriting about a person they know. We encourage our students to experiment with written expression, to try out many written forms, to fool around with writing. Instead of demanding an impossible perfection, we encourage trial and error and an attitude of try-it-and-see-what-happens. We encourage students to work beyond their zones of comfort in writing, to start with what they know and like, but then to move into less familiar territory in their writing. In this way, students expand their language and writing repertoires. They are expanding their thinking and learning.

The Journal

One indispensable tool in helping students expand their language and writing repertoires is the journal. We talk more at length about the journal in the next chapter, but we mention it here because the journal provides immature writers with some of the regular practice they need to become comfortable with writing.

In the journal and in the class, the student's experience with writing should be a *daily* affair. Quite simply, the student—especially the one just starting out as a writer—*needs to write every day*. No matter how good the assignment and no matter how inspired the teaching, students cannot develop as writers if they write only once in a long while.

Now before you panic at the idea of a mountain of journals to grade every weekend from 150 or more kids who have written their hearts out every day in your class, calm down. It doesn't work that way. Journals are not designed to be—and should not be—red-penciled. The idea of journal writing is to develop fluency and to eradicate fear of writing. Correcting every error that students make in their journal writing will not promote those goals.

Instead of being corrected, journals need to be read and celebrated and responded to by a real audience—you, the teacher, and fellow students. Peer reading and responding is one way to take the pressure off of you, and the reactions and comments of peers will often mean more to the new writer than will yours. You'll need to develop procedures for peer responding in your classroom. Dawn tells her students that specific comments are more valuable than are generic "good job" responses. She models specific comments such as, "I like the part about . . ." and "I could really relate to the part where you talked about . . ." and "When you mentioned getting your sister's room after she went off to college, I remembered. . . ." *Sharing* writing is important for its own sake and is a powerful motivator for further writing. And if you work it right, peer reading will help you alleviate some of the paper load.

With most classes, Tom required at least five pages of journal writing, a page a day, and collected journals weekly. Dawn usually requires four pages a week and collects them four times during a semester. Of course, the idea is that students will write more than the minimum. Regardless of how often you collect journals, the idea is to feature lots of opportunities for sharing journal writing in class before the journals are collected. We ask for volunteers during the first few minutes of class to read something pithy or funny or thought-provoking from their journals. We provide opportunities for response groups during class, and we have students read to us from their journals during conferences. Because working with journals is so integral to our classes, we know at any given time what each student is writing and the progress she is making with her latest effort.

We do not read papers at home at night, and we do not grade journals on the weekend. We have learned to read during breaks in our day, before and after school, and on the train during the morning and afternoon commutes. We have learned to read fast, to skim journals for the gems of writing that we always find there, and to respond briefly with a question, an exclamation point, or a concise but meaningful comment. Of course, some parts of the journal will connect with you, and that's when you'll respond with more detail and depth, but responding to journals is a way to encourage writers, not note their every nuance. The task is not impossible.

We do assign grades to journals, and we do hold students accountable for the number of pages assigned for the journal each week. We count the pages and give them credit for the percentage of the minimum number of pages assigned that they completed; if they completed the full number of assigned pages, they get full credit. We don't give full credit for half-pages, and we don't give full credit for pages that have exorbitant margins or quadruple spacing just to fill the page. We redirect students who aren't getting the point or following directions. Their journal work is important, and we make sure that students know how and why their journals are important writers' tools. We take time with getting journals started and with making sure everyone is on the right track, we praise the writing, and we make sure that we're hearing from everyone regularly in class during those sharing times before the journals are due. This combination of praise, sharing, responding, and credit for journal writing has been successful for us, and the journals have been invaluable writing tools for our students.

Getting Personal Writing Started

The activities we suggest are designed to help beginning student writers get their thoughts, words, and ideas down on paper, perhaps for the first time. These explorations will help students to become more fluent writers. The emphasis is on the students and on what they have to say in their own voices. These activities are intended as a catalyst to get you and your students started, to give you some initial ideas, and to stimulate your own thinking. Some of these ideas have been around for a while, so you may recognize some of them. In fact, one of our colleagues said to us recently, "Good grief! You're *still* using that old activity? It's such a seventies thing." Well, it may be, but, guess what? Our students, except for some of the ones in college, weren't even alive in the seventies, so it's all new to them—and maybe to you, too. Plus, we have success with these activities and our students respond well to them as writers. Again, select what you like and what works for you, but try out several of them. You just may be surprised with the results.

Freewriting

Freewriting is the bread and butter of the writing classroom. We use it frequently with our students. It is the writer's first and most basic tool. We go back to freewriting whenever students seem threatened by a new assignment, stuck in their thinking, or otherwise in need of limbering up their minds.

Have your students write for ten minutes without stopping or thinking about what they'll say next. The important thing is to keep the words flowing across the paper. They are not to worry about spelling, punctuation, or usage. If they can think of nothing to say, tell them to write "I've got nothing to say" over and over until something occurs to them. This exercise should be repeated for several days initially so that freewriting becomes almost automatic for students and so that they can do it without balking.

High-school students generally enjoy freewriting, probably because it's a nonthreatening way to write, and it removes the restraints. After a while with daily practice, patterns in their writing begin to emerge and individual voices begin to grow distinct. That's why we usually don't assign a topic for freewritings; they are *free*.

Freewriting Variations

Once the students are used to the idea of freewriting, we like to have them play around with some possibilities as they write.

Ask the students to *listen* carefully as they freewrite, recording the sounds they hear around them, or ask them just to concentrate on listening while they keep their writing going without paying particular attention to what they're putting down until the ten minutes are up.

Have them freewrite to music, and use different kinds of music to set different moods as they write. Students particularly enjoy this stimulus, perhaps because they like to ridicule our music choices. Freewriting to rock music changes radically if you switch to jazz and changes even more radically with Beethoven and Tchaikovsky. At first we use only instrumental music so the lyrics will not distract the students, but later we have them freewrite to songs also, reacting to the lyrics as they write. We discuss how the lyrics and musical arrangements of Alanis Morrisette or Billie Holliday or Nora Jones make us feel; we discuss tone and voice and style, all tools of artists, including singers and writers.

For students practiced at freewriting, read them a poem or a brief prose passage and have them freewrite about it without planning or preparation of any kind. This activity is a way to get those gut-level reactions to a piece of writing down on paper. The purpose is to get feelings and ideas out that can then sometimes be ordered, with more thinking and talking, into a more complete paper.

Tom likes the way that Tom Dickinson, a social studies teacher, uses focused writings. His students keep journals in the classroom, and he never lets them take them home. Tom D. is a challenging teacher who asks a lot of questions and never lectures. He likes to work with the whole class. He might stop discussion abruptly in the middle of a heated debate with a well-chosen question and the instructions to "Give me five minutes." Out come the journals, the room is suddenly quiet, and Tom D. and his students write furiously for five minutes. Then he quickly calls on one student after another to read. They cannot comment; they must read what they have written. At some point he will read his, with no more nor less fanfare than he gives each kid in the room. And the questions and the argument continue. Dan starts a new class by asking students to freewrite about *writing*. The results are sometimes surprising. Focused freewriting has almost endless uses in the classroom. It's a learning tool you will want to explore.

Some criticize the disconnectedness of freewriting, but the idea is for the writer to explore a range of ideas and to see what surfaces that is promising for future and further work. The following ideas get students going with writing and with freewriting. Then, periodically, have students cull their journals for pieces worthy of further work and development.

Spontaneous Writing/Quickies

During the first days in class, get students into the daily habit of writing by having them write a Quickie—a half page of writing in ten minutes or less—at the beginning of each class. Personal subjects work well for these. Here are a few suggestions.

1. Given the choice of one, and only one, of these things, which one would you choose? Money, Fame, Friends, Love. Why?

2. Tell about one thing that makes you happy.

3. Tell something that makes you sad.

4. Talk about something you hate.

5. What *color* do you feel like today? Talk about why you picked that color.

6. Tell about your favorite song.

7. Plan the menu for the school cafeteria for a week. You may include anything you wish.

8. If you were a character from a television show, who would you be? Tell about what you would do in one episode of the program.

9. Imagine that you stayed out of school today. Where would you go? What would you do?

10. You are an artist painting your masterpiece, the painting that will make you famous for generations to come. What is the painting? Describe it.

Movie Sound Track

Many short videos are available to teachers that feature particularly well-done or unusual sound tracks with no narration or dialogue. Three of Tom's favorites for this exercise are *Which Is My World*, *The Ways of Water*, and *Homo Augens*. Explore your educational video library and local video store for others.

Many movie sound tracks are available on CD for purchase. Music is being used in lots of creative ways in moviemaking. Many movies are now using popular music as a montage to complement the action of the movie. Additionally, many movie sound tracks are now composed by contemporary artists such as Elton John and Tim Rice, Sting, or Phil Collins, artists whom your students will likely recognize. One of our favorites in this *genre* is Bryan Adams, who composed most of the songs in the movie *Spirit*. Music like that by the artists that we've mentioned in these examples interprets the script, enhancing the visuals of the movie and perhaps even suggesting the visuals. In order to capitalize on this type of composing, play the CD *before* showing the video and have students write an imaginary script to match the sound track. Or they can freewrite using the sound track as the stimulus. Then show the video and have students turn their papers over and record their reactions on the back.

Memory Writing

The purpose of this exercise is to encourage student writers to use their best resource— themselves—as the material for narrative writing and to impose some controls on that material.

Tell the students that they are to concentrate on capturing the essence, the particular detail and feeling, of each incident as they do the activity and not to be concerned with grammatically perfect or complete narratives.

The students are on a fishing expedition into the past, with the following instructions:

You are to go back in time to capture four incidents in your life. Each incident may be important or trivial, but it should be one that stands out in your mind. Record it as briefly as you can, but make it as real as you can.

1. Go back in time twenty-four hours. Remember one incident from yesterday. Record it.
2. Go back in time a week and remember something you were doing on this day seven days ago. Record it.
3. Go back a year for this one and record an incident you remember from about the same time of year. Concentrate on the particular details.
4. Now concentrate really hard and go back as far as you can. Record your first *clear* memory.

We have students look for concrete details and vivid verbs in this writing. How did they make the memory live on the page? What connections do they see among the experiences?

Then and Now

This is another memory exercise with a different twist. Have students look back into their memories and compare a person or place they remember *then* with their perceptions of the same person or place *now*. Here are a few suggestions of good then-and-now subjects.

1. Your backyard when you were six years old and now
2. Church then and now
3. School then and now
4. The family car then and now
5. A close relative then and now

Remember to keep the writings short unless the student gets involved in a memory and wants to continue it. Your purpose at this point is to provide the stimulus to get students started as writers, not to demand long expositions.

Here and Now[3]

You may want to pick a time for this exercise when your students are particularly agitated about something or one of those days when the room seems to buzz with excitement or sinks into a gloomy silence for no particular reason. Ask the students to record the date and the time and write four words that say how they're feeling here and now. Tell them to think about the four words they have recorded and to expand on one or more of them. For example:

March 15, 2003, 3:40 PM. Tired. Anxious. Hungry. Excited. I'm anxious today thinking about the book and whether I can do this right or not. Will people want to read it? This is the second time I've tried to rewrite this chapter. Maybe if I call Dan he can pull me out of it. A deadline coming soon. Besides, what am I going to do with that third period class tomorrow?

It's a good journal exercise, or you may want to do it as a Quickie. However it's used, it helps students get in touch with themselves and gives them something real to say in their writing.

Try several Here and Nows, and choose the best one from each student to be expanded, edited, and published.

People Photos

This activity is a verbal snapshot; it is intended to involve quick, perceptive writings.

Have the students create a number of word pictures of interesting people in interesting situations: the student being admonished in the hallway by a teacher, the President at a press conference when asked a question he didn't like, the kid standing in a rainstorm alone waiting for the bus that is late, the younger sister watching a funny cartoon—whatever. These written photos should be brief, accurate, and as precise as possible. You may want to collect these writings for several days; then, select the best ones to share. Tell students to concentrate on letting their eyes be the camera and their paper the picture.

CIA

This eavesdropping activity is a favorite with students, but do caution them about the types of situations in which eavesdropping may—and may not—be a harmless activity.

Instruct students that when they are in other classes and interesting places around the school such as the front office, the auto repair shop, or the gym, or when they are in other venues with lots of people, such as malls, parks, bus stops, and grocery stores, that they should eavesdrop on the conversations around them. Remind them to be nice, polite, and unobtrusive—just as a CIA agent would need to be.

They are to collect in writing several conversations that they overhear, recording what is said as accurately as they can. You can also expand the activity to include phone conversations. Tell students to eavesdrop on only appropriate conversations, nothing high-stakes, threatening, too private, or too risky. Have your spies share their best conversations.

As a follow-up activity, you may have students take the raw material of their collected conversations and edit the best one into an effective dialogue or vignette.

Portrait

This exercise also encourages close observation and recording details. Have each student observe one of his classmates but without letting that person know he's the subject of the exercise. Tell students they are to concentrate on details that make their subject unique and interesting. Then they are to paint a verbal picture of their subject *without using his name*. Read these verbal pictures aloud and guess the identity of the subjects.

Walking Composition

Dan mentions this activity in Chapter 3, but here's another variation. It's a favorite with students, but it may require administrative approval before you use it.

Give students a choice of three itineraries with specific instructions on the route they are to take from your room to an interesting place on campus and back to the room. Remember to set specific time limits for the walks and for when the students are to return to class.

One of the walks that Tom has used with his students, for example, takes the student down one hallway, around the third wing of the school building, up to the gym where the students are to stay for ten minutes, and back to the classroom by a different route.

Ask students to take the walk alone, or at least not to talk to one another as they walk along and observe. Tell them they are to soak up what they see, hear, and feel, especially watching for the interesting and the unusual. They should make brief notes about their observations.

When they return to class, have them share their observations. Discuss differences in individual perceptions. This activity provides a nice segue to journal writings or short descriptive papers.

Sensory Tour

This activity is a variation of the Walking Composition, but it is less structured.

Send your students out on campus with a definite time limit and the following instructions:

1. What mood are you in?
2. See something smaller than your hand.
3. See something bigger than you are.
4. Hear something far away.
5. Hear something very close.
6. Feel something soft.
7. Feel something rough.

8. Bring back several items that caught your eye.
9. What mood are you in now?

Dan uses this activity to set the tone for nature readings and writings or just to shift subtly the mood of a grumpy class.

Listening to a Place

This simple variation of the Walking Composition can also give good results. Again, alert colleagues and administrators about this activity, or expand it to be an activity that students complete on their own in their neighborhoods.

Ask students to follow these instructions in order:

1. Go to a place you like in or around the school.
2. Do not talk while you do this activity.
3. Listen for ten minutes without writing.
4. Close your eyes for two minutes and concentrate on what you hear.
5. Rapidly write your impressions of the place.
6. Eavesdrop on the people around you and write down some of the things they're saying.
7. Bring your notes back here and we'll turn them into something.

Cemetery as Classroom

Cemeteries are interesting places for writers. Take your students to the local cemetery or instruct them to go there on their own. Then, have them try the following suggestions:

1. Explore, move, and meditate among the living and the dead.
2. Enter some observations and thoughts into your journal.
3. Try a ten-minute freewrite, using something you see or feel to get started.
4. Take a word picture. Photograph a tombstone with language.
5. Using a name you find here, write a first-person narrative or a monologue in which you become that person.
6. Collect some sensory experiences—touch, see, hear, and smell the environment. Capture these stimuli in short phrases.
7. Pretend to interview one of the permanent residents. Ask him or her questions and jot down your answers.
8. Look inside yourself; examine some of your feelings about being here.

The Name Piece

This activity is a favorite with Dan and Dawn, who extensively explore memoir reading and writing with their students. This is the first piece of writing that we usually do within a memoir framework.

First, we read several excerpts from published writers in which they have written about names. Tobias Wolf has a good piece in his memoir *This Boy's Life* about his name, Toby, and about how he once wanted to change his name to Jack. Sandra Cisneros has a piece about the names of her characters, Esperanza and Magdalena, in *House on Mango Street*. Scott Momaday has a piece about tribal names in *The Names: A Memoir*. The Name Piece is out there in published literature; go looking for it.

After we have read and discussed these name excerpts, we ask students to take a sheet of paper and to write each of their names across the top of the page so that each name is a separate column. Then, as in the excerpts, we ask students to jot what they know about each of their names. Who named them? Are they named after someone? Do they like their names? Do they have nicknames? Do their names show up in songs? And so forth. We keep the jotting going for a while, and we complete our name chart on the board as students write their own charts. Then, we briefly discuss the jottings on our name charts with the class. Next, we put students in pairs to tell the stories of their names, too.

After this sharing of about five to seven minutes per partner, we debrief as a whole class. What was particularly interesting in the partner discussions? Did we mention anything similar to what one of the published authors mentioned?

Next, have students write a draft piece that tells the whole story of their names. The next day in class, we share and respond to our drafts. The discussions are lively. Then, we file the draft in our Writer's Notebook (see Chapter 5) for possible revision later and for possible inclusion in our longer memoir pieces.

Not surprisingly, some students don't know a lot about their names. They may need to do some family interviews or conduct some research. The following is a name piece by a student who did just that to find the information she needed to write a rich piece about her name.

Sadiqa Adero Ihsan Edmonds. Isn't that a mouthful? I love my name but it took me a while to be able to say it all at full speed. I first blessed the world with my presence on a Friday, March 2. I was born at 610 Albert Court around noon.

Even though I was born on a Friday, I wasn't named until Saturday, March 10. Of course, my dad had already picked out my names before I was born, but my parents made the decision to name me in a very special African naming ceremony. African names are believed to be very meaningful in a person's life by the people of certain African tribes, so my parents decided to use a variation of the naming ceremony used by one of these tribes.

That Saturday, March 10, a lot of relatives and friends of the family came to participate in my naming ceremony. The first thing that they did was sit in a circle on the floor. My parents were at the head of the circle and everyone else sat around from the eldest to the youngest, the eldest being by my father, and the youngest by my mother. My parents talked about my birth and how my being born would help us as a family. My father whispered my name in my ear, and then announced it to the people in the room. So other than my father, I was the first person to hear my name.

After this my father passed me to the eldest person, who was my Aunt Ossie. As each person passed me around, they each would whisper some words of wisdom in my ear. In the African villages, this was done to show the baby's acceptance into the community. By doing this, my family showed that they accepted me into the family. After this was finished, everyone had a big dinner of certain foods.

The names my dad gave me were *Sadiqa*, *Adero*, and *Ihsan*. *Sadiqa* is my first name. It's Arabic for "friend." My dad chose *Sadiqa* as my first name because he believes that the essence of a relationship both outside and inside the family is a friendship, and if friendships can be formed inside a family it makes the bond stronger than just having the same blood.

My first middle name is *Adero*. It's from East Africa and it means "life-giver." Dad chose this name because he wanted me to breathe life into everything I do and everyone I meet. My second middle name is *Ihsan*. It's also Arabic and means "performer of good deeds." My dad chose this name because he wanted me to do pretty much what the name says, perform good deeds.

My last name is *Edmonds*. I acquired this from my dad. My great grandfather's name was Tony Edmonds but everyone called him Papa Tony. Although his father was a slave owner named Bardlin Edmonds and his mother was an African princess removed from her African village by force and sold into slavery, Papa Tony was not a slave. His mother was given the name Susie Robison by her slave owner.

Although she was subjected to the pursuit of her slave owner, she still had children from the mate of her choice.

Papa Tony was a man who built his own businesses. He built a school and a church for black children to attend. The church is still attended. I was able to see it. The school has been torn down after integration but my dad was able to visit it.

My parents chose to give me African names and to celebrate my joining the family by an African naming ceremony so that I'd have a full appreciation for my African as well as my American heritage. They want me to appreciate what my forefathers have done to overcome their oppression.

—*Sadiqa*[2]

We especially like this starter activity and use it at the beginning of each new writing class for several reasons. One, it helps all of us to learn each other's names. Two, students know more about their names than we do, so they are writing from authority and expertise. Three, this activity is modeled after real, published writing, but remains personal and contextualized within our study of memoir. Four, sometimes students want to learn more about their names, which can lead to Internet research on genealogy websites, looking at the family Bible, or conducting some Action Research on their names by interviewing family members. (See more about Action

Research in Chapter 13.) This piece is a hit with students, who love to write about themselves; they usually spend time revising it, indicating that they value the piece; and the Name Piece almost always makes it into the finished memoir, showing us that it resonates with students.

By the way, the naming ceremony mentioned here in the piece by Sadiqa is very similar to the one portrayed beautifully in a children's book by Deborah Chocolate entitled *On the Day You Were Born.* We recommend that book along with the other sources we named here as good exemplars for use with your students.

Pulling It All Together: The Life Map

Becky Flanigan, a teacher at Westover High School, in Albany, Georgia, took Dan's Road of Life exercise in Chapter 3 and with Tom's collaboration, elaborated it into an effective starter activity for her ninth graders. She began by showing students her Life Map, done on a large sheet of art paper, and briefly told them the stories that went with each drawing. Then she passed out the construction paper and markers, and students did their own. Because hers was carefully done, students took some time making theirs. (A Life Map by Tom is included in Figure 4–1 to illustrate the activity and the kind of detail that can be a part of it.) Then students talked at some length about their Life Maps, telling stories and laughing a lot. The talking was one of the highlights of the class. As usual, only those pictures on the map about which each student wanted to talk were shared. (No, Tom will not explain his to you. Come join his writer's group, and maybe he'll talk about *some* of it.)

Becky modeled this kind of selective storytelling, too, but she didn't stop there. When the Life Maps were displayed around the room, she used them as the basis first for an Anatomy writing and then as a kind of visual card file of memories that could be used for several more writings. Any time students were out of good writing ideas, they could go to their Life Maps.

Becky accomplished a lot in those first three weeks that she and her students worked with the Life Maps. She created a positive, working atmosphere in her writing classroom. She started each student with a major piece of writing that was successful and celebrated by the class. She modeled the working habits of a writer. She got students to laugh and talk to each other and feel good about themselves and to begin to see themselves as a community of writers. For some of the students, it was the first time they had ever been applauded by their classmates and their teacher. Everyone needs that sometime.

Who Owns the Writing?

Once students see that they can write—and that can be a big job itself—what we hear almost at once from some of them is, "What do you want us to write about?"

Figure 4–1. *Life Map*

Years of conditioning have taught them to rely on the teacher for this information. When we tell them that they are the writers, they don't like it. "I don't have anything to write about!" they cry, and the tug-of-war starts. Students try to give the authority for their writing to the teacher. Refuse to take it.

In her observations of classes, Dawn found that students are adept at getting teachers to do some of their work for them. She observed one student say to a teacher, "I don't know what to write." The teacher read what the student had written so far and then made detailed suggestions for what the student should write next. The student, being smart in more ways than one, proceeded to write what the teacher had suggested. The teacher loved the paper. While this is a humorous, if bittersweet story, it points out the overreliance that students have on teachers as idea-givers and as those who control the writing. Break this habit in yourself and in your students if you want them to author their own, authentic writing instead of just churning out your assignments.

This chapter gives you some of the starters we have used to make the job of finding something about which to write less threatening. We have found that these activities are generally catchy and interesting to adolescent writers, but we remind students that these activities are intended to give them practice and to help them find things on their own about which to write. Without that intention and attitude, these activities can become as artificial and arbitrary as those dreadful summer vacation essays. Remember that *the writing belongs to the writer.* Imposing a topic, even a good one, doesn't help the growth of young writers. Your curriculum may demand certain kinds of writing, and you may have to compromise, but there are usually ways to give students some control over the writing while still teaching them how to be successful on the mandated tests required by most districts.

Another notion that may help you is not to be too concerned with originality. Writers steal from other writers. Consciously and unconsciously we copy ideas, techniques, novel twists, even vocabulary we like when we read the works of others. It is natural and healthy for your students to borrow from each other and from their reading. Good ideas are catching, and they should be.

Tom has taught an entire class using no other approach to stimulate writing other than daily freewriting with his students and the journal, along with whatever reading was interesting to them. Read Ken Macrorie carefully and try it sometime. You'll be amazed.

We try to grant our students the authority of the writer over their own writing. We maintain our authority in managing the classroom so it is a safe, friendly place in which to write and share and talk about writing. We also insist that they do write, and we set deadlines. But our only real authority derives from being a writer with more experience than they have who is willing to show them how. Their writing belongs to them.

Notes

1. Richard Poston was a student at Gainesville High School, Gainesville, GA.

2. Jonathan Tholen and Sadiqa Edmonds were students at Albany High School, Albany, GA.

3. The exercise is adapted with significant changes from Sidney B. Simon, Robert C. Hawley, and David D. Britton. 1973. *Composition for Personal Growth: Values Clarification Through Writing*. New York: Hart.

Works Cited

MILLER, JAMES F. JR. 1972. *Word, Self, Reality: The Rhetoric of the Imagination*. New York: Dodd, Mead.

MILLER, JAMES E. JR., AND STEPHEN N. TCHUDI (formerly, Judy). 1978. *Writing in Reality*. New York: Harper & Row.

MORRISON, TONI. 1998. "The Site of Memory." In *Inventing the Truth: The Art and Craft of Memoir*, edited by William K. Zinsser. Boston: Houghton Mifflin.

5

The "J"

I wanted to keep my writing—all of it—in one notebook at a time,
because I was interested in figuring out who I was. I wanted to study
my own mind. I wrote down my mind in the notebook and then read it
later. It was a way to digest myself, all of myself. In the spiral
notebook, my poems were intermixed with my complaints, my
disconnected afternoons, my restlessness—with everything I had to say.

—NATALIE GOLDBERG, *Long Quiet Highway*

The journal is one of those phenomena of English teaching: an instant hit with teachers everywhere. It zoomed like a skyrocket through every instructional cookbook and conference. Seven million teachers used it with their kids on Monday. Like the collage and the "write your own commercial" activities, the "J," as our students affectionately refer to it, has been used and abused at one time or another by most English teachers. Some teachers swear by it; some swear at it. Some do both. As one veteran teacher confided in Dan late one afternoon, "I love journals, but it beats the hell out of me to keep up with 'em." This chapter is dedicated to renewing your interest in the journal and to giving you some ideas for using it without slashing your wrists or filing for separate maintenance.

Simply stated, the journal is the most consistently effective tool for establishing fluency that we have found. True believers swear that the J works on some mystical principle because nonfluent, nontalking, and apparently nonthinking students have blossomed so dramatically through journal writing. We are true believers; growth in fluency sometimes comes dramatically for students who get hooked on the J.

It is possible that students become more and more engaged in journaling because they write about subjects that are important to them. The journal provides opportunities for students to write through their questions, experiences, and imaginings. The writer may feel freer in this place where spelling, punctuation, and usage will not be red-penciled. This is the chance for students to think for themselves, and their writing shows how enthusiastically they accept the challenge.

Look at this example of growth in a before-and-after comparison of a typical low-achieving sixth grader, Claude.[1] Claude's first journal writing was halting and hostile:

I feel good just to be living but
I feel like killing someone
I want to kill someone who
boss me around

One of Claude's last journal entries was in response to a picture. Claude speaks as the character in the picture:

I just got my job being a lawyer. Every Friday we get our pay. This Friday I was happy. I got a raise on my check.

I used to get 150 dollars. Today I got 190 dollars. With my money I went to my car and got in. I was going home and a man stopped my car and pulled a gun in my face. He knew I had some money. I told him I only had two cents. He didn't believe me. He shot me in the wrist. I fell on the ground holding the two pennies. I was out cold. I woke in the hospital. My arm was hanging.

One week later I got out and began work as the same.

Claude's words come easily. He packs his writing with detail. He even includes an ironic twist, "holding the two pennies." The journal has drawn Claude out and changed more than his writing ability. Claude loved the journal and worked faithfully in it.

Why the Journal Works

There are several reasons why the journal works so well for many students. Let's go back to an earlier premise in Chapter 1: All kids have language inside their heads. That stream of feelings and remembrances and hurts and people and successful moments and colossal failures is all up there in their heads. The journal, because it's a private, protected place, becomes an invitation to open up, to explore, to dip into that stream of language. Good journal writing is like fishing in the river of your mind.

Because the J is less structured and more subjective than most school writing assignments, many students find it instantly inviting, even seductive. This seductive quality means that many students will write more frequently and for longer periods of time. This practice effect certainly accounts for much of the journal's magic.

Second, because students use the journal to write about those things in which *they* are interested, they often write with clearer, more powerful language. For all of our careful attempts to choose good topics for students, somehow student writing usually comes off better if the motivation for writing and the topic ideas well up from within the students themselves. The J is an idea market, a place where students explore ideas that interest them alone. They dance their own dance.

Another important feature of the journal is that it is intended for an audience of one. We tell students, "The journal is for you; please yourself." Of course, they invite us to look over their shoulders to see if what pleases them also pleases us and has the potential to please many others. But basically, when students write in the J, they are talking to themselves. Because most school writings pose the teacher as sole audience, the journal represents an important shift. The J-writer becomes the most important critic. Some students who will slop any old thing together for the teacher will take pride and pains to make their journals attractive. Being allowed to write to please oneself is a rarity in school. Developing a distinctive, discernible voice in one's writing demands practice in careful listening. As writers develop this voice, they also develop a heightened sense of audience. By writing and reading and reworking their writing in the J, student writers can make startling progress. When kids first read their journals, they act the way they did the first time they heard their voices on a tape recorder: "Is that me? I didn't know I sounded like *that!*" Becoming comfortable with your own voice in your writing and then working to make it more powerful and understandable is the beginning of important growth as a writer.

Of course, many students fail to find the journal an irresistible place to talk to themselves. Maybe they aren't introspective enough, or maybe they just feel silly doing it. For many of these students, the joy of the journal comes because it gives them a chance for a dialogue with the teacher. A sensitive adult who really listens and seeks to help the writer further explore and clarify thoughts and feelings may be a rarity in the lives of many of our students. We're not suggesting that the teacher become a psychoanalyst or succumb to giving advice or preaching. The journal as a dialogue demands that the teacher be a good listener, nodding occasionally, encouraging, asking for clarification, smiling at attempts with humor, and even acknowledging ambivalence or confusion. Many of our students love to talk. They'll tell you more than you ever wanted to know about anything. The journal is a great place for conversations, and students warm to honest dialogue.

Students also rarely get to know teachers on more than a superficial level, and they rarely reveal much of the core of themselves to adults in positions of authority. The J is an opportunity to connect as people without losing the roles of student and teacher. We can respond to students honestly, personally, and in a caring manner that reveals pieces of our personalities, values, and ideas without taking over those of the student. Students can reveal what they really care about and think without fear of correction, ostracism, or humiliation. The personal level of the journal makes it a dynamic instructional tool without crossing boundaries of student-teacher roles.

What's in It for You?

Let's face it; reading and responding to journals takes time. Even the most dedicated types get burned out on the J. "It's nice to see the students enjoying themselves talking my leg off in the J, but what do I get out of it?" For us, the J is a great source of information about how we're doing as teachers. Even after decades of teaching, we still need feedback on how the class is going and how the students are perceiving us. Students volunteer all kinds of evaluative comments about the English class, and they usually do it in ways we can accept and profit from. You won't need to pass out a class evaluation form if you use the journal—or if you do, you probably won't have many surprises. The students will keep you posted on the good, the bad, and the ugly.

Second, the journals keep us *with* our students. We hate to be in the *out group*. We want to know what's *in* with students; even if we don't want to talk as they do, listen to their music, or wear those clothes, we still want to know those up-to-date allusions and references to use in the class. The journal is a potpourri of new sayings, new looks, new loves, and old feelings. We feel more in touch with our students and their culture (or lack of it) when we read their Js. One thing is sure: It beats reading *Cosmo Girl* magazine, watching MTV, or attending Eminem concerts.

Four Journals

We have been using the term *journal* as if the J appeared as a well-defined, readily agreed-on form. In fact, one of the joys of using the J as a teaching tool is its versatility. A journal is not just a journal, as an examination of the journals of William Byrd, H.D. Thoreau, Mary Hemingway, and Hugh Prather illustrate. More and more journals of writers, artists, naturalists, and housewives are published each year. Check out Ellen Gilchrist, Joan Didion, Anaïs Nin, John Barth, and Loren Eiseley for starters. Put a collection of excerpts together and read these with your students. Doing so will help them find new ways to use journals, and it might give you ideas for classroom assignments as well. Here, we suggest four different journals for four different purposes.

The Writer's Notebook

Most good professional writers keep a notebook, a place where they store ideas, observations, and insights for later use. A Writer's Notebook—we call it the WNB—is a place where writers can add something new every day. The notebook becomes the writer's workbench. The writer returns to the notebook periodically, reviews what's there, selects a project or two, and then works and reworks it. The notebook is a place to save things: a word, a phrase, an unrefined thought, the title of a poem or song. The title of this book and many of the ideas for chapters and activities in the book first surfaced over twenty years ago in Dan and Tom's Writer's Notebooks. In fact, as Tom and Dan reviewed those early entries in their WNBs, it became apparent to them that a book was growing somewhere in those journals even without their knowledge. That's how the first edition of this book was born in 1981. The Writer's Notebook is a miniature greenhouse. If you keep planting seeds and nurturing the ideas stored there, good things happen and the results are sometimes surprising.

The Writer's Notebook does not look much like school writing a teacher could collect and grade. It is often marked by idiosyncratic systems of organization. Writers frequently use codes, shorthand, sketches, and bizarre notations. There's almost always some system of organization to it, but the writer alone may know the system. The key to a good Writer's Notebook is that, like yogurt, it contains active cultures.

Good writers throw nothing away. They put it all in the pot to let it work a little. Maybe only 1 percent of that stuff in the Writer's Notebook will ever be shared with anyone else, but the notes become a record, a chronicle of the winding journey of the writer's mind.

We also want to point out that the habit of writing daily and of storing that writing somewhere to be reviewed at a later date is a fine habit to foster in developing writers. Part of learning to become a writer is learning to work as do real writers (see Donald Hall for a detailed account of how a real writer works), and keeping a Writer's Notebook is a small, but significant, step in the right direction.

The Writer's Notebook has been used most frequently in the schools by creative writing teachers and their students. Because the thing seems impossible to grade and because *creative* is often synonymous with the frivolous or chaotic, teachers have shied away from using it with their students. Actually the Writer's Notebook has good potential even for struggling students, and we believe all students need to experience the joy of the Writer's Notebook somewhere in their schooling. The teacher will need to provide many of the stimuli and be much more active in getting students started and keeping them going, but all students can use the Writer's Notebook with profit.

If you must grade the Writer's Notebook, we suggest using a credit system similar to that discussed later in this chapter for other journals, one that credits students on a check system (check, check plus, check minus) on number of entries or pages, or on creative, thoughtful effort.

Suggested Activities for a Writer's Notebook
- people watching—laundromat, bus stop, bowling alley, skating rink, elevator, cafeteria
- unobtrusive eavesdropping—listen to the public conversations around you and re-create them in the WNB
- observing/describing
- new words/vocabulary
- themes—loneliness/kindness
- poetry—original and published favorites with responses
- dreams
- tag lines
- coinages
- slogans/advertising's false claims
- analogies
- metaphors
- minutiae
- fabul*ous realities*
- *ironies*
- *newspaper stuff*

- *contrasts: light and dark/old and young*
- *dream journal*
- *nature journal*
- *work journal*
- *first lines or titles for stories or poems*
- *reflections*
- *ideas for other pieces*
- *cool quotes*
- *paradoxes* and absurdities

Practice improves performance. Journals provide a place for writers to rehearse and to experiment with subject matter, voice, and form. From these practices, the seeds of essays, fiction, or poetry may sprout. To encourage students to recognize the journal as a source for topics, give some in-class time each week for reworking journal material. Comment on style *and* content. Look for potential. Publish good stuff.

The Class Journal

If you subscribe to the "Write Three or More Times a Week Club," as we do, the class journal (CJ) is a teacher-saver. At the beginning of each grading term, we instruct each of our students to buy a notebook. The notebooks are kept in the classroom, and the students do most of their writing during the regular class period. This journal forms the basis of a daily work grade and simplifies evaluation. We usually start the week off with fifteen minutes of writing on Monday, called Weekend Update. In this assignment the students look back over the weekend, commenting on any significant events or talking about anything they feel like. In the last part of the entry, students may say something about the week ahead. For the remainder of the week, the CJ comes out at the drop of a hat. If we show a video, the students respond in the CJ. If we have a particularly vigorous class discussion, we ask them to do a wrap-up in the CJ. If the principal announces a new policy or if the students feel a recent test was too difficult, out come the CJs so that they can explain their position fully.

The CJ works particularly well for responding to literature. Class discussions are much more enlightening if students have first logged a response to the selection in their CJs. Reading, writing about reading, and then discussing become habits in our classes.

The Dialogue Journal

We have had good success with dialogue journals (DJs). Students write their questions and reflections on a particular work of literature to a partner. Partners read and respond to each other's journals, often engaging in lively exchanges. We find that they get past teacher questions to the heart of the issues that are important to them. Here's a sample of dialogue journal entries from Heidi and Darin. Darin writes first of his reading of Barry Lopez's *River Notes*.

D: This Lopez guy is definitely strange. Is he on something or what? He lies down by the river for two years to get to "know" it. I love that passage where he says, "I place my hands like frogs beneath the water. . . ." Wow! Great metaphor! Do you think he is a naturalist? I mean did he really go out and carefully note how the river comes around the bend? Or is he a poet? He uses so many metaphors. Or is he trying to create myth here with all of his allusions about the heron?

H: I can't quite figure out why we're reading this. Lopez isn't strange, Darin, he's downright WEIRD. I couldn't make any sense of why he was lying around with his ear to the ground until I started thinking about how he was probably trying to hear the pulse of the earth. In metaphor it would be something like listening to the heartbeat of the river. Or is he listening for something more general? I was just wondering if he wanted to hear the heartbeat of nature. I think he is a naturalist. His metaphors all come from nature like the one on hands as frogs that you pointed out. What is the difference in a simile and a metaphor? I thought "like frogs" was a simile? Is the heron a metaphor to something that becomes mythical? I thought it was interesting that you thought it might be mythic. I hadn't thought of that.

D: I've read a little more of this stuff and I'm kind of getting into it. I was really interested in his Log Jam chapter and how he linked all those little stories together. More on that later. Okay, Heidi, always the purist. Yes, technically a simile is a comparison using like or as, and a metaphor is an implied comparison, but that's English major stuff. I think of metaphor as any connection you make. mmmmm . . . O.K. heartbeats of the earth. I am impressed with how carefully Lopez listens to the earth. . . . "the sound of birds' breath rolls oceanic. . . ." Wow![2]

Dawn particularly likes to use a two-column format for DJs. That way, students can more directly see the part of the entry about which a partner is responding.

DJs can also be used effectively by students to respond to readings completed for a research paper (see the following section on project journals) or to current events and issues being discussed in the class. The versatility of the DJ makes it a valuable variation of the standard journal.

The Project Journal

One of the frustrating responsibilities that inevitably accompanies the assignment of a project, novel, or research paper is all of the elaborate checking the teacher must do to see that students are doing the work. That old human instinct to leave everything until the night before it's due is particularly strong in adolescents. Most good teachers reluctantly assume the responsibilities of setting deadlines for note cards, rough drafts, and progress reports. We have found the Project Journal (PJ) to be an efficient way to keep students on track during a project that stretches over several weeks.

GROUP PROJECTS Asking students to work together in a group to prepare a presentation is still a worthy idea. The problems for the teacher are obvious, however. Are they really getting anything done? Who is responsible for what? Is everyone carrying a fair share of the load? The Project Journal can answer most of these questions. Ask each member of the group to keep a PJ throughout the project. Ask students to log their participation in the project, their work dates and hours/minutes, their responsibilities, and their evaluation of the group's effectiveness and progress. Collect these each week, and you have a quick check on how the group is doing. The final entry in the PJ can be a summary essay commenting on how well the project was done and what things the group might do differently. This final essay increases students' awareness of their own effectiveness as a group member, enhances their self-monitoring and metacognitive skills, and gives you some indication of how to evaluate the group's efforts—all valuable information.

NOVELS AND PLAYS Teaching a class novel or play offers another good opportunity to use the PJ. Students enter responses to their reading *as they read*. The responses may be personal observations, questions, feelings, and even digressions. Reading student responses gives the teacher some idea of the thoroughness and the level of comprehension of the reader. The PJ substitutes for frequent threats and pop quizzes and sermons. Collected once a week during an extended reading assignment, the PJ gives you a written record of the student's effort and understanding of the work.

More important than its efficiency as a check on student performance, the PJ gets students to *respond in writing as they read*. You can structure the responses any way you wish. We typically ask for the following types of entries:

- Record new words for vocabulary study.
- Jot down memorable quotes.
- Speak directly to the character and/or author.
- Make guesses about what will happen (making predictions) or what might have happened (making inferences by filling in background information not provided directly in the text).
- Speak as one of the characters.
- Digress into personal experiences similar to those of the character (connecting literature to real-life experiences and showing how literature is a record of life experiences).
- Ask questions, questions, questions.

In other words, encourage interesting and varied responses to the work. Don't let it become a drag. One final incentive: Tell the students you will let them use their PJs to answer your essay questions on the end of the unit exam. Students are then motivated to write more complete PJ entries, and you can expect more detailed responses—maybe even including supporting quotes and page numbers—on your exam.

RESEARCH PAPER: RESEARCH LOGS We hear a groan or two out there at the mention of the research paper. Yes, it's alive and as problematic as ever in schools everywhere. Most veteran teachers who must teach the research paper every year have worked out an elaborate survival scheme with deadlines and checks and handouts. Beginning teachers frequently stumble through the process, vowing to do it differently next year. If you're still looking for a manageable system to teach the research paper, try using the PJ. Because every assignment in the classroom must have a name, we call this a *Research Log*. We ask students to get a loose-leaf notebook and divide it into six sections:

1. A *working bibliography*. Each potential source is entered in complete bibliographic form and briefly annotated, if you'd like. More elaborate notes come in section number two.

2. *Notes and quotes*. This section takes the place of the old note cards and is keyed to section one.

3. *Working outline*. Because it is virtually impossible to outline anything until you know what you want to say, this is a tentative outline that may change weekly as new ideas and materials surface.

4. *Flashes of brilliance*. This is an ideas section. If a student gets a good idea for a beginning or an ending or wants to be sure to remember something, this is the section for such entries. We encourage students to have their own thoughts about the research topic. Cutting and pasting encyclopedia and *National Geographic* quotations is not serious research.

5. *Weekly summary*. Each week the student logs time spent on reading, writing, looking, and thinking. The student and the teacher have the opportunity to observe how research time is spent.

6. *The rough draft*. Ideally, a rough draft grows over time. This section encourages students to write parts of the rough draft whenever they are ready. Sometimes the ending comes first; sometimes a student is ready to write one section before another. Encourage reading and writing *during* the research phase of the project.

Encourage students to share their insights, questions, and discoveries with a classmate as the research paper forms. A live audience helps the writer search through and explain information. This valuable practice gives the researcher a preliminary rehearsal before drafting sections of the paper. One way to do so is to use the Dialogue Journal here. Have students respond to each other, especially for items pulled from sections two, four, and five. Students learn from each other as responders and as fellow researchers, promoting students' growth as thinkers and as reflective researchers. It also shifts some of the burden for idea-sharing and thoughtful response to the students themselves.

We think using the Research Log as part of the process associated with writing the research paper encourages students to do more thinking and writing before the final draft. It also gives the teacher a clearer idea of the students' progress and potential problems during the research process.

Reflections on the "J"

Students anticipate the opportunity to respond to classroom activities and exercises in the J. If we forget or decide not to have them respond, they frequently remind us with a "Hey! Don't we get to write about this in the J?" The J is particularly effective for getting students comfortable with writing as a way of responding. They frequently like to share excerpts from their Js, so writing facilitates talk and vice versa.

As we read journals, we block off sections of writing that speak to us and that resonate with the tenor of the week's in-class discussions. Then, we write "Share?" in the margin. Each week, we invite students to share these highlighted, short, pithy sections with the class. Lively discussion usually follows, and we comment anew on skillful writing techniques or key insights. We also make a point to write "Share?" in each student's journal every two to three weeks, at least, so that no one is left out of the discussion and recognition process.

In addition to being a lively discussion point, the J also holds writing that might be worth a revisit for a longer or more polished piece. Provide some time each week for revision. For Dan, Fridays are rework time. He asks students to select an entry from the week and work on it. We focus on different strengths and weaknesses of their writing each week. Sometimes the focus is on proofreading—working to eliminate surface errors in spelling, capitalization, and punctuation. Sometimes it's on beginnings or endings. Sometimes it's on a particular function of writing: telling, arguing, or describing. Sometimes it's on rewriting for a different audience—the principal, your best friend, or a parent. Sometimes there is no focus; we pick something from this week and rewrite it.

The J is a weekly record of a student's responses to the class. Most of the entries are short and can be read quickly each week. The piece the student selects to rework is read more carefully and evaluated, based on a particular focus. The student writes often; the teacher reads all of it, but spends grading time on only one short selection each week.

The J has taken us away from book reports and pop quizzes and other frustrating devices. If we want to know whether students have done the assigned reading or if they are prepared for class, we ask for a response in the J.

Suggestions for Using the Journal

Because journals are not for all teachers in all situations, we want to make some specific suggestions and reiterate some cautions. Using the journal effectively requires some patience, persistence, and expertise on the part of the teacher. The collected wisdom of teachers who consistently use the journal tells us:

- Journal reading and writing are time-consuming.
- Begin using the journal on a small scale. Set a time limit; two or three weeks is a good start.
- Use the journal in only a couple of classes at any one time.
- Stagger the collection date so that you receive only one class set at a time.
- Use "journal starters" to get your more reluctant students going. Use quotes, posters, poetry, a personal story, song lyrics, or recent events as stimulation.

The journal is a good way to begin the school year or a new class. Or use the journal during a particular unit such as the short story or a Shakespearean play. Find a context for the journal; work it into the normal class routine. We have found that journals work with all levels of students. We have also discovered that when we write a journal *with* our students, we get a better feel for just what it takes to keep a journal. Some tireless veterans always write a journal with their students, sharing entries right along with them. When we do keep a journal going alongside that of our students, we find that we actually enjoy the time within our teaching day to gather our thoughts and write for ourselves.

Other helpful pointers for using Js include:

- Differentiate the journal from the diary—clearly. Use past anonymous students' beginning entries as discussion points.
- Set aside regular class time, such as the first ten minutes of class, for journal writing. We have established a routine that has students enter the room, pick up their journals, and start writing.
- Stimulate journal writing—put quotes on the board, posters on the wall, read poems to them, discuss a recent happening, tell a personal story, play a song you like, or ask their opinion about a class activity.
- Encourage extra entries and digressions in the journal. More is better.
- Include personalized touches in your journal responses that let the students know you're reading them closely. Insert a cartoon or newspaper article that relates to ideas that the student shared in the journal entry.

Responding to and Evaluating the Journal

"But how do you grade the thing?" Sometime during most of the workshops we do with teachers on the journal, somebody raises this question. Grading and the journal are two apparently mutually exclusive processes. Our best advice is to work out a point system (5, 4, 3, 2, 1) or a check system (+, √, –) that gives students credit for their thoroughness, or simply assign a certain number of pages per week. Above all, use a system that deemphasizes evaluation and is quick and easy for you.

Our experiences tell us that some systemized way of evaluating journals will simplify your life and give students a clear idea of what you expect in the journal. We use a simple system, a three-point check. The three criteria for journals in our class are *truthful, thoughtful,* and *thorough.* That may sound like the Boy Scout oath to you, but it works well for us. We use excerpts from the students' own writings to illustrate the criteria. We collect the journals weekly and give each journal a 1, 2, or 3 rating. Unusually good journals get five-star ratings, journal of the week awards, or copious verbal praise in class. We believe such a system is positive and encouraging to journal writers and not overly burdensome to the teacher.

Tom works with a specified number of pages. He requires three to five a week. He offers extra credit for motivation to do more, 2 to 5 points per page. He says, "It's entirely possible for a student in my class to make up a major test score by being involved enthusiastically in the journal. I do pages because it's a quick way. Even if I can't get it all read, I read beginnings and ends and spot-check throughout."

Another idea is to give up on grading and responding to journals altogether. Instead, pair up students to exchange journals and hold partner conferences. Writers mark two or three entries that they would like their partner to notice particularly. Give class time for the pair to discuss the entries and share reactions. Keeping a journal partner for an entire grading period establishes intimacy that pays off in the quality of responses given. The partner conferences wean the students from the "I only want the teacher to comment" syndrome. Some students may still want teacher comments, so you can agree to read one or two pages more carefully when a student especially wants your response.

How you *respond* to student journals is much more important than how you *grade* them. The whole idea of journal writing is to stimulate internal motivation for writing. Our students care much more about the comments a reader makes in their journals than evaluative numbers or letters because they are writing to communicate thoughts and feelings.

Suggestions for Responding
- Be an *active* reader.
- Encourage the student to share excerpts from the journal with classmates.
- Suggest future topics. Notice profitable digressions.
- Ask for permission to publish good stuff to share with other students.
- Be truthful yourself. Respond genuinely as *you.*

- Write an extended response, a short poem, or ask questions.
- Avoid empty comments like "interesting," "nice," or "good idea."

Problems with the Journal

Veteran users of the journal have no doubt encountered all of the following problems. One good piece of advice is to talk with an experienced journal user before you begin using journals yourself. If you've never tried the journal before, however, you may appreciate a short digression about potential pitfalls.

PROTECT THE PRIVACY OF THE JOURNALS Don't ever read them aloud to other teachers or students and don't ever publish excerpts without the author's permission. The surest way to lose the honesty and openness of journal writers is for them to find out their trust has been violated.

BE HONEST WITH STUDENTS Sometimes students tell you more than you want to know. Detailed accounts of sexual adventures, drinking in the parking lot, and smoking dope in the restrooms may be honest writing, but when a parent finds his child's journal with such entries and sees your nonjudgmental comments in the margin, you may get called on the carpet for failing to uphold conventional morality and maybe even some laws. Whenever students tell us things we don't want to hear or use unacceptable language or make obscene offers, we tell them to "cut it out."

CONFIDENTIALITY Some students begin to see the journal as such a personal vehicle for writing that they almost forget your forays into their journals for class purposes. These students may be writing about very personal matters that they don't want you to read, and quite frankly, that you'd just as soon not read. Offer students the option of folding such a confidential page in half—maybe even stapling it—as a way of signaling you not to read that page. Naturally, we caution students to use this option only occasionally, and we honor the bond of the folded page.

We suggest that you very explicitly and clearly remind students that teachers—including you—are required by law to report to the proper authorities certain breaches of laws and of students' safety. Cases of abuse and of certain sexual encounters, for instance, must be reported to the appropriate agencies in most states. Encourage students to seek professional help and the proper interventions for serious problems in their lives. After all, this is an English class, not psychotherapy.

LOOK FOR SOMETHING GOOD Sometimes you get journals from students you don't like. These kids' values are quite different from yours. Their writings rub you the wrong way. Try to find something positive to say. Don't give up on the kids. If they are writing, there is hope. If they lean back against the wall in sullen isolation, you don't have much of a chance to help them.

AVOID SARCASM It's easy to get discouraged with students when you know they're doing only the bare minimum. You know they have ability, but they slop any old thing in the journal and you see very little happening. Don't make nasty comments in the journals. Be patient; stay with it. They may have more ego involvement in their journals than you think. We have found that consistently and persistently responding as a real person to students' writings eventually lures most students into a genuine exchange.

TAKE A BREAK—AVOID BURNOUT If the journals start getting stale or if you find yourself running out of enthusiasm, stop them for a while. Don't burn yourself or your students out on the journal. It's too valuable in the writing class to kill through overexposure. Similarly, if you're burning out on responding to the journals, but your students are still enthusiastic about writing them, switch to using students as responders as described under the Dialogue Journal and/or Evaluation sections discussed earlier in this chapter.

A SUCCESS STORY Teachers are a strange lot. They are masters of delayed gratification, and the happy ones have found ways to let a few dramatic successes cover the sadness of their failures. Dan's favorite journal success story comes from a former student, Charles. As a first-year teacher, Charles found himself in a very difficult teaching situation. His students were openly hostile and the administration ineffective. He decided quite idealistically to win his students over with the journal. Charles tells the story in a letter:

> I wanted to start the quarter off with something really different and catchy, but I quickly found out that so many things I considered fun and exciting were considered a bore by the kids. Luckily, I decided to use the journal. The results those first days were fantastic. I encouraged complete honesty and emphasized that I would not hold any cuts about me personally against the student. The kids were really puzzled about this journal bit. Obviously, they had never heard of a journal. But I could not believe the response I got. After they found their work was strictly confidential and that I honestly would not hold anything against them and that I did not grade them as such and even resisted the strong temptation to correct their spelling and grammar—a temptation you will probably feel in reading this letter—they began to really get into the journal. I honestly believe that I know more about many of my students and their feelings than other teachers who may have known them for years. Also, the journal gave me much feedback on the impression I was making and the teaching job I was doing. In addition, I think I may have discovered a "basic kid" who is a gifted writer—though I will admit my inexperience in making such judgments.
>
> After my first week I took all the journals home. I was exhausted spiritually, physically, emotionally, and mentally. I had been through a living hell. I picked up a journal. It said "Our new teacher is so dumb! He gave a stupid vocabulary test, and everyone cheated like crazy, but he has such a big nose and is such a midget that he could not see. This class is such a bore." I wanted to cry. Instead I wrote back. "Thanks for sharing your thoughts with me. I appreciate your honesty. I wish I could get in the circus with my giant nose, but I have been unsuccessful. Anyway I enjoy teaching and enjoy having you in my class." I put a smiling face at the end. The next week this girl wrote on Friday in her journal, "Good-bye! I am really going to miss you

this weekend." Later the next week her parents came to Open House and said, "Margaret said 'Mother, you will *really* like Mr. Walker!' "[3]

Similarly, Dawn is always amazed at students' enthusiasm for the journal and at their appreciation of the ways in which writing the J helps them to grow as thinkers and writers. Every semester, Dawn asks her students what aspects of the course content and assignments she should consider omitting and which she should definitely retain. Overwhelmingly, students tell her to retain the journals. Even the students who didn't always write all of the required number of pages or who struggled with their Js want it kept in the course. Here's a typical comment from a student:

> I really like the journal because I get to think in there and I can write what *I* want. I feel good when you write neat comments back to me, and I like how my peers responded to my writing. Sometimes I did it at the last minute, but I was always proud that I wrote that much, and now I can read back over my journal and see what I was thinking. It's going in my drawer with my high school yearbooks and photos. I'm really, really glad I did it.[4]

We are, too.

Notes

1. Claude Patton was a student at Clarke Middle School, Athens, GA.

2. Heidi Anderson and Darin Weyrich were students at Boise High School, Boise, ID.

3. Charles Walker. Personal letter to Dan Kirby.

4. This comment came from a student, who asked to remain anonymous, who was in Dawn's Freshman Composition class at the Metropolitan State College of Denver.

Work Cited

GOLDBERG, NATALIE. 1993. *Long Quiet Highway: Waking Up in America*. New York: Bantam Books.

6

Different Voices, Different Speakers

Voice is at the heart of the act of writing. As the writer moves from talking into writing, she tries to hear clearly the flow of language in her head and capture it on the page, hoping you will hear her talking to you and be moved by what she has to say. That tension between *I* as writer and *you* as audience, created by the distance between writer and reader, is the dilemma and the generating force of every writing act. *I* write because *I* have something to say to *you*. This chapter concentrates on the *I* of the writer.

When you read good writing, you *hear* the sound of another human being talking to you. A writer's *style* is the *sound* of a voice on the page. The natural place to start with a beginning writer is with his or her own voice. Early on in working with writing processes, beginning writers need to learn how they sound when they write. Our job as teachers is to help student writers find a voice in each piece they write. Alice is a young writer who has found a voice with a clear tone in this moving and personal piece.

> I once felt like writing a poem about the moonlit door. Or the wooden lady whose face holds more secrets than her mind can speak. Or since silent spring never leaves, spring will always come.

I once felt like writing about broken colored glass lying on a clear floor with the sun sparkling. I thought of mysteries with passwords to unknown hideouts. And human detectives with houses of dreams where there lives an old-fashioned girl that is someone's little princess. And when she glimpses that girl in her mirror, her wonderland through the looking glass will hold love for little men and little women.

I once felt like writing about closing doors and opening windows, learning to pretend, to live in fantasy, of courage and war and love that I have not felt but that will be tomorrow's poem. For then it will be today and I will learn of love to come. For tomorrow is the future of today.

—Alice[1]

Alice is able to use voice very effectively for so young a writer. There's more involved here than just using the first person "I" in the writing. Unlike Alice's "Babysitting" piece found elsewhere in this book, this prose poem has a more serious subject, pondering the mysteries of growing up; it's a little melancholy, but hopeful, even though her irony flickers in places in this piece, too. Her two pieces are very different, but Alice has been able to find a voice for each that we hear clearly when we read them. The voices are individual and identifiable as Alice's in both writings, and she has found the right voice for each experience.

Hal demonstrates his sensitivity to voice in this short piece.

Staying Alone

I know when I left that I left the light on. And that paper wasn't on the floor. Someone is in here, I know it.

Oh, don't fool yourself, no one got in.

I guess you're right. I'm just nervous. I'll just lock the door, the windows, and check under the beds and in the closets. No one got in.

I know I heard a voice when I finished washing my face and hands. And I know someone is here.

Ah, you're doing it again, no one got in.

No one got in. That's easy for you to say. You're just me, I'm you. And I'm scared. I guess I'll just watch *Saturday Night* and fall asleep.

No one got in.

—Hal[1]

Hal talks to himself with one voice that is afraid, the other reassuring—and both voices are his. "You're just me, I'm you." We hear throughout the piece the sound of a fallible, very human person.

Our approach to writing instruction helps students to discover and strengthen their individual voices in their writing. A great deal of practice writing about subjects close to them and important to them is necessary. Giving them choices in the writing class, the freedom to explore their own expressions in their own way, is also important. Your genuine, positive response to the good in their writing is essential, more important than anything else you do. In your responses to their writing, listen for students' effective voices and point out for students indications of their effective use of unique, authentic, and personal voices in what they have to say in writing. Watch for opportunities to make comments to your students such as, "This is *you*," and "This *sounds like you* talking" as you read their work. Mark their papers to indicate where they sound real, genuine, like themselves. Use every opportunity in class to point to passages in their writings that clearly reveal their voices. Have students ask themselves after they have completed a piece, "Does this sound like me? Can I hear myself in this paper?" Do whatever you can to create an environment in which students are aware of, and encouraged to use, authentic voices in their writing.

Because being aware of their voices in writing is so important to young writers, we don't believe you should try to move student writers away from personal expression too early in their development as writers. Don't be too anxious to get them through the personal stuff and on to the "serious business" of *real* writing. Any writing that is *real* to the good writer is personal. Accomplished writers do not remove themselves from what's important to them. Even a writer as formal as Henry James had this advice for young writers:

> Oh, do something from your point of view; an ounce of example is worth a ton of generalities . . . do something with life. Any point of view is interesting that is a direct impression of life. You each have an impression colored by your individual conditions; make that into a picture, a picture framed by your own personal wisdom, your glimpse of the American world. The field is vast for freedom, for study, for observation, for satire, for truth. (1889)

Encourage students to write from their own point of view, to use the unique expressions of their individual voices so that they can create their pictures of experiences with their written words.

Hearing *All* of the Voices

Each student in our classes is unique. They have differing opinions, looks, perceptions, religions, cultures, experiences, mannerisms, and methods of expressing themselves. Some of them are monolingual; some bi- or trilingual. Some speak English as a native language; some don't. Whatever the student knows from personal experience impacts what he writes. The language that flows inside his head impacts what he writes. Whatever he reads impacts what he writes. His dreams and aspirations and values and beliefs impact what he writes. It's the same for all of us. We are unique, and our writing rings with authority when we delve into what we know and what we care about for our writing.

The diversity in our classes is a source of richness. Tap students' varying experiences and languages and cultures and viewpoints and knowledge bases to enrich the conversation and then the writing in your classes. When students bring the full force of their complete backgrounds into their writing and into the conversations that surround their writing, their voices ring with greater authority, the writing resonates with

78

readers, and the power of the written word again asserts itself as a powerful tool for learning and for human expression.

As you read the remaining sections on voice in this chapter, ask yourself how you can help each writer in your class tune his unique voice, express himself from the power base of his culture and language and experiences, and use his voice to connect with his readers. When students feel that authority and power, they understand the value of becoming writers—not just for today and not just in your class—but for life.

Tuning Your Voice

Although mature writers have a voice on the page that's relatively constant throughout their writing, they adapt their voice in a particular piece of writing to their purpose and to the anticipated demands of their audience. In a way, the workings of purpose, audience, and voice are so inextricably mixed in the act of writing that they can't be separated. However, it's important for us to focus on voice as the aspect of writing closest to the writer. Once they begin to find their voices in writing, student writers further need to find out the range of their voices and what their voices can do.

It's more difficult to talk about a writer's use of voice and exploring ways of using voice than to show it in operation. Listen to this:

> The legend of Junior Johnson! In this legend, here is a country boy, Junior Johnson, who learns to drive by running whiskey for his father, Johnson, Senior . . . and grows up to be a famous stock car racing driver. . . . Finally, one night they had Junior trapped on the road up toward the bridge around Millersville, there's no way out of there, they had the barricades up and they could hear this souped-up car roaring around the bend, and there it comes—but suddenly they can hear a siren and see a red light flashing in the grille, so they think it's another agent, and boy, they run out like ants and pull those barrels and boards and sawhorses out of the way, and then—ggghhzzzzzzzzhhhhhhggggggzzzzzzeeeeeeeeong!—gawdam! there he goes again, it was him, Junior Johnson! with a gawdam agent's sireen and a red light in his grille! (Wolfe 1963)

There is no mistaking the voice of Tom Wolfe. Like the voices of other traditional classic and modern classic writers, his voice rings true decades after it was written. The excitement, the feigned innocence, even the sound effects make us hear the experience as though we were sitting around in a North Carolina country store, listening to a backwoods orator tell us about "The Last American Hero" and how he fooled the revenuers that time. But when Tom Wolfe talks about Las Vegas, his voice changes.

> This is Raymond talking to the wavy-haired fellow with the stick, the dealer, at the craps table about 3:45 Sunday morning. The stickman had no idea what this big wiseacre was talking about, but he resented the tone. He gave Raymond that patient

arch of the eyebrows known as a Red Hook brush-off, which is supposed to convey some such thought as, I am a very tough but cool guy, as you can tell by the way I carry my eyeballs low in the pouches, and if this wasn't such a high-class joint we would take wiseacres like you out back and beat you into jellied madrilene. (1963)

This time the pace is slower, and we hear the deliberate sarcasm of a jaded crap dealer, a "very tough but cool guy."

The voice is always Tom Wolfe's; it is his trademark and not to be duplicated. Yet, he alters his writing voice to put us closer to one experience or the other. He adapts his voice automatically to suit his purpose. That's what skilled writers do; that's what makes their writing resonate with readers across time; and becoming flexible and adaptable with their voices is what we can teach our student writers to do, too.

Exercises for Tuning Your Voice

Too much of what we teach in school is not a voice people want to read; it's only one expository voice, and a limited, restricted one at that. Compare, for example, the five-paragraph formula theme with the exposition of Tom Wolfe. The activities that we suggest here will encourage your students to grow stronger in their own voices, to be more aware of what their voices can do, and to move away from that impersonal school voice that James Miller classically calls "the prose in the gray flannel suit" (1972).

One caution is in order, however, when you use these activities. They're not merely clever activities for students to do that you take up to read and return with a grade. The emphasis in the class should be on "hearing" the sound of the voice in the writing. That means that the writings need to be shared *aloud*, and they need to be *discussed in some detail* in class. A great deal of reading aloud and much open discussion about what is distinctive and interesting, moving or funny, personal and unique are necessary if these activities are to be helpful in showing student writers what their own voices can do.

A supportive atmosphere in the classroom is absolutely essential when you talk with students about their voices in their writing. Remember that the point of all of the activities in this chapter is exploration and experimentation. The point is to work on fine-tuning writers' voices, *not* to produce a finished product. Think of the singer who warms up her voice prior to the concert; that's what we're doing here: warming up student writers' voices.

We'll talk about this first short writing activity in some detail to show you how we approach the subject of voice with our students.

Mad Talking, Soft Talking, Fast Talking

This activity has its origins in a book by Gunther (1978). The purpose of this activity is to let students experience something of the range of their writing voices, their capabilities, and to see inductively that they use a variety of stylistic devices in their writing, automatically adjusting them to the use to which they're putting their voices. It shows them how purpose influences voice in specific ways.

Unlike most activities, we don't begin this one with an example of the kinds of writing we ask students to try. The idea is to show students the techniques they use automatically and intuitively in their own writing. We want to start with what they do, and we draw examples from their writings as we discuss their inductive knowledge of voice in writing at the conclusion of the activity. The three short writings in the activity are done quickly as freewrites.

Mad Talking

We ask students to think of someone or something that makes them very angry. "Who is someone who really makes you mad? Don't say the name out loud; just *think* of the person. Or maybe there's some *thing* that makes you madder than any person—your neighbor's aggravating dog, inconsiderate drivers, people with full grocery carts who try to go through the express checkout lane, something like that. Think of it. Or maybe it's a *situation* that really steams you—like some rule here at school, or maybe something you've seen on the news that's going on in the country or the world. Think of that." We give them a few minutes to pick a specific subject. We ask them to close their eyes for a few seconds to see their subject and feel mad about it. We even ham it up a little—"Concentrate *hard!* Grrrr—Oh, that makes you sooo mad!" Then, we give them five minutes to say in writing the angry things they feel about that person, thing, or situation.

Soft Talking

Next, we ask the students to think of a person or thing in need of comforting. "You know, someone who's been hurt or who is in trouble or who is suffering in some way. Or maybe it's an animal—a pet hit by a car, or one that's sick—or even something not alive that you feel sorry for. I feel sorry for my old car lots of times. Concentrate on that person or animal or thing and feel sorry." We have them close their eyes again and visualize their subject for a few seconds. Then, they write for five minutes to comfort that person or thing.

Fast Talking

The third writing we have students do during the class period is to persuade someone to do something or to believe something. "Think of somebody you want to talk into doing something. Maybe you want your parents to buy something for you, or maybe there's somebody with whom you need to argue in order to win them over to your side. Maybe you need to explain that last grade report. Be irresistible. Be seductive." We have them visualize their subjects and concentrate on winning them over. Then, for five minutes, they write their most persuasive argument to that person.

Follow-Up

With this activity, talking about the writings is the key to its success. We have students share their writings with a partner and talk about what they hear in the different voices to match each rhetorical situation. Then, we call for a few volunteers to read aloud a piece or two, and we discuss how the voices change and differ in each situation. We make three columns on the board for *Mad Talking*, *Soft Talking*, and *Fast Talking*, and we list under each the stylistic devices used in each kind of writing as they appear in the papers as they are read. We concentrate on only one or two outstanding examples in each paper, and we try to include as many students as possible in the sharing and discussion, without intimidating the shy students. Our point here is to show students inductively that they all use a variety of techniques as part of their writing voices.

Some of the stylistic devices you can expect to hear in the three kinds of writing follow. These examples are taken from one ninth-grade class.

MAD TALKING loaded language, abrupt sentences, repetition of key words and phrases, sometimes invective, sometimes profanity.

> I hate you, you little shrimp. You think you're so good at everything, but everyone knows how stupid you are. You're always trying to copy someone else, but it never works. Everyone hates you because they're saying things behind your back and always talking dirty about you.
>
> —*Kevin*[2]

> I hate this person. I think he's a pain in the butt. He makes me downright sick. He is so ugly, and he has greasy hair. He never takes a bath. He stinks all the time. I hate him so much. I think I'm going to puke. Just thinking about him makes me sick. He thinks he's really cool. He even thinks he's good looking, and he also thinks I like him. *Yuck!*
>
> —*Karen*[2]

SOFT TALKING repetitious, rhythmical sentences linked with conjunctions and little punctuation, a slower pace, often empathy and reassurances.

> Bill, you don't need to run! You broke the law and you need to admit to that. You're old enough to understand what I'm saying. I've tried it and it doesn't work. Please confess to the court and I'm sure that they'll understand. See, if you stay then the judge will know for certain that what you say to him is true. Just tell him what really happened and he'll understand, I promise. Everything will work out and I know it will if you'll just face it. Please. . . .
>
> —*Lisa*[2]

> Pussycat, it's going to be all right and your leg won't be broken forever. It will heal. Now you lie down and rest for a while. I'll bring you some food later after you wake

up again. It's OK. The cast will be off in about two more weeks and by then you will be able to walk on it. You just stay right there and go to sleep now.

—*Patti*[2]

FAST TALKING logical, parallel sentence patterns; strong, active, or imperative verbs.

This is only a mid-term progress report. It will get better by the end of the quarter. I will start doing more homework. You don't know how hard it is. Just because you're so smart doesn't mean I should get straight As. Teachers are a lot harder now. I've been trying real hard. I can't try much harder. Just because my sister has so much homework doesn't mean I should. I have different teachers, you know. I promise these grades will be better at the end of the quarter. If you ground me, it won't help my grades.

—*David*[2]

Momma, please let me go out with him. You said yourself he was a nice guy. If he's such a nice guy, why don't you let me go out with him? Don't tell me I'm too young and I can't go out until I'm 16. I know, but I still want to go out with him. We won't do anything. He just wants to take me out. Please let me go, *please!* Well, what if Sheila and Jill and their boyfriends go out with us? Then will you let me go? Please, you just got to let me! *Please!*

—*Karen*[2]

As you do this activity, be aware of metaphor, kinds of repetition, rhythms, onomatopoeia, sentence length, and verbs. Ask your students to listen to differences among the kinds of writing and the various voices of their classmates and to describe the differences in their own way. Often, they'll catch features of the writing that distinguish each voice and each style.

Evaluation

Because we deal with students' personal voices in a quickly done first draft in this activity, we don't grade the papers. However, we do take up the writings and point out more of the outstanding stylistic devices in our written comments. Or sometimes we simply underline examples to share with the class the next day.

Talking Back to Yourself

Read Hal's "Staying Alone" to your students and talk about the two voices he uses—one afraid, one reassuring—rather, the *two sides of his own voice* arguing with each other. Tell the students they're to write a dialogue in which they say something and talk back to themselves. Help them brainstorm ideas for the dialogues. Here are a few ideas to get them started:

1. You're about to do something you know is wrong.
2. You have just wrecked your father's car.
3. You're going to ask that special someone for a date to the school dance or to the movies.
4. You have money for a new CD, but which one will you buy?
5. You skipped English class yesterday. Debate with yourself about what you'll tell the teacher today.
6. Your parents expect you home at a certain time on Saturday night. You're *two hours late*. The lights are on, and you know they're up waiting for you.
7. You've just been kicked out of class and are waiting in the assistant principal's office.
8. Your girlfriend is pregnant.
9. The police have just pulled you over for speeding. The officer is walking up to your car.

Here's a dialogue with herself that Tami, a ninth-grade student, wrote on a different subject.

Here comes the teacher, she's passing out the report cards now.
I know I'm gonna get an A, I've gotta get an A.
  What if I get a B or C?
  Naw, I'll get an A. I did all of my homework. Most of it. Well, some of it. Homework's not important anyway. Besides, this class is a snap and the teacher likes me, I think.
  She's coming over to this side of the room. It's gotta be mine. Whew! Thank goodness. But here she comes again. She's coming toward me, she's looking straight at me. It's mine!
  She handed it to me folded. Should I look at it?
  Yeah, I better. What if it's bad? I'll die.
  It's gotta be good, at least a B.
  If it's good why did she fold it?
  I'll look, good or bad. I gotta look at it sometime.
  An *F!* I got an *F!* I knew she hated me. God, what am I gonna do?
  I'll lose it on the way home.
  Naw, with my luck my little brother would find it and take it home.
  Man, I'm getting out of this class next quarter. My dad's gonna kill me!

—*Tami*[2]

Have students write the papers quickly (thirty minutes is usually sufficient to draft them), and use the remaining time in the class to follow up by having some of the papers read aloud. Talk with your students about the two voices in the papers and how they are different. Discuss how they shift registers as they change point of view.

Have students put the papers in their Writer's Notebook for possible revision later.

How to Say "I Love Thee"—Let Me Count the Ways

The idea of this activity is to explore ways of saying the same thing in different forms and media. Ask students to express "I love you" in these forms: a poem, a song, a brief essay, a letter, a telegram, a drawing, a greeting card, a film script, and/or a collage. Share some of the results, and talk about how voice and form change with the medium.

An alternative is to say "I hate you" in the same range of media suggested.

Trying on Other Voices

Even though most of us cannot truly write as do our favorite authors, even when we try, we can learn much about voice, style, and the craft of writing when we study closely what published writers do, how they connect with their audiences, and how they establish their signature styles. Therefore, a time-honored method of good writers in perfecting their own style is to model their writing after that of authors they admire. We're definitely not suggesting that we go back to the copy books of an earlier age, nor are we suggesting that students learn to write by following the examples of Milton, Swift, or Franklin; but there's nothing wrong—and much to be learned—with having students' trying out the techniques of the masters.

Select a favorite passage from a classic work or from a contemporary classic. The passage might include pithy dialogue, vivid descriptions, intense emotion, vibrant action, or some other hallmark that students can identify. Discuss the style of the author with students. What makes the writing work? What makes it *classic*? How do audiences today view the author's style as compared to audiences during the time when the work was first written? After this analysis and discussion, have students select a subject about which the author might have written and try to write in the author's style and voice, but not in the author's exact words.

Dawn has found that memoir and nature writers work well for this activity, as do authors who write about more controversial topics, such as Mark Twain, Toni Morrison, Alice Walker, Henry Louis Gates, Jr., Sojourner Truth, Norman Mailer, or Truman Capote, just to name a few. Of course, this activity also works extremely well for students as they work on multigenre papers. (See Chapters 13 and 16 for more on the multigenre paper and resources.)

Contrasting Voices

Another technique accessible to students for stretching their voices is putting on the voice of someone else. Ease them into creating a *persona* with this exercise.

Remember that the point is again the experience and not a polished, professional product.

Give students these instructions.

Write about a *situation* twice, as two different people in that situation would see it. Each time you are to be one of the persons in the situation and speak with that person's voice. You may put your people into any situation you like, but here are some choices of characters for you to use:

1. A local and an out-of-towner
2. A man and a woman
3. A young kid and an old person
4. An impractical idealist and a down-to-earth realist
5. A worker and the boss

Your students, of course, should be free to suggest their own contrasting characters. Tell them first to visualize each person in the situation and to imagine that person talking before they begin to write. They'll also find it helpful if they use the first sentence of each contrasting voice to set the scene and get into the character. As they write, check to make sure they're using the first person. Often *I* will switch to *he* or *she* before they finish a piece. Emphasize again that they're speaking with the character's voice.

The finished pieces should be read aloud in groups of three or four students. Instruct the members of each group to underline the words and phrases that indicate that the author was speaking with the character's voice.

Keep realistic expectations. Even professional writers find it difficult to keep a *persona* in character and sounding authentic. Your students will enjoy this kind of writing, but they'll require a great deal of practice before their characters begin to have a personality of their own. The point is for students to stretch their own writing voices, not to become novelists.

Getting into Another Speaker

Ask students to interview an older person whom they know (a grandparent, an aunt or uncle, or a family acquaintance). Brainstorm with them a brief list of questions to ask to get the interview started before they go hunting with their tape recorders.

Once the interviews are taped, tell the students to write a *monologue* based on the tape, or at least part of it, in which the *speaker* is the older person interviewed. In the monologue, the student writer should try to capture the personality of the interviewee by trying to catch the sound of the speaker's voice.

This activity usually works best when students work in pairs—one to handle the tape recorder and one to conduct the interview. Sharing ideas and perceptions also helps in writing the monologue.

Collecting Dialogues

Another activity for partners, this one concentrates on careful listening to speakers and writing for an audience. Send students out in pairs to do some eavesdropping around the school. Or, for homework, ask students to go to the mall or to hang out at a fast food restaurant to do their eavesdropping. Instruct them both to take notes for better accuracy and to collect several real dialogues that are funny, interesting, or bizarre. Then they're to write up their best dialogue. They may make it longer, more dramatic, funnier, or stranger than it was in reality. But they're to write only the dialogue, leaving space for needed exposition to be filled in later.

Each pair of writers then reads their dialogue to a listener recruited from the class. As they read the piece, they're to supply information the listener needs to understand and enjoy the dialogue. Groups can cooperate with one another by swapping listeners and taking turns reading dialogues for reactions.

The fourth step is for the partners to add to their dialogue whatever explanatory notes, scene setters, speaker identifications and descriptions, and stage directions that an audience needs. In essence, they turn the dialogue into a little drama by adding whatever exposition is needed.

Finally, the finished products may be performed for the whole class. The object is to observe, collect, and create authentic conversation, not to write a play.

On the Phone

This activity is a different slant on Collecting Dialogues that Dan has used successfully with his students.

Give your students a week to collect one side of a telephone conversation. Tell them to position themselves unobtrusively near a phone at home, in a coffee shop, or some other public place—anywhere the phone is likely to be used a lot and they can eavesdrop without being obvious. Or, they can frequent a busy spot in town, such as the food court at the mall, and eavesdrop on cell phone conversations that they overhear. Suggest that they have paper, pencil, and books with them so it will appear they're doing a school assignment. They should sit with their backs to the phone or to the person talking, if possible, so they can listen and take notes without being observed.

At the end of the week, have the students bring their collected conversations to class. They are to select their best monologue and then put together a complete one-sided phone monologue to read to the class. Tell them to add whatever exposition is needed for the piece to be clear and effective, such as scene-setting descriptions, pauses or long silences, and mannerisms of the speaker—"She listened breathlessly," or "He twisted the phone cord nervously." However, they should take out or change any names in the monologues to avoid identifying their subjects.

Share the papers, reading them aloud and talking about the way authentic voices are captured in writing.

This activity, like others in this chapter, can be used as a preliminary to more sophisticated writing tasks later, and students usually enjoy doing it. But more important, as they listen carefully to the sounds of voices around them, try to capture voices authentically on paper, read their attempts aloud, and hear the voices again in the reading, they're building their own intuitions as writers through practicing the basic skills of writers.

Who Owns the Voice?

This activity leads students into the rather sophisticated techniques of *tagging* a character. It requires the skills of detail selection, repetition, dialogue, and pacing. For that reason, we suggest you use it after your students have had a good deal of practice with voice in writing and are beginning to have an intuitive feel for voice when they write.

Have students write a brief piece, trying to capture the voice of someone known to the entire class, such as the school principal, the football coach, the Latin teacher, a TV personality, a famous politician, or a local radio personality. Ask them to pick someone with distinct speech mannerisms. They're to write the piece as a short monologue using *I* and assuming the voice of their subject. Then, read the papers aloud without identifying the speaker. The class tries to guess who owns the voice.

Follow up the activity by selecting two or three of the best or most interesting monologues and asking *what the clues are* to the speaker's identity in each case. Make a list on the board of key phrases and word choices that identify the speakers, and point out important uses of repetition in the writings.

Then use a recording or a videotape of an impressionist and talk about how an impressionist works. Point out how they *select* and *emphasize* certain voice qualities and mannerisms. Also talk about what impressionists do to create a character that a writer can use—selection, repetition, and exaggeration.

Next, show students a video clip from the classic television show *Taxi* in which the character Jim is featured, or show them a video clip from the television show *Seinfeld* in which the character Kramer is prominent. Ask students to notice Jim or Kramer's mannerisms. (They are quite distinctive.) Help students understand how Jim and Kramer's mannerisms, dress, movements, facial expressions, hair, clothes, speech patterns, intonations, and word choices all distinguish or *tag* the character by asking them some questions such as: What's distinctive about the way he talks? What are a few details about each character that are exaggerated and unique to that character? What is his speech pattern? Does he elongate some words and misuse others? What are his unique mannerisms? Does he wave his hands or thrust them through his hair? Analyses such as these indicate how a few repeated and exaggerated characteristics are used to tag a character.

Additionally, students can examine passages from literature for similar ways in which authors make characters come to life on the page by tagging them. For example, look at descriptions of Boo Radley in *To Kill a Mockingbird*, Willy Loman in *Death of a Salesman*, Shug in *The Color Purple*, or Lennie in *Of Mice and Men*.

Finally, ask your students to write about a character they know, including dialogue, in a few pages. Tell them to be particularly aware of the person's voice and mannerisms, to concentrate on *seeing* and *hearing* the character as they write. After they have the character captured on paper in a first draft, then they can go back and *emphasize* the characteristics of voice and action to make their creation stand out. Share the finished characters aloud with the class.

Multifaceted Self-Portraits

Students are to try to see themselves as others see them, and to explore different perspectives at the same time. Ask them to write a multifaceted portrait of themselves consisting of several sections, each one from the point of view of one of these people— their mother, a brother or sister, a close friend, an enemy, a teacher, and one other person who knows them well. Ask them to write each section in the first person as though they were the person describing them. Then, have the students conclude the self-portraits with a brief section on *the real me* from their own perspectives.

Collect the papers and read aloud excerpts of the voices. The class will enjoy guessing who the subject is, and it gives the teacher an opportunity to point out examples of well-done voices and the way voice changes with perspective.

As students tune their writing voices and try on other voices, as they practice and stretch themselves, they naturally will speak as the *I* of the growing writer to the *you* of their audience. This chapter has concentrated on the *I* and on ways to make it stronger and more flexible. The next chapter looks closely at the *you*. Working with these two related and basic demands of writing helps students to become skillful and versatile writers who are confident of their ability to tell you what they know on paper.

Final Thoughts on Voice in Writing

Voice is easy to demonstrate in your students' writing if you are sensitive to it. Skilled student writers will already be exhibiting some control and agility with their written voices. All you need to do is point out to them their effective uses of voice, and they'll probably catch on. Whether you are an experienced or a novice teacher of writing, your students will probably like doing most of these activities. We have generally found that students think they are fun, and they learn lots about their range of voices as they do them. These activities do demonstrate voice to students in obvious ways. They also show students powers they have as writers.

Not all of the students who enter our classes are skilled writers; they may not exhibit control over a wide range of voices, their own or those of others. Novice writers need help distinguishing, controlling, and manipulating voice and other stylistic features in their writing in order to achieve their full potential as writers. These activities hone the ear of novice and experienced writers to voice.

Dan has often commented on how important narrative is in all of this business of teaching writing. "Narrative is the language of world-making." That's the way he put it. Narrative is important to us as writers and as teachers. What we really want to do is to tell you a story. That's what most of us want to do—tell our stories and tell them well and tell them to a captivated audience. That's what student writers want to do. Writing starts with telling stories. It's in their stories that you'll probably first discover your students' voices. Show them the power they already have in their expressions, written and oral, where their voices are genuine and strong.

We are always amazed, and a little amused, at the relief in students' eyes when we tell them, "You may say *I* and *you* and use contractions when you write." Of course they may. The question is, who has been telling them they shouldn't—and why? Forget those tired models of writing. Formal essays are written only in English class and only then as an excuse to "get them ready for college" or to "pass the assessment test"— which can usually be passed anyhow with a piece of writing that exhibits a fresh, lively voice, along with some control of language, form, and the traditional conventions of written expression.

Who are the writers you most enjoy reading? Bring them into class—when you can and still keep your job. Who are the writers your students like best? Bring those into class, too—again, when you can and still dodge censorship issues. What are those favorite authors' voices like? When you share favorite writers, you enhance writing and reading. Try it. It works better than threats of not passing the test or of not getting into college any day of the week.

Notes

1. Alice Murray and Hal Silcox were students at Gainesville High School, Gainesville, GA.

2. Keven Davenport, Karen Smith, Lisa Toler, Patti Tyson, David Van Laeys, and Tami Beaver were students at Stone Mountain High School, Stone Mountain, GA.

Works Cited

GUNTHER, DEBORAH. 1978. *Writing: A Sourcebook of Exercises and Assignments.* Reading, MA: Addison-Wesley.

JAMES, HENRY. 1889. "A Letter to the Deerfield Summer School."

MILLER, JAMES E. JR. 1972. *Word, Self, Reality: The Rhetoric of the Imagination*. New York: Dodd, Mead.

OLSON, GENE. 1972. *Sweet Agony: A Writing Manual of Sorts*. Medford, OR: Windyridge Press.

WOLFE, TOM. 1963. *The Kandy-Kolored Tangerine-Flake Streamline Baby*. New York: Farrar, Straus and Giroux.

7

Growing Toward a Sense of Audience

When students write only to teachers, they often end up writing not as the act of communicating to people but as performing for a grade. . . . If you never play the violin except for your teacher, you will probably find it unrewarding before long, but if you are playing for yourself and others, playing for the teacher is helpful and rewarding.

—PETER ELBOW, *Everyone Can Write*

One of the most desirable sensitivities to cultivate in growing writers is a heightened ability to *feel* an audience as they write. As writers continue to develop their skills, they experiment with their abilities to create a distinct voice, to control readers through their words, and to choose precisely the right words to convey their implicit messages to readers. As writers develop increased skill and agility with techniques needed for crafting their writing to suit the rhetorical demands of form and audience, they also continue to develop a sense of audience. They work on word choice, organization, imagery and metaphor, and on the messages that are implicit and explicit in their writing. In short, they are learning the craft of writing, and they are perfecting their sense of audience. As part of learning this aspect of the craft of writing, classroom teachers can provide opportunities for student writers to develop a growing sense of audience.

As student writers become more confident with their writing and with their unique voices, they also become more confident and more able to share their writing with a variety of audiences, not just the teacher and a few peers. Remember, most student writers will not be experts, yet, at meeting the demands of a variety of audiences. They are still making discoveries about what exactly to do in their writing to exert more control over audience. Each writer must keep writing, trying out and testing the results. Each writer will begin exercising independence as she develops confidence in predicting the ways readers will respond to certain effects. That's where you, the teacher, come in.

Begin by reminding yourself and them to think again about the communication process. When a writer begins to write anything, that process is set in motion. The piece of writing is written to be read by someone. The writer attempts to provide certain rhetorical conventions and techniques needed by the audience for comprehension of the writer's message, and the audience in turn agrees to read the work closely, carefully, and with an enlightened eye. The writer, the writing, and the reader are linked in a cooperative relationship that inevitably changes each of them.

Some theorists call this link the *rhetorical triangle*, and some refer instead to the transactions that occur between text and reader. Whatever you call it, the link exists and can be strengthened by a skilled writer and by a skilled reader. That's why both reading and writing are considered active, meaning-making processes; both are acts of composing; and both can be taught effectively. As we explain in Chapter 12, we don't separate the teaching and reading of literature from the teaching of writing in our classes, but we talk about them separately here for the sake of clarity. Effective literature connects and resonates with its reader, so we read literature with a *writerly* perspective; that is, we read the text closely, becoming active readers who study the writing in order to see how the author connected with her audience and to see what techniques the author used that we, too, might use as writers. Then, we write with a *readerly* perspective—with the readers' needs in mind—to include the details, formats, and conventions of text that our readers will need in order to understand our texts. Without a doubt, one of the keys of effective texts and therefore of effective writing is an ability to connect with the intended audience.

Successful professional writers have a well-tuned sense of audience. They don't know the individual minds of their readers, but they have a feel for shaping language that connects with that audience. That *feel* often seems almost mystical to the novice. You can help student writers understand that there is more than mystery by bringing into the classroom excerpts from published writers' discussions of their work. Professional writers trust that an audience will imagine, laugh, cry, and live momentarily through their words. An acute sense of audience is one of the hallmarks of a mature writer.

A well-developed sense of audience comes through experience. Unfortunately, a chapter on audience or a few exercises on word choice will not be all that developing writers need in order to hone their sense of audience. More than that, you will need to provide many opportunities for students to adjust their writing for real audiences, letting the interplay of writing and audience teach indirectly what no direct teaching can do. Encourage students to practice and fool around with audience, to test their writings on a variety of audiences, and to learn by doing.

Let's face facts. In schools, most writing is done for the teacher, as we have discussed earlier in this book, and the very structure of schooling limits the possible audiences for students' writings. However, the classroom atmosphere *can* support opportunities for writers to develop a sense of audience, and there are some ways to introduce new audiences into the classroom. Throughout this book, we discuss some of these expanded audiences, such as having students write for peer response groups, for the school newspaper or literary magazine, for younger students in the neighborhood elementary school, for the local newspaper, or for the school or class website. Nonetheless, students will continue to seek your opinion about their writing, and having you as a sophisticated and caring responder may actually benefit students' progress in writing. The key is to be *one* audience, not the *only* audience. When you help students find a whole range of audiences for their writing, you need not apologize for your role as one responder/audience/teacher for students.

Initially, beginning writers should write for themselves as audiences in journals and personal writings, listening for the sound of their own voices. They may choose to share these writings with friends and helpful teachers to see if what pleases them personally also pleases those close to them. Beginning writers also can experiment with audiences less well known and further removed from them. Encourage these audience experiments while providing responses and evaluations that are gentle and positive. Adjusting subject, language, and voice to other audiences is sophisticated writing behavior, and our approach to developing such sophistication is simply to encourage experimentation and exploration.

Explore audience options and examine reader–writer relationships that span the range of possible audiences. Help students to write for audiences that include, among others, themselves; a trusted adult; you as the teacher and/or the evaluator; larger known audiences such as peers, younger children, or older relatives; and general unknown audiences such as congressional representatives, corporations, and the general public. Note the continuum from self to general public. As the audiences become more abstract, a greater degree of writing skill is necessary in order to bridge the increasing distance between the writer and the reader and in order to meet the needs of the audience.

Gaining experience with a variety of audiences matters for developing writers. Here's a list of possible audiences for student writers; be sure to add your own and students' ideas to our list.

Peers
- in class—notes and messages, persuasive papers, explanatory papers
- in other classes—letters, journal entries, inquiries
- in other schools—letters, class magazines, surveys, opinion polls
- pen pals or email partners
- famous peers—fan letters, question letters
- generalized peers—children of the world
- school newspaper—editorials, opinion letters

Teachers
- to encourage a teacher
- to make a request of a teacher
- to share relevant personal information with a teacher

Larger Known Audiences
- parents

- parents' friends
- older relatives
- family friends
- principal

General Unknown Audiences
- newspaper editor
- heroes
- authors
- athletes
- TV and movie personalities
- corporations
- unknown offenders (the person who threw all the trash on the highway)
- citizen groups
- governmental bodies
- information sources
- listserv subscribers
- website visitors
- chat room participants

Imaginary Characters
- in books
- on TV
- on videos
- in films

Talking Directly to an Audience

In addition to varying the kinds of audiences for whom students write, many other audience experiments are possible. Some students have a flair for talking directly to their readers as they write. Use the following models to illustrate the technique.

The Author's Voice

Authors use unique voices to draw readers into their writings. Student writers can learn this technique and use it to their advantage.

> Or is the author trying to ease you into something here, trying to manipulate you a little bit when he ought to be just telling his story the way a good author should? Maybe that's the case. Let's drop it for now.

But look here a minute. Over here. Here's a girl. She's a nice girl. And she's a pretty girl. She looks a bit like the young Princess Grace, had the young Princess Grace been left out in the rain for a year.

What's that you say? Her thumbs? Yes, aren't they magnificent? The word for her thumbs has got to be rococo—rocococototo tutti! by God.

Ladies. Gentlemen. Shh. This is the way truth is. You've got to let those strange hands touch you. (Robbins 1976)

That's Tom Robbins, involving you personally with Sissy Hankshaw, and with himself. Kurt Vonnegut also knows his audience. He touches us with his fine and scathing irony.

[This book] is so short and jumbled and jangled . . . because there is nothing intelligent to say about a massacre. Everybody is supposed to be dead, to never say anything or want anything ever again. Everything is supposed to be very quiet after a massacre, and it always is, except for the birds. . . .

I have told my sons that they are not under any circumstances to take part in massacres, and that the news of massacres of enemies is not to fill them with satisfaction or glee. (Vonnegut 1969)

Ask your students to try talking to the reader directly in their writings much the way they may have been doing in their journals. Tell them to use their author's voice to inform the reader, to cajole the reader, or to involve the reader.

Anticipating Audience Response

Writers' choices of voice, language, and content are often influenced by their informed guesses about audience response. Particularly when the writer's intent is to influence or persuade a hostile audience, the writer tries to anticipate possible audience rebuttal. Dan's son, Matthew, when he was younger, tried to convince Dan for some time that Matthew needed a minibike. Partly from frustration and partly from his knowledge of parent psychology, he put the following note on Dan's desk. Notice how Matthew's intuitions about audience response guide his word choices, his specific information, and even the organization of his piece.

Dad—
This is about a minibike. Chris is only nine and his parents let him have one.
[Peer pressure—anticipates Dan's "you're too young" argument]
I would be real careful and only ride it when you're there to watch me. I would always wear a helmet and watch out for cars and trees.
[Anticipates Dan' concern for his safety]
I will always put it in the garage. And I could ride it to soccer practice and I wouldn't bug you about being bored and I would learn how to take care of something.

[Anticipates Dan's concern for responsibility]

I'll save my money and maybe we can find a used one cheap. I'll read the want ads. It saves gas. Dad, you could ride it to work.

[Anticipates Dan's "we can't afford it" final line. And involves Dan in the last line]

Ask your students to draft an appeal to one of their parents. They should try to persuade that parent that they need something. Tell them to anticipate parental response. Suggest that they actually write anticipated responses in brackets as they write their papers, as in the previous example. Have the writers try out the piece on the parent and report to the class how accurate their hunches were about their intended audience.

Writers also alter their voice with strategy that is based on their perception of their audiences' vulnerabilities. Sometimes a writer moves an audience with an emotional, evangelistic appeal. Sometimes a writer shames the audience by choosing accusatory and preachy language. Sometimes a writer supports the audience by using warm, understanding language.

Ask students to draft three different pieces in which they ask a teacher to change a grade on a recent assignment. Tell them to blame the teacher in one piece, to be humble and ingratiating in another, and to be coldly logical and businesslike in the third.

Speculate with your class as to what kind of teacher would be influenced by each piece. Compare the three pieces, talking about similarities and differences. With which voice are they most comfortable? This follow-up time is important. Involve your writers in a discussion about their audience strategies and ask "why?" questions.

Personalizing an Audience

You may find that a more direct approach to audience awareness works better with less sophisticated writers. Prewriting discussions about a potential audience and their uniqueness is certainly always appropriate. Asking students to think about and even to describe their audience may help them refine their intuitions. Brainstorm with your students specific questions about their audience before they begin writing, and have them jot the answers in an effort to familiarize the student writer with the potential audience members. Some sample questions to use with students for this activity include:

- How old is the potential audience?
- Where do they live? City? Rural area? Another country?
- What is their education?
- What do they believe and value politically? For example, for whom did they vote for President? Why?
- What do they believe and value philosophically?

- Where do they work? What position do they hold at work?
- What are their personal interests and hobbies?
- Where do they go for vacations? Why?
- What is unique or unusual about them?

When developing writers can more clearly envision members of the audience to whom they are writing, they can better evaluate how to appeal to the audience's interests and needs as readers.

Rewriting for Different Audiences

Advertisements and commercials are interesting sources for a consideration of audience strategies. Most of us have heard of or used instructional lessons in which students conduct detailed analyses of the logical fallacies and types of appeals used in commercials and ads, but we may have done so without thinking about how all that is related to writing. Survey your students to find out what they think are some particularly effective commercials. Videotape them for classroom use, if possible, and analyze them with your students. Discuss the assumptions these advertisements make about their intended audience. Discuss how a particular commercial might change if the product were directed to another audience. Ask your students to rewrite a commercial for a different audience. For example, they might sell sugared cereals to 40-something adults, oil company stock to environmentalists, pick-up trucks to female college professors, or bubblegum to grandmothers. Discuss audience strategy with your writers, focusing on the audience-directed changes they make in their sales pitch.

Follow this frivolity with a more extended writing assignment. Ask your writers to design and write ads for a class publication or design and produce a commercial to sell the principal on assigned parking spaces for seniors, the PTA on the need for an improved and updated gym, the county commissioners on the need for a new recreation center, the local theater manager on the idea of offering student discounts, or the city council on the feasibility of building bikeways. Brainstorm with your students for real products, real potential audiences, and effective audience strategies. Complete the activity by videotaping the final products or creating PowerPoint® presentations, and then presenting them to the intended audience.

Writing for Younger Children

Your writers need direct contact with their audience. If you can work out the logistics, elementary school children are an excellent audience for student writings. Find a second-grade teacher somewhere and take your class over for a visit. Have your students interview the younger children—in person or via written exchanges—to find out what kinds of stories they like. Help your students to analyze their second-grade audience, and then turn them loose to write some children's literature. You can make this experience as elaborate as you want. Some teachers ask students to illustrate and bind their books. Some teachers spend time examining and talking about picture books and their importance in the education of children. But the most important follow-up is the chance for students to read their stories aloud to the younger children so that your students can experience their audience personally. If getting the two groups of students together isn't possible, videotape your students reading their stories aloud, send the tapes to the younger audience members, and ask for written or videotaped responses to the stories. The key is to get the two groups to know each other's responses to writing better.

Dawn has also had great success with journal exchanges. Her college students read the same young adult novel as did eighth-grade language arts students. Then, they discussed in exchanged journals what they liked and disliked about the book, including character development and author's style. At the end of the nine-week exchange, the two groups met for a discussion of the book and of the personal insights they had gained about each other by reading their journal entries. These students then understood the literature and the audience of their journal partner much more fully. Remember, the more personal the connection between the two groups, the better for helping your student writers understand the real needs and genuine responses of an authentic audience.

Audience Adaptation

Good writers make subtle, often almost invisible, adjustments for their audience. Maybe an unsubtle and obviously rigged assignment will illustrate the point. In order for students to create different audiences for a piece of writing, ask them to write letters giving the details of an automobile accident, in which the writer was hospitalized and the car was totaled, to the following audiences:

- a relative or loved one of the driver
- your friend, Officer Lopez, who suspects reckless driving as the cause of the accident
- the automotive company to discuss their car's performance and crash index ratings

Follow this role-playing demonstration with real letters to real people. Have students try writing three letters to people they don't know well. For the first letter, they should find something around their house that has never worked properly or that has failed recently because of a manufacturer's error. Have them draft a letter detailing the product's defects and ask them to suggest a reasonable remedy. For the second letter, have students locate people around school or town who seldom receive recognition. Have the students write letters of appreciation to them. Send copies to the local newspaper and the persons' employers.

Finally, have students try a "Why?" letter. "Why?" letters ask people to explain a position or a recent decision. Why does the swimming pool close at eight? Why are students never invited to the school board meeting? Why did you vote against reduced bus fares for the elderly? The intent of such letters should be to give the addressee an opportunity to state fully a point of view. Letter writers need to choose a voice and a vocabulary that do not create defensive responses. The intent is to draw out the addressee and open a channel for dialogue.

Ask students to share their letters. Discuss specific audience strategies: voice, syntax, and word choice. Talk about problems inherent in writing to people whom you don't know very well.

Real Audiences

It's not easy to design writing assignments that specify diverse, real audiences. Many so-called audience assignments are not real writing situations, and they don't teach students very much about actual writing problems. Two important sources for real audience experiences are all around you: performance and publication. Students need to read their writings aloud to other classes, to PTA meetings, on local television and radio shows, and even in local shopping centers. Publish their work in classroom magazines, in school newspapers and newsletters, in local papers, in children's magazines, in literary magazines, and on the Internet on your class' website. Encourage students to submit their products to contests and commercial publications. Look constantly for new outlets. Remember, nothing you can do in class will teach your writers as much about audience as will a firsthand experience in performance or publishing. Going public with writing broadens students' audience intuitions and builds their motivation. Design occasions that open the dialogue between writers and readers.

A Final Note

We are rather well convinced that writers write for themselves first. Meanings are personal, self-constructed, and homemade. Maybe the best kinds of practice in writing for other audiences that we can give to our students is lots of practice struggling with tough ideas and lots of opportunities to share those struggles with other writers. That we can do in our classrooms. We can help students find important topics about which to write, and we can encourage them to test those ideas by reading and sharing with fellow writers. It's the community of writers in our classrooms that will ultimately teach our students about audience.

Works Cited

ELBOW, PETER. 2000. *Everyone Can Write: Essays Toward a Hopeful Theory of Writing and Teaching Writing*. New York: Oxford University Press.

ROBBINS, TOM. 1976. *Even Cowgirls Get the Blues*. New York: Bantam.

VONNEGUT, KURT. 1969. *Slaughterhouse Five*. New York: Dell.

8

Responding to Student Writing

You have to love what they do; try to understand what they do;
and not be promiscuous with what they do.

—Quincy Jones[1]

Writing in isolation without lively response is like other solitary activities: singing in the shower or dancing in a coal mine. They may be pleasurable diversions, but without some response from an audience, they do not get much better. Most writers, and particularly your students, need the reactions of other human beings both during and after they write.

More to the point, they will demand to know what *you* think about their writing. Thus, the critical moment in any writing class is when beginning writers put their words in your hands. "Well, what do you think?" "You don't like it." "It isn't very good, is it?" They watch your eyes. You can't fool them with facile praise.

Over the years, students have developed a kind of self-preservation instinct in writing classes. They try to figure out what teachers want and then give it to them. They have also learned to insulate themselves against the criticism of the writing teacher. If you're successful in drawing them out, in getting them to take a chance with language, then you must also accept the burden of bringing them along with sincere and measured response.

The secret of building good writer–responder relationships lies in the *touch* of the responder. Overly harsh, picky, and niggling criticism will spook any writer. The *only* way to help writers improve is to draw them out slowly with honest encouragement and support. We hear a little murmuring out there from those who label this kind of responding as softheaded because it doesn't discriminate enough between good and bad writing. The successful writing teachers we have observed are an idiosyncratic bunch, it's true; but they have one strong similarity. They draw out writers by searching for the good in their writings and by looking for potential with the same vigor some composition teachers waste on the great fragment hunt. Successful writing teachers never sit around in smoke-filled rooms ranting about how badly their students write or reading the latest collection of fault-ridden papers to horrified listeners.

Good writing teachers have a positive mind-set. Good writing teachers, because they have a backlog of miracles, know that students' writings are full of clues to hidden potential. Good responding technique is at least 50 percent mental. Get your mind right, put your hand on this page, and resolve: "I will look for the good. I will go with anticipation to my students' writings."

Responding as a Person

You may need to spend some time practicing this responding business. Teachers are frequently unaware of the extent to which they respond as correction machines rather than as people. Your response should be essentially a shared reaction. Participate with the writer by sharing your own thoughts and feelings as you read the writing. Look at the following student papers and Dan's responses to them.

Piece #1

My horse was painted red. The eyes and the bridle and saddle were painted on with black paint. I could ride that horse for hours. When I was mad or excited—I'd hop on that horse and ride it so hard that it would leave the floor and bang back down with a wonderfully loud wood-on-wood, spring-breaking ka-plam! One thing that really pleased me then was that the horse was always in the same mood I was. If I wanted to ride her hard—she seemed to want to fly and crash on the floor—if I was tired and rocked very slightly back and forth—she sometimes went to sleep before I could rest my head on her neck and "rest my eyes." She died one day in a fire at my aunt's house—but then I was "too old" for my horse and too young to be told about the fire.

—*Rita*[2]

RESPONSE #1 Your horse story brought back memories of an old, yellow horse that used to stay on our screen porch. He, too, was always ready for a rough ride. He was especially good at getting me over a serious pout. I particularly like the way you captured the sound of the horse hitting the floor: "wonderfully loud, wood-on-wood, spring-breaking ka-plam!" The irony of your last line "too old" and "too young" is also well done. Maybe you could do something with that in another paper.

Piece #2

My teacher was Irish—long black hair and icy blue eyes—the same color as the ocean in the Spring when it's glassy and I can see my toes. She always wore sexy clothes, tight skirts and sweaters that showed her breasts at the top. She always sat on the steps during recess watching us play, a sailor cap with the rim pulled down over her eyes, her skirt pulled up to her thighs revealing long perfect suntanned legs. The boys were crazy about her. They fought over that cherished place next to her on the steps daily.

—*Shirley*[2]

RESPONSE #2 Ah, those Irish teachers. . . . I remember falling heavily for Ms. O'Rourke in the third grade. She still has a part of my heart. Nice job with the details: "icy blue eyes, sailor cap with the rim pulled down." You have a nice touch with people descriptions. Any more memorable characters in your past you could recall for us?

Piece #3

We moved from Lincolnton to Louisville the summer before I was in the fifth grade. I didn't know anybody. My mom had told me that the girls across the street from us had a "Man From Uncle Club." She said that they wore sweatshirts with "The Man From Uncle" written on them. This seemed strange to me. I had been used to Barbie dolls and an occasional exploration of the woods behind our house. "The Man From Uncle?" The first day that we were in Louisville, I cried all day. Why did we have to come to this stupid "Man From Uncle Place"?

—Sheri[2]

RESPONSE #3 Your piece brought back vividly the traumas of moving during elementary school. How I hated that first day in a new school! Your piece is good because you remembered specifics. The "Man From Uncle Place" is perfect. You've got a good ear for conversation. Try using dialogue in your writing. Let your mother speak.

Dan's responses are personal and specific. We're not suggesting that you should use every student paper to tell a story of your own, but you do need to find a way to let the writer know the story has touched you personally. Recounting a personal memory, arguing that you felt differently, or simply saying, "I can really tell you feel strongly about this," are all ways of letting the writer feel the impact of a personal reader.

Looking for the Good

The most significant role any teacher/reader can play is that of skilled responder, offering concrete, helpful suggestions about specific stuff in the writing. To respond means simply to react—orally or in writing—first as *reader* rather than as teacher. If we've got to look for the real reason kids don't learn to write, it's right here. Most teachers are not practiced as responders to students' writings—editors, proofreaders, critics, raving lunatics, error counters, yes. But responders? No. Most kids never hear any specific, human, teacher-as-responder comments about what they write. First, teachers must discover the power of responding. Forget grading and evaluating for the moment. That kind of responding is less than helpful with beginning writers. Real responding differs from evaluation because it is personal and shared. It is here-and-now feedback. It is not a list of things the writer should do next time, but an immediate response to what the writer is saying *now*.

The goal of the responder is to help writers discover what it is they want to say, and then to challenge them to say it as powerfully as possible. Modeling is very important at this point. Showing them good examples from their own papers encourages them. Sit down with those papers and look for the good stuff: a word, a phrase, a fresh idea. Then mark it; circle it; say, "I like this because. . . ." Excerpt the parts from the students' writings that you like and bring them to class on a handout. (Don't identify the student writer on the handout. See Chapter 5 for more on when to and not to identify student writers.) Show the excerpts to your students. Say, "Look at what great stuff I found in your writings."

Yes, you will have to look through a world of chaff to find the kernels. Yes, there may be far more bad writing than good. But you start by rejoicing over the good rather than haranguing over the bad. Never lie to your students. Tell them, "I had to mine the slagheap looking for the gems." Sometimes we laugh with our students about the lengths that we will go to in order to find something good in their writing, but this positive psychology in the writing class changes dramatically the students' willingness to work at the job and improve.

If you have not tried "mining the slagheap," wait no longer. Look at this piece of writing by an eighth grader.

If I Were Older

I would like to be older than I am now. Because when I get sixteen I could drive a car. When I get eighteen I could buy beer. When I get twenty-one I could drive a transfer truck. I want to become a trucker because I have been on trips with my daddy and I had fun talking to all those trucker's. Once I talked to a lady trucker. Her handle was "The Lady Buttermilk." She had came from VA. headed toward Big 'A' town (Atlanta) with a load of frozen food. We was her frontdoor until she got behind schedule and she put the pedal to the metal. Then she passed us and she became our frontdoor. One other time I was with daddy on a trip and we was in the rockin' chair. The old "Yellow Jacket" was at our frontdoor and the old "Halk Eye" was at our backdoor. We was just riding along because when ever a smokey was coming, my good-buddies would call for me over the old radio. Then we would slow down to double nickles (55 m.p.h.). We stayed in the ol' rockin chair until we got up to ol 'Sparkle City (Spartenburg South Carolina). Boy we had fun that day.

Dylan[2]

Maybe all of those run-ons and fragments and usage errors catch your eye first. Maybe you're tempted to label this a hopeless case. But you took the pledge. You said you would look for potential. Plunge in. First, look for *anything* you like about this writing. There's a lot to like. Personally, Dan liked the trucker talk and the fact that the student is the expert and the teacher is the novice. Dylan seems comfortable with writing. You could suggest that the writer give you a dialogue between "The Lady Buttermilk" and old "Yellow Jacket." Point out the expressions you like. Skip the bad stuff. Listen to what the writer—as a person—is trying to tell you. Stay with him. Point out the good things in his writing and be patient.

As we discuss in Chapter 9, *good* in writing is not a static quality. *Good* is a growing thing. *Good* for the halting writer is different from *good* for the fluent writer. *Good* for the unpracticed writer is different from *good* for the effective writer. Goodness in writing is not an absolute standard and does not have a moral equivalent.

Teacher's Response

There's no way to escape it; your response to your students' writing remains very important to them. In a traditional class, your response is important because you control the grade. Whatever your response ("submit this in word-processed format"), students who want a good grade do what you tell them and the rest check out. We don't think that the teacher should be the only audience for all student writings because having only a single audience focus is inhibiting to a writer's development. When the teacher becomes the only audience for student writers, many will learn to give the teacher what he wants, but then they can't write for the next teacher, the next year. Additionally, some Genghis Khan types who teach writing can damage students' motivations and development. But we don't think that teachers who are merely insensitive responders do irreparable damage. One writing class with a skilled teacher/responder can restore confidence and awaken latent language talent even in the oppressed. Teachers' responses are absolutely critical to student writers, and such responses do not necessarily stifle and enslave students. Our observations of successful writing teachers confirm this point. They move students to make insightful observations and to offer helpful criticism of writing by example, by talking students through the processes of writing firsthand.

Students need to hear your opinions, and they expect you to deliver content knowledge to them. They need your sophisticated and caring responses. Grow better student writers by sharing your knowledge and responses with them.

What Kind of Response Is Helpful?

The writing teacher has to be willing to play a number of different responder roles, changing these roles as the writer develops. At the fluency stage, the writer needs attention, encouragement, and support. Responding at this level means seeing potential, drawing out, spotting future topics, learning more about the student, and rescuing nuggets from the slagheap. Responding to beginning students' writings demands more than merely putting gold stars on the papers. Almost immediately, the teacher must respond as an informed reader, pointing to what works in the students' writing. Three skilled gurus of writing instruction give us clues about what works in most writing. For Ken Macrorie, strong verbs, vivid detail, inventions of all kinds, ironies, oppositions, and a strong, personal voice are signs of development (1984). For Peter Elbow, "cooking" is hopeful (1999). For Donald Murray, an abundance of information, sense of order, clarity, and an air of authority are the most important initial indications that a writer has potential (1985). See Chapter 9 for our list of good stuff in writing. Better yet, make your own list, perhaps drawing from state and national standards for writing for ideas. Create your own examples of good stuff. Publish excerpts and demonstrate to students what you're talking about. Look for things that work at the word, sentence, paragraph, and whole discourse levels. Keep the classroom awash in examples of good writing.

Try giving your students the task of making their own list. Ask them to work in small groups with a stack of student writings that represent a complete range of struggling to skilled pieces. Have students sort through the writings, putting the papers in piles to help them identify and categorize the criteria for good writing. The discussion, arguments, and questions that ensue help students find their own voices as responders to each others' writings. Have each group compose a classroom chart that represents their criteria. Display these charts in the classroom as reminders of response topics.

Later in the year, ask students to compare their categories with the Kirby-Liner chart (see Chapter 9, Figure 9–1) when the peer groups are more skilled. Or, give students simplified versions of the standards used in your state for writing. Ask students to compare their criteria to the published ones. While student labels for the criteria may vary from the professional models, it has been our experience that students identify the same broad categories—interest and technical expertise—as well as many of the same subpoints. Such similarities give students confidence that they know lots about what makes writing work.

As the student writer gains confidence and a sense of personal voice and worries less about getting words on the page, your role changes gradually to that of editor. Our best editors have not been insensitive authoritarians who want us to write it only one way; far from it. Rather, as editor, you offer support to the writer and help writers express as powerfully and effectively as possible what they have to say. Your responses should often be phrased as questions or as take-it-or-leave-it advice. A responder uses a very different tone from that of authoritarian or grade-giver. The writer is in control of the writing; the responder sees alternatives or offers a second opinion, being careful not to take the piece away from the writer.

This is not to say that there won't be times when writer and editor are at an impasse. Several summers ago Dan worked extensively in a residential version of the Whittenberger Writing Project in Idaho. One of Dan's favorite kids, crazy Ed, was struggling with a piece about growing up in Northern Idaho. Basically, he had a strong piece about riding up in the cab of his dad's log truck and how that gave him such a sense of importance and power as a kid. Nice piece. But in the opening paragraph, Ed describes the scene of coming into town in the truck; and right in the middle of this rather solid descriptive stuff, a panther runs across the road. Now, the panther never returns in the story, plays absolutely no role in the guts of the piece, and Dan found it distracting, a random detail. Dan said to Ed, "Oh, this panther doesn't really work for me, Ed." Dan gave him some other feedback, and Ed wandered off to the computer to grind out another revision. Ed's back in twenty minutes with a new draft, and the panther is still in there. Repeat scene one. "Ed, about the panther, I think he ought to go." Ed does eight or nine drafts and the panther never leaves that first paragraph. Finally Dan is adamant. He's ranting, "Ed, the damn panther is hurting this piece!" Calmly Ed replies, "I read it to four other kids and they all liked it."

So much for the teacher-as-editor. The important point to make here is that the teacher-as-editor is not the same as the teacher-as-God. The give-and-take—the healthy dialogue between teacher and student writers about specific stuff in the kids' writing—is a worthwhile activity regardless of where it takes the piece of writing.

With confident writers and advanced writing classes, your role as responder may be more to function as a critic, arguing fine points of diction, asking for a more consistent point of view, and challenging the writer to return to rework the piece. Even as critic, the teacher/responder realizes that the writer and the writing are closely related. The criticism must clearly be to improve the piece, not to punish the writer. It will be much easier to function as careful critic if you yourself are a writer. Teaching writing from inside out builds expertise and credibility, but more important, such inside experience gives you a knowing empathy for the difficult task of the writer.

You may be thinking, "Well, sure, I could teach writing if they would put overachievers in my class." We hear you. We know that you aren't teaching private writing lessons to one student at a time. You've got the usual 150-plus students in five or six or more motley classes. Fortunately, this book is about teaching writing well in impossible situations. The key to providing enough response to student writers is, of course, to involve the students themselves as responders. Student response is often more forceful than your own and certainly may carry more weight. Okay, you tried that and nothing happened. You brought in some student papers and said, "What is good about this writing?" And the kids looked the other way. Responding takes practice; it's new to students. Don't be surprised if it takes a little time to get them going. Model the kind of response for which you're looking. Lead them. Cajole them. But don't give up on them.

Developing Effective Writing Response Groups

We give students lots of practice at working as responders, but first we teach them very directly how to be effective responders. Here are the keys to such work, as developed by Dan.

1.   **The teacher's response to student writing establishes the ground rules for the responses of all others.** Your appropriate modeling is the key to effective response groups. Whether orally or in writing, how you handle the words of your students will signal to your students how they are to talk and respond to each others' writings.

2.   **Establish a "No Hunting" rule for your responses and enforce that rule with students' responses to each others' work.** The rule basically means no cheap shots at writers as they try to express their ideas. Avoiding judgmental and unkind remarks toward writers must be a value in an effective response group or workshop situation.

Similarly, gratuitous and insincere or inaccurate comments about students' writings are not helpful.

3.   Appropriate response generally begins by trying to understand what the writer is trying to say. Summarizing the piece or restating the message or story lets the writer listen to what the audience has made of the piece. Talk about the piece as a whole. "I like the order of events," or "I like the way you wrap up this piece."

4.   Finding things to like in the piece is important. Point very specifically to things in the piece that work: "I like this opening," or "I like this verb right here." Point to where you think the piece is going well: "I like the voice in this passage," or "Nice transition here."

5.   Making suggestions for how the writer can elaborate on what is already written is probably the most helpful editing posture. Rather than suggesting that the writer make changes or correct errors, find places in the piece that have potential for more development. Through a series of questions to the writer, draw out elaboration possibilities. "Is there any more to this story?" "What happens next?" "I'd like to hear more about this." "I'd like to see and hear more of this character."

6.   The reader's questions and voiced musings are also very helpful. "I wonder. . . ." "What if . . . ?" "If this were my piece, I might. . . ." "I notice. . . ."

7.   Question the writer about what he or she plans to do next with the piece. "What will you work on next?" "Where do you see this piece going from here?" "Is this piece related to any other thing that you've written?"

8.   Give the writer the chance to ask the responder questions. The writer will no doubt want to clarify response comments, ask advice, and seek counsel about what to do when returning to the piece.

9.   Always focus on the piece rather than on the writer. It's easy to be sidetracked by the emotional content of the piece. Don't be tempted to become the writer's analyst, priest, or rabbi. Continue to focus on *how* the experience is rendered in writing rather than on the experience itself.

Students as Responders

Students can become expert responders to the writings of fellow students if you take the time to teach them how to do so. In addition to the ideas mentioned elsewhere in this book on how to have students interact with each other and respond to each others' writings, here are some ideas for how to model responding for students and for teaching students to give constructive responses to their peers.

Helping Circle

Begin demonstrating the art of responding to students by using your own writing. When students are first asked to talk about each other's work, it's basically one incompetent talking to another incompetent. "Well, wha'd ya think?" "Oh, I liked it." This type of response is far from helpful for improving writing.

So hand out a piece of your own writing and ask them to give you some help. Tell them to point to good stuff first and then ask you some tough questions about your piece. What does it need more of? What to leave out, what to leave in? Take notes on what they say. Be accepting of their comments, not threatened. Listen; don't talk back to them in defense of your own written words. Then, bring in successive drafts of the same piece, showing them how you have incorporated their suggestions; invite further response and questions. It doesn't take much of this kind of modeling to have a dramatic effect on the quality of students' responses in peer editing.

The next step in the *Helping Circle*, a term coined by Macrorie, is to move from public critique of your writing to that of students' writings. We usually begin with a student whom we've asked in advance to be the first public participant, someone who is a rather confident—but not arrogant or defensive or necessarily perfect—writer. Because leading a group of students through public responding to other students' writings is a bit frightening the first time or two, it's important to begin with some rules or structures and then be prepared to enforce them. Our basic rules are simple: Be positive; be helpful; assume nothing—if you're unsure, ask the writer; be as specific as you can.

Sharing a piece of writing with a large group is definitely growth producing, but it may also be very frightening. Lessen the tension by making public miniresponses a routine part of your class structure. Spot good writing in the student's Writer's Notebook (see Chapter 5) or folder, and write a note encouraging the student to share it with the group. Some students are understandably reluctant in this setting, but if you can get them to try it once, the thrill of seeing thirty-two heads bobbing up and down in response to their writing will get them hooked. The key to this type of responding is the teacher's skillful enforcement of rules and sensitive attempts to help the novice through the experience.

Publishing Excerpts from Students' Writings

The best way to teach the group to be skilled responders and to point out good writing is to publish weekly or twice-weekly excerpts from their own writing. Dan frequently begins the week (because he can prepare the handouts over the weekend) with cuttings from student writings. He reads quickly through the writings for the week, looking for particular pieces that work. The excerpts are kept anonymous. He reads them aloud and asks for comments. The group members feel free to open up because they do not know the identity of the writer. We focus our comments on what makes the piece work and what, if anything, the piece needs. Students look forward to the excerpts and take genuine pride when they "get published."

Partners

We have gone almost exclusively to response partners in our writing classes. Partners are so much more efficient than are larger groups. There's a debate about whether the teacher should choose the partner pairings or let the students choose their own partners. We've done it both ways and have success with both methods. We usually mix the two methods within the same class, sometimes assigning partners and sometimes letting students choose their partners. The key is that they're being productive. In order to promote productivity, Dawn has students prepare for their partner time. Each writer composes three to five specific questions about his piece of writing, questions that cannot be answered by a simple "yes," "no," or "maybe" response. After the writer reads his piece aloud to the partner, the partner offers responses to the piece, and then the writer asks his specific questions. The questions extend the discussion and help the writer to generate ideas for dealing with troublesome spots in the writing.

In order to build some self-reliance within the partnerships, we delay answering most of the tough questions kids ask about their writing by saying, "Check with your partner on that," or "What did your partner say?" Students soon realize that the teacher is not the first line of response in our classes, thereby empowering the authority of the student writers in matters concerning their own writing. We give "partner of the week" awards and generally celebrate good collaborations. Of course, some kids prefer to work alone, and that has to be okay, too; but we generally continue to encourage them to seek out a partner.

Standing Groups

Small, supportive groups that function well together can be a comfortable place for a writer to get helpful responses. The key is to build groups who have confidence in one another and then keep them together for the tenure of the class—or at least for an entire grading period or completion of a major paper—letting them meet on a weekly basis. The group gives the individual writer a home base and a comfortable audience on whom to try something on before it goes "public." In our experience, the respect and caring attitudes that form among these standing group members as a result of their prolonged work together is really quite remarkable.

Occasionally, groups will cease to function well. At that point, consider reassigning group members, especially at the beginning of a new grading term, unit, or major paper. Or, sit in with that dysfunctional group and provide some modeling, again, about how to work together as effective responders. Despite the occasional pitfall here and there, we like the use of standing groups because of the varying responses (that is, more than just the teacher's opinion) that emerge about the writing and because they help students to develop greater courage to take on new audiences/responders.

Editorial Boards

If you're a well-organized type who doesn't mind an involved set of procedures for responding, the editorial board approach may be helpful. Appoint groups of five or so students who are responsible for selecting good writing and suggesting editorial changes. The board's problem is to publish an excerpts edition by a certain deadline. All student writers are required to submit a finished piece to the editorial board. The board reads the submission, selecting pieces that have potential and notifying authors of their editorial decisions. Authors whose pieces are not selected are sent "rejection" notices. By simulating the actual process writers go through to become published, the teacher takes some of the mystique out of it, and students learn firsthand the joys and pains of getting published.

Rotate the editorial responsibilities among your writers so that each of them can experience the processes, responsibilities, and pressures of editing someone else's writing.

Holistic Ratings

Tom experimented quite successfully in his advanced placement classes with a structured approach to responding and rating. He divided his class into groups and appointed a group leader. The groups read the papers from another group, responding and rating with a holistic rating guide. This approach is especially well suited to advanced placement classes because the essays that students write when they take the advanced placement test are graded holistically. Specifically, each member of the group reads each paper, underlining examples of good writing and writing helpful and positive comments in the margin. The reader also makes general comments on the effectiveness of the piece, suggesting changes to the writer or simply asking the writer questions.

The entire group rates the paper on a five-point scale. The rating is assigned to the paper, and the group writes a brief defense of the rating. Such cooperative response develops the students' abilities to recognize effective writing, and it shifts much of the burden of careful response from the teacher to the students. As students continue to practice pinpointing the good in others' writings, they begin to transfer those successful techniques into their own papers. Our goal is to make students more independent of our help. By relying on us less and on themselves more, students hone their confidence as writers and their own sense of what constitutes successful writing.

Some Final Thoughts on Responding to Writing

We think it's important to vary response modes and strategies to keep the whole business as fresh as possible. Kids can get lazy as responders, or they can get into ruts with formula responses. Jog them every once in a while with a look at the quality of their responses. Spend some time evaluating student response as a whole class, talk again about what kind of responses are helpful, and challenge them to read closely and ask good questions of the writer. When these factors are in place in your classroom, the skills associated with quality writing and responding show marked improvement.

Notes

1. National Public Radio Interview with Quincy Jones. 1997. Jones was discussing how to work with artists as he produced the Grammy Awards televised show, but we think his comment applies to responding to writing, also.

2. Rita, Shirley, Sheri, and Dylan are fictitious names of student writers who preferred not to be identified.

Works Cited

Elbow, Peter. 1999. *Writing Without Teachers*. New York: Oxford University Press.

Macrorie, Ken. 1984. *Writing to Be Read*. Porstmouth, NH: Boynton/Cook.

Murray, Donald. 1985. *A Writer Teaches Writing*. Boston: Houghton Mifflin.

9

What Is Good Writing?

Quality . . . you know what it is, yet you don't know what it is. But that's self-contradictory. But some things are better than others, that is, they have more quality. But when you try to say what quality is, apart from the things that have it, it all goes poof! There's nothing to talk about. But if you can't say what Quality is, how do you know what it is, or how do you know that it even exists? If no one knows what it is, then for all practical purposes it doesn't exist at all. But for all practical purposes it really does exist. What else are the grades based on? Why else would people pay fortunes for some things and throw others in the trash pile? Obviously some things are better than others . . . but what's the "betterness"? . . . So round and round you go, spinning mental wheels and nowhere finding anyplace to get traction. What the hell is Quality? What is it? . . .
A person who sees Quality and feels it as he works is a person who cares.

—ROBERT M. PIRSIG, *Zen and the Art of Motorcycle Maintenance*

We know good writing when we read it. So do you. But what Robert Pirsig says about quality, and our perception of quality in our lives, is also true of writing. Knowing that writing is good is one thing. Determining exactly what *makes* writing good is more difficult. Perhaps it's a sense that the writer took care with what she wrote, as Pirsig suggests. *Good writers* care about their writing and take care in writing it. Or perhaps a feeling for good writing has more to do with what James Dickey said he looked for when he read a new poet. "I wish merely to be able to feel and see and respond to what the poet is saying, and with as much strength and depth as possible" (1968). Considered in this way, good writing is writing that touches readers on a personal level. It's writing to which readers can respond. And the stronger the response, the better the writer?

Well, that's part of it. Still, that's not much help when you're faced with a stack of student papers. You know what you've done before to mark and correct and grade the papers has made no difference you can see.

One reason we have not been as successful with student writers as we could have been is that, too often, our only criterion for quality in student writing has been correctness. It's a tenuous thread when the "goodness" of the writing of students hangs by whether the students can avoid a narrow range of errors in spelling, punctuation, diction, and formal usage. Teaching writing with correctness as the only criterion is deadly. Worse, except for a very few students who manage to write well in spite of our intimidation, the error-avoidance approach to teaching writing produces uniformly bad writing.

We maintain that you can find and nourish quality in the writing of your students without scouring their papers for surface errors. Donald Murray uses a classic phrase we like when he talks about the "listening eye" of the writing teacher (1979). This listening eye is the sensitivity the teacher must develop to see the good aspects of the writing of even the most immature student writer. One of our first jobs—and maybe the most important one—is to look for potential in the often-stumbling attempts our students make. Murray points out that some sign of skill in any area in a paper is hopeful. Perhaps it's only a few words in the whole paper, but we can begin to build from that strength.

Listen carefully with your eyes when you read those first attempts of your students, and train yourself through practice to be sensitive to the good things that are there. Peter Elbow reminds us that "a person's best writing is often all mixed up together with his worst. It all feels lousy to him as he's writing, but if he will let himself write it and come back later he will find some parts of it are excellent. It is as though one's best words come wrapped in one's worst" (1999). What our students need first is for us to help them see their best words that are usually hidden by their worst. Skip the detailed criticism and offer, instead, encouragement in those areas where it will do the most good.

Sometimes improvement comes almost spontaneously from practice and sustained praise. Your persistence in insisting on some writing being done every day and your open, receptive attitude will probably bring out more potentially good writing and cause more real growth in your student writers than anything else you do, but you still have to have a clear idea of what you're looking for when you pick up a student's paper. Otherwise, even your best intentions, carefully planned writing activities and opportunities, and most positive reactions are random, perhaps confusing, and finally ineffectual.

After you have gotten your students started writing and after they're used to writing daily, then you'll need to approach their writing systematically, looking for the best aspects of what they are doing and helping them see the good and how to grow with it. First, you get them writing; you can't do anything until they're no longer afraid to put words on paper. Then, the work of growing good writers begins by growing the good in their writing.

So what is good writing? What are the criteria we can use in the classroom?

In a classic definition, Ken Macrorie says, "Most good writing is clear, vigorous, honest, alive, sensuous, appropriate, unsentimental, rhythmic, without pretension, fresh, metaphorical, evocative in sound, economical, authoritative, surprising, memorable and light" (1984). Whew! That kind of list almost takes your breath away. What we propose is working criteria for good writing in the English classroom, touchstones that will give you a systematic review of the most important qualities of good writing that you can identify and encourage and build on in student writing.

There's nothing really new about the categories we give you in Figure 9–1. The criteria on this list will probably resonate with you; you'll nod your head in recognition of some of the criteria for which you have looked in the writing of your students. You may recognize similarities with national and state standards for writing and with the criteria for good writing that are used in your area to evaluate high-stakes tests. While we didn't look at standards or test evaluation categories as we composed our list, we'd simply say that any similarities do indicate that professional writers and educators have some tacit and overt agreement about what constitutes good writing.

The criteria are listed more or less in order from the most basic to the most sophisticated. That fact does not necessarily mean, however, that your students will demonstrate that they can write in a recognizable human voice before they begin consciously to use words rich in sound effects and imagery. Nor are the categories mutually exclusive. In the act of writing, many things happen at once, and the mental processes are incredibly complex, especially when the writing is going well, which makes any linear tracking of writing processes and development faulty. The criteria are listed in a linear fashion for convenience, clarity, and for an indication of the most common developmental patterns that you might find in your students' writing.

We believe that you can expect to find these qualities to some degree in the writing of *all* your students in *every* set of papers you read. It's not only the exceptional paper written by the rare and brilliant student that has good writing in it.

There are two main attributes of good writing, to which all other qualities are related. Good writing is interesting to read, and good writing is written with technical skill. Good writing is fun. The first and most basic requirement we make of anything we read is that it interest and/or entertain us. Without that, it becomes drudgery. Good writers create and keep the interest of their readers. This aspect of writing is where we need to begin in teaching quality in writing to our students.

A reader's interest cannot be sustained for long, however, unless the writer demonstrates some skill with the techniques of writing. The craftsmanship with which words, sentences, and paragraphs are manipulated in an essay—or such aspects of writing as dialogue in a short story or imagery in a poem—these affect our judgment of a work and either frustrate us or add to our pleasure as we read. Therefore, the two important questions for us to ask when faced with a stack of student papers are: What are the qualities that make writing interesting? and What are the attributes of technically skillful writing?

The examples in the following section were all culled from students' writings in one of Tom's classes on an average day. By using these typical papers, we are trying to emphasize that quality shows up in all students' writings, not just in those pieces that are high-stakes.

The Kirby-Liner Working Criteria for Good Student Writing

Good Writing Is Interesting

1.	Voice	One human being talking to another
		Makes the reader believe
		Strong, recognizable imprint of the writer
2.	Movement	Words building/pull the reader along
		It goes somewhere with variety
		A sense of order
3.	Light touch	Writer doesn't take himself/herself too seriously
		Even-tempered
4.	Informative	Important
		Has substance/says something
		Adds to our experience
5.	Inventive	Unique experience
		Something new/or something old in a new way

Good Writing Is Technically Skillful

6.	Sense of audience	Makes contact with the reader
		Anticipates reader's needs
		Compliments the reader with meaning
7.	Detail	Concrete
		Photographic
		Selective
		Words that put the reader there
8.	Rhythm	Words that sing
		Sounds effortless
9.	Form	How it looks on the page
		What it looks like in print
		Presentational style
10.	Makes sense	Thoughts are communicated clearly
		Organization aids meaning
		Makes a point and develops it effectively
11.	Mechanics	Observes conventions of spelling, punctuation, and usage
		Enlightened control

Figure 9–1. *The Kirby-Liner Working Criteria for Good Student Writing*

What Makes Good Writing Interesting?

1. Good writing has a voice. Good writing talks to you with a real voice; it has the recognizable imprint of the author on it. A lot of rhetoric and composition texts talk about *style*. A writer's voice on the page *is* his style. That human sound is what makes a piece of writing real for us. That's the reason bad translations are so frustrating to read, and that's why bestsellers are not written like doctoral dissertations. Notice the human contact and individual voice in this piece:

> I looked down at the terribly small piece of chicken on my plate—somehow there just didn't seem to be any justice—I always received the smallest piece possible.
>
> The girl sitting next to me looked at me for a slight moment as though I was a creature from another world and then turned back into her own small world—herself. She laughed a high inhuman laugh that seemed to pierce the whole room with sound.
>
> First I thought she was laughing at me and my measly portion of chicken—but only of news of how her ex-boyfriend had received a blow in the eye which now wore the colors black, blue, green, and a tinge of red.
>
> I thought how she would look that same way but then another devilish thought entered my mind.
>
> "I hope she gets fat!"
>
> —*Tracy*[1]

Tracy is beginning to find her voice as a writer, and in places in this paper we hear a very human voice talking about an irritating neighbor in a crowded school cafeteria. There is a hey-I've-done-that-too kind of feeling about the piece that gives it its humor. We share experiences and feelings with the writer because she speaks in her own voice.

To have a real voice, a piece does not necessarily have to be written in first person singular.

> Waiting eagerly behind the dark stage wings for her music cue to enter into brightly colored spot lights. Lights with cool and warm colors. Nervous, tense muscles, and pounding heart. Thinking over her part before darting on stage to do her dream ballet.
>
> —*Lynn*[1]

Good writing is *honest* writing. Lynn takes a chance with her reader, sharing something very important to her. There's no mistaking that the "nervous, tense muscles, and pounding heart" are hers. If a teacher's only remark about Lynn's paper is to put "FRAG/–30%" in the margin beside that phrase, then the teacher will have proven to be an insensitive pedagogue and a poor rhetorician. Published writers frequently use fragments for effect in their writing. Student writers can do so, too, but the effect needs to contribute to the tone and mood of the piece, not just result from sloppy punctuation. Such latitude helps students develop their written voices and produce effective writing. Lynn risks herself a little with her reader. Our responsibility as teachers and as readers is to be receptive, to *listen* to the writer's voice, and encourage the writer to use her voice when she writes.

If you want your students' writing to have a real voice, then you will have to accept their individual voices and be accepting of what they have to say. We realize that our students' voices will differ from those of each other and from our own adult voices. Some students have fluent knowledge of another language; we encourage them to use that knowledge in their writing. If a phrase can't be effectively translated, use the Spanish or Japanese phrase, giving enough context clues to help the reader figure out much of the meaning. We fully support the notion of multiple voices in our classes. Everyone's voices are different, and it is the combined variety and impact of those voices that will enrich our classrooms' learning environments.

If students submit papers that are stilted and dead, ask them to "tell me about it" when they next write. Structure ways for them to *talk* about it *before* they write it. Help them find their voices by freewriting often. In fact, the only way that students will find and refine their voices in their writing is to practice using that voice on the page regularly, preferably *daily*.

2. Good writing moves. Good writing starts here and goes to there, and it pulls the reader along with it. Whether it's a narrative or an elegant argument or a poem, there is movement and order to it. Good writing also gives us enough variety, enough changes and twists and turns and sometimes surprises, to keep us interested and reading.

A sense of order appears in student writing first as the straight chronological this-happened-first-and-then-this-and-finally-this order of the narrative. Lynn's piece has less than fifty words, yet it shows this kind of order—a ballerina waiting, her nervousness growing, and the beginning of the dance anticipated.

You will also find that students will begin to place special emphasis on the first and last sentences of their writing. They feel the movement and order of the piece and are looking for ways to strengthen it.

> She was in a bad mood anyway. He kept on bugging her, so finally right before the curtains opened she agreed to go and buy him popcorn. Secretly she had a crush on him, but he was sitting next to another girl. It was a very scary movie, when she came back the theater was silent. She walked down the aisle with a big bucket of buttered popcorn. He was sitting directly behind her, when she started to hand it to him, both of their hands slipped. In the silence of the movie, all there is to hear is—"DUMBASS!"
>
> —*Kathy*[1]

Kathy's opening sentence is particularly effective. With a casual and natural sounding ill will, it starts moving us toward the climactic ending of a too-loud and embarrassing vulgarity uttered in the silence of a dark movie theatre. Tracy's writing about the frustrations of the cafeteria has a similar movement, but there the action is all in the flow of thoughts and feelings of the writers.

Fairly early you can expect your students to begin playing around with more complicated movement.

> Holding his hand, I was anticipating the shock. Slowly and smoothly the music flowed. Mouth agape, Henry stared blankly at the screen. As the girl opened the closet door, Henry's grip tightened. Suddenly the dead man's body rocked back and forth through the doorway. With a shriek of terror Henry's hold on my hand was like a tourniquet.
>
> —*Beth*[1]

Macrorie talks about creating oppositions that bring surprise, and Beth does something like that in this piece. It's a narrative, of course, and therefore chronological. Beginning and ending are stressed as in the other examples, but the movement zigzags back and forth from the boy holding her hand to the action on the screen, building tension in a short space that is released in the last sentence with Henry's shriek.

Some students' writings seem to begin anywhere and end nowhere, with no sense of order at all, but a close reading shows that most have some kind of movement somewhere in the paper. As young writers grow, some of their writings will become very complex. The place to start to develop a sense of movement in writing is with simple narrative order and with the invitation to "tell me about it."

3. Good writing has a sense of humor. Good writing often laughs. Laughter keeps us sane and helps developing writers take themselves less seriously, which helps them to develop a more even tone in their writing.

Three of the four examples we have already read from the set of papers treat their subjects with humor. Sustaining humor is as difficult as sustaining high seriousness.

Babysitting

Babysitting. . . . Cleaning up the toys and papers and clothes and baseball cards and the bubble gum stuck to the rug, the half burnt pots of spaghettios and the dried grape juice on the white counter. The boys you thought were God's sweet angels turned out to be the dirty dozen instead. One thinks he is the six million dollar man, but is the fifty dollar hyperactive midget, who is working for the CIA on figuring out if babysitters are the backbone of the U.S.'s economy crisis. *Everyone* needs babysitters, at least I think everyone needs them.

Babysitting. . . . Fighting over Hogan's Heroes and Gomer Pyle, compromising on Sesame Street (Well, I guess Stalag 13 deserved a rest). A moral came from an animated fable called "The crow and the pitcher." This show can be found to be very stimulating, but don't you dare tell anyone I said that. They all think I'm spastic already, and I really don't want to visit my friends in Milledgeville on anything but a social visit. One of my friend's daddy is the Chief of Security for the *State Hospital*, and he told me I can have a room at half-rate. Laugh. It was a joke. I *think* it was a joke.

Babysitting. . . . Mr. Rogers blaring on the screen, the phone ringing, the door bell buzzing, and the already burnt spaghettios burning again, only all at once this time, and just when you are on the verge on taking that room at the State Hospital, the dirty dozen comes in and says, "Hey, you're not such a bad sitter." I've won the first half—score Dirty Dozen 14, Tired Tyrant 20. Yet, the second half is coming, and I don't think my reinforcements can take bathtime *and* 8:30 bed check. I thought I enjoyed kids. But Jekyll and Hyde here seem to want to change my mind, and I have to admit the offer is tempting.

Babysitting. . . . The tired tyrant was just accused of uncalled for brutality since no extra time is scheduled past the routine 8:30 bed time. She will be sentenced to die at 3:30 Wednesday afternoon (the next time I sit for the Rat Patrol). I would prefer daisies and forget-me-nots to carnations. You can't afford roses or baby's breath, because life is cruel to English Teachers who should be guru prophets or Yamaha dealers.

Babysitting. . . . Life is ending so it doesn't matter what a few generous words that "Spazz" may have left, except I would like to get a kiss from the whole muppet gang, especially the Cookie Monster. I will also sue them for all they are worth (which is quite a lot) if I get that incurable disease "Manikin of the Mouth."

The End

—Alice[1]

Alice's rambling essay about the perils and joys of babysitting is successful, in part, because she laughs at herself and because of the real voice we hear talking to us.

Good writers don't take themselves too seriously even when they're writing about a serious subject.

As I gain the crest of the mountain I see in the fading light the solitary figure of my father as he loads his muscular arms full of firewood. I walk up silently expecting not to be heard but his keen ears catch the noise of what I thought were silent footsteps. He turns and with a quick dodging motion I barely escape a flying piece of wood. He laughs and I open the door for him.

No words are spoken until he notices that my hands are empty of game.

"Where's the meat?" he says as he throws another piece of wood on the fire.

"Still in its skin, I guess." I laugh at my remark and he looks at me sternly and I get the message that he'd rather I keep my remarks to myself. A silent period takes place as we sit down to eat supper.

—Billy[1]

This excerpt shows a relationship between a boy and his father handled with a light touch.

Laugh with your students when they are funny. Keep your silence when their humor falls flat or misses the mark. Encourage them to write in their own voices and not to take themselves or any subject too seriously.

4. Good writing is informative. Good writing *says* something. It adds to our experience. Good writing adds up and makes the reader feel that her time has been well spent. Good writers grow from the author's unique experiences and knowledge, from the writer's individual areas of authority.

He's a large one I thought as I saw the track in the soft mass that ran beside the creek. I unslung the battered 30-30 Marlin from my back and even as I did it I could see the moss rising back from the track. I clicked the safety off, this track was fresh, very fresh. I had no intention of running into a big brownie at this time of the evening. The sun was setting and the woodland around me was taking on the murky shapes of coming night. I turned silently and started away slowly and carefully with my rifle still cradled in my arms.

—*Billy*[1]

Billy's area of authority is hunting. He writes about it well because he *knows* it well.

All writers, even the most inexperienced student writers, have their own areas of authority. Tell your students that they have unique experiences about which to talk. Teach them to reach into their memories for those experiences that will say something to their readers.

Backstage at a ballet performance is one of the most hectic places imaginable. Costumes are hanging everywhere. The smell of hair spray, sweat, and ballet bags fills the room. The make-up lights are hot and very bright which practically causes your make-up to run before getting it on. People are nervous, fidgety, scared. I noticed that some were very quiet, going over steps in their minds, and others were nervously chit-chatting, trying to take their minds off being scared. The excitement in the air is thick. Curtain is in 5 minutes.

—*Susan*[1]

Susan, like Lynn, is an aspiring ballerina. She gives us a glimpse into that world and shares her feelings about it that only someone with her experience and perspective can. She gives the readers information.

Billy and Susan also ask something of us. They challenge us to move into their worlds, however briefly, and take part in their experiences. As readers, we derive meaning from what they have written.

5. Good writing is inventive. Good writing says something new, or it says something old in a new way. Writing is infinite in its possibilities. The perception, emphasis, voice, concerns, and, perhaps most important, the *imagination* of each writer are different from those of every other writer.

Alice's writing is certainly inventive, and Billy's way of presenting the relationship between his father and himself is not what we would have expected. Even quieter writings, those that have almost no overt action involved, may suddenly flash with the writer's inventive phrasings.

Photoscript Final

An older man, about fifty years old, sits at a roundtop table. A cup of de-caffeinated coffee, sipped noisily at one minute intervals, is in front of him to the right. A pack of cigarettes rests, at an angle, on the plate-sized, half-full, ceramic ashtray to his left. His rugged, aged semi-line-creased face is covered from the cheekbone down with a salt and pepper beard. His upper lip is invisible in the multi-earth-colored mustache. He sits with his right elbow resting on the table with his fore-head planted in his palm. The smoke stained fingers are visible in his dark brown fine hair. On the table in front of him he reads the words off of the paper that he has written. He destroys the still image, in what seems only a split second, to light a cigarette, sip the coffee, clear his throat, then he resumes the position. His smoking cigarette strategically and instinctively finds its place in the right hand, between the yellow fingers.

—Richard[1]

Richard's description is static, until there is a brief flurry of activity that returns to stillness, which emphasizes the statue-like quiet of his subject. It's finely done with a subtle touch that makes the piece memorable. Tom particularly liked the cigarette that returns, as though by itself, to the smoke-yellowed fingers of the man reading at the table—and ends the piece with quiet emphasis. This is pretty sophisticated writing for a student writer.

What Makes Good Writing Technically Skillful?

6. Good writing has a sense of audience. Good writing anticipates its audience. The writers are aware of their readers and their needs as the writing progresses. Writers sometimes directly answer questions readers might ask; at other times, writers talk to the *you* who is reading the piece. Writers pay their readers a compliment when the writing contains allusions or an intricate and well-formed argument because they trust that their readers will comprehend their points and appreciate their techniques. Good writing always conveys the feeling of *contact* between a real person writing and another real person reading.

Sometimes the writer plays with the reader. Alice writes for an audience of one—"I would prefer daisies and forget-me-nots to carnations. You can't afford roses or baby's breath, because life is cruel to English Teachers who should be guru prophets or Yamaha dealers"—but the joke is really for the entire class who knows Tom's reputation and the fact that he enjoys motorcycles. Even in a private piece, the feeling for a reader out there sharing the experience of the writer adds to the enjoyment of the work. This next piece by Richard was intended as a personal writing, perhaps one that others would not even read.

Cocoon

I float in peace in my cocoon—fluffy cotton walls, not visible to sight but soft to the touch. Air sweet. Sweeter than honey to the taste. Being suspended as I am in total weightlessness my mind is free, free as the wind is free to blow and take residence any place it pleases. Having this freedom I travel to the limit of boundless thoughts—Here I can be sad but not cry, happy but not smile, wonder but not be confused, find answers to questions not asked, war with the real, be at peace with fantasy. I have been shaken and torn away from my cocoon—I want to return—I never want to leave. If you see me but cannot find me—*that* is where I shall be . . . I was really there—

—*Richard*[1]

Although it's private, Richard cannot resist a playful nudge to his reader as he ends his fantasy. One of the most important steps in the growth of the immature writer is when he becomes aware that there is an audience out there. Richard seems to have reached that awareness.

7. Good writing uses detail, but not too much detail. Good writing is selective. The writing evidences the selection of just the right details from the chaos of sensation that threatens to overwhelm the writer; the writing particularizes the experience for the reader. The details are vivid, they suit the piece of writing and the audience, and they create clear images in the reader's mind. Along with the writer's voice, perhaps it's the selection of detail that makes what is said more *real* to us.

> As I was sitting in the library, I noticed an old man at the table beside me. He looked like a retired soldier. His face was old, dark, and wrinkled as if from the worries of war. He was rather fat and very tall. He was dressed in a khaki shirt and pants, and the pants were tucked into a pair of old boots. The boots were faded green and looked like they'd been through hell. He was reading *Douglas Reenan*. It looked like a rather boring book. His briefcase before him was stacked full of books and old papers which were yellow at the edges. His glasses were lying on top of the briefcase. There were more books lying on the table—*American Espionage* and war books. His eyes began to droop. He put down the book, rubbed his eyes and leaned on his knees with his elbows. Then he picked up another book and began reading in the middle of it.
>
> —*Susan*[1]

Susan particularizes the old man with his khaki shirt and pants tucked into boot tops; she includes the titles of a couple of books he is reading, and she includes the detail of the glasses lying on the briefcase. Her description has a photographic reality because she chooses to include small details that help the reader visualize the man.

Look at these telling details from the examples of student writing[1] used in this chapter:

> . . . the colors black, blue, green, and a tinge of red.
>
> —*Tracy*

> Mouth agape . . .
>
> —*Beth*

. . . the toys and papers and clothes and baseball cards and the bubble gum stuck to the rug, the half-burnt pots of spaghettios and the dried grape juice on the white counter.

—Alice

His rugged, aged semi-line-creased face . . . the mutli-earth-colored mustache. . . . His smoking cigarette . . . finds its place in the right hand, between the yellow fingers.

—Richard

The student writer who is beginning to find a voice and who has a sense of audience will be able to use details effectively with little trouble. Sometimes, we just have to alert the writer to the impact that using such details adds to her writing. We show students many models, pointing out effective uses of details and vivid verbs and evidence of a fine eye at work. We encourage as much close observation for writing as possible. If they are ready, such instruction helps most student writers to notice more details and to improve their use of details in their writing to make it feel more real.

It is much more difficult to teach students to cut and edit their writings. Economy with words seems to be an ability that comes very late in the growth process of writers. Many writers, especially student writers, are reluctant to throw away any of the words they've worked so hard to put on the page. With only one exception, all of the student writings in this chapter would improve with some careful cutting. The economy in Lynn's piece about the ballerina about to go on stage probably comes as much from her subject as from anything else.

It seems that student writers need to be comfortable in using detail before they are able to learn what they need to edit out. A Hemingway's ruthlessness doesn't come along very often. Any real success we've had teaching students to tighten their writing has been done individually and almost word by word. That kind of revision is complex and subtle and demands careful work done in conference.

8. Good writing uses words that sing. Good writing is rich in imagery and associations, strong in rhythm and repetition, and filled with wordplay. The skillful prose writer uses the language resources of the poet, choosing words that are effective in sound and metaphor. This is sophisticated stuff for most student writers, but you'll find that some of your students show signs of skill with wordplay.

Look at these words that sing from the examples of student writing[1] in this chapter:

Rhythm, Repetition, and Variation
Laugh. It was a joke. I *think* it was a joke. . . . Mr. Rogers blaring on the screen, the phone ringing, the door bell buzzing, and the already burnt spaghettios burning again. . .

—Alice

Paradox, Words That Play with Each Other

Here I can be sad but not cry, happy but not smile, wonder but not be confused, and find answers to questions not asked, war with the real, be at peace with fantasy.

—Richard

Imagery, the Dramatic Scene

As I gain the crest of the mountain I see in the fading light the solitary figure of my father . . .

—Billy

The smell of hair spray, sweat, and ballet bags fills the room.

—Susan

Association, Metaphor, and Simile

His upper lip invisible in the multi-earth-colored mustache. . . . He destroys the still image. . . . His smoking cigarette strategically and instinctively finds its place in the right hand . . .

—Richard

Emphasis, the Right Verbs and Nouns and Adjectives

Mouth agape, Henry stared . . .

—Beth

. . . the fifty dollar hyperactive midget . . .

—Alice

Sounds of Speech, Real Dialogue

"Where's the meat? . . . "
"Still in its skin, I guess."

—Billy

Good writing seems to flow. There's nothing halting or awkward about it. It *sounds* easy. Like a good gymnast or archer or guitar player, the good writer makes a very difficult task seem effortless to the audience, and like them, achieves this apparent ease through practice, through caring about what is done, and through careful attention to detail. As James Dickey puts it, "I work it over to get that *worked-on* quality out of it" (1968).

Working it over—and over, and over again—and listening with a practiced, sensitive ear each time is the only way we know for your student writers to make their words really sing.

9. Good writing has form. Good writing is graphically well designed. It has a presentational sense. In this criterion, we are ultimately concerned with the writer's ability to visualize the work *in print* or as part of some multimedia presentation that may include print.

A feel for form in writing is most obvious in a student writer's poetry.

So came the night;
It dropped down upon me
I was blanketed by purple blackness
    and everything was dry
    and everything was wet
    and everything was cold
And my head fell forward in sorrow
    But it was useless.
I saw it in the shadows, in the
    corners, behind every tree, every
opaque object; but I still saw it.
It creeped behind me and my
    spine melted in the heat
    of Death's passion.
It grabbed me and held me
    squeezing my last breaths
into the fog.
    and everything was dry
    and everything was wet
    and everything was cold.
            —Lynne[1]

Lynne has learned to use the line in her poetry—line endings and beginnings for emphasis, and line indentations to build her refrain. She *sees* the poem as it would appear printed and manipulates its form accordingly (and rather surprisingly in a few lines). She wants the poem read straight through, for example; there is no stanza break to create a pause.

With the advent of computers, more and more writers now compose on a computer, opening up even more possibilities for the manipulation of form and of how the writing appears in print. We call this new range of possibilities that a writer possesses about the appearance of a piece of writing a *presentational sense*, or a writer's sense of presentational options and enhancements. Writers may easily insert clip art into their written products, use font style and size and color for effect, or even enhance the finished products with shadings, borders, tables, bullets, or print overlays. Perhaps the finished product will become part of a PowerPoint® presentation. Writers can post their products on websites and add animation to them. The possibilities are endless and far exceed conventional print. The use of computers by writers will only increase. We think that it is important for teachers to sponsor and encourage writers who enjoy making print and graphic options a part of their meaning-making process.

Concern with form is properly the last, or one of the last, aspects of writing that you'll take up with student writers. To insist on too rigid a concern for form alone will only teach students to create a hollow shell or to consider form and appearance before substance. Some students seem never to have a feel for it, although most have at least some sense of form. They know to write in paragraphs, for example—unless, like Alice, they create new forms to suit their treatment of a subject.

Form-finding is legitimate writing behavior even for young writers. Encourage your students to experiment with form and presentational options.

10. Good writing makes sense. It is clear. We get the message. The writer knows what she wants to say and is able to communicate her ideas and her points clearly to the reader.

In all of the student examples that we have seen in this chapter, and even in the entire book, we see the sense of what the student writers are trying to say. We may want to word the ideas differently or put them in a different order, but those are mainly stylistic considerations. The meaning that the writers are trying to convey to readers is present in their writings.

When writing makes sense and is clear, all of the previous elements of good writing that we have already mentioned in this chapter work together in concert to convey and to develop the writer's point. The writing is interesting and skillful in ways that contribute to the overall message of the written piece.

Writing that makes sense leaves us with an "Aha," not a "Huh?" In fact, when students wander in their writing, lose their way within the direction of a sentence, or move inchoately from one idea to the next, Dan and Dawn often just write "Huh?" in the margin. The writer gets the point ("I'm lost here.") and knows that this is a section of the piece in which her writing has become muddled. In conference, we work together to determine how to recapture the flow of ideas—by word choice, sentence structure, the inclusion of more details, or a more effective ordering of the ideas.

We have found that having students read their writing aloud to a partner helps them determine places in the writing where clarity and sense fade. When readers hear their words and attempt to read the words actually written—not just the words intended—they can pinpoint what needs to change in the writing to improve the sense of the piece. Short of that, a responder can say, "Do you mean . . . ?" again letting the writer know what is and is not making sense to others.

The idea of making sense is basic to good writing, but achieving sense is not always as easy as it sounds. We think in convoluted, interwoven ways so that our precise thoughts and ideas are sometimes difficult to capture in clear form and diction and order. *We* know what we mean when we write; why don't you? Nonetheless, genuine responses focused on helping the writer to express ideas clearly will eventually improve the writer's awareness of her ability to make sense in writing.

11. Good writing observes the conventions of mechanics and usage. Finally, good writing observes those social conventions of written discourse that are expected by literate readers. Punctuation, spelling, and consistent usage are the most obvious. Notice that we list these conventions of *correctness* last in the criteria because we believe that eliminating surface errors is one of the last aspects of writing that student writers should consider. Once they are accomplished to some degree as writers, they need to know that their readers will judge what they have to say by their ability to spell, put commas in the right place, and select the right endings for verbs. There's nothing wrong with insisting that competent writers also become competent proofreaders.

Oh, yes, there's one more category. It may be the most important one.

12. Good writing is what you like (and what the writer likes). We believe that our working criteria can be of practical value in your classroom, but we realize that you're the expert in that room. You're the final authority for your student writers, and you have the responsibility for teaching them to write as well as possible in the time you have with them. Don't be afraid to trust your own judgment about what is good and bad in their writing. Make your own list of criteria to use with them—referring to district standards, if you must—think about that list, and talk about it with your students; revise it frequently, but use it systematically.

Finally, what we're trying to teach student writers is to recognize and pursue the good in their own writing, to make sound judgments about what is effective human expression and what is better changed or discarded. What we're trying to do is to make them the judge of quality in their own writing—to help them become people who see and feel quality, and who care.

Thriving as a Teacher of Writing in an Atmosphere of High-Stakes Testing

We are teachers of writing with attitude. We teach writing to every student who walks into our classes, we teach it well, and we love to teach it. What's more, our students learn and they write often and they understand why writing is valuable—if not downright essential—to them.

It's deplorable to us that legislators, commissioners of education, and politicians can't think of much else to do with writing in any official way other than grade it, score it, assess it, or make a contest out of it. We can think of lots more wonderful things to do with writing, beginning with sharing it, celebrating it, talking about it, crying over it, maybe even cussing it when necessary. Mainly *enjoying* it and *struggling* with it together. Together. That to us is what teaching writing is about. As we've clearly shown in this chapter, however, that doesn't mean that we're soft on quality in writing. We're not. We just think there are different—and better—ways to achieve and reinforce quality than through high-stakes tests, the results of which are published in the local paper for public criticism.

We'll stand by the criteria in this chapter. We like them just fine, thank you, mainly because they are the criteria of a writer. You may have different words for how you look at your writing, and that's fine too. Share them with your kids. Don't use them to grade. We grade too many papers anyway. Use the words you have to help your kids look at their writing as writers and then to see the quality that is there.

Yes, the quality is there. Our job is to give students the vocabulary for talking about what they do well and the confidence to assert their capabilities.

When we look at our own writing—and we put off judging it critically for as long as we can—we ask ourselves three questions before we ask somebody else, "What do you think?" We look at it hard and ask, first, Does it tell the truth? In other words, is the piece as *honest*, as true to emotion and experience and sense and logic, as it can be? Once past that question, the other two questions are usually asked and answered quickly: Does it say enough? and then, Does it say more than it needs to say?

What we expect from all of our students is that sooner or later they—every one of them—will read something to us and to the class that will knock us off our feet because it's so honest and revealing—and surprising. We wait for that moment when our students write something better than they know or expect. Then we begin to talk about voice and movement and a light touch and all of these other things writers need to talk about together. When we work together as real writers and when we write what is real and honest and when we write for authentic audiences and in authentic contexts, students learn—and their test scores on any test that any politician or administrator can throw at them will show their growth as writers and their efforts to learn. Period. End of story.

Note

1. Tracy Tate, Lynn Aaron, Kathy Owen, Beth Murray, Alice Murray, Billy Sailors, Susan Carpenter, Richard Poston, Susan Hayes, and Lynne Moore were students at Gainesville High School, Gainesville, GA.

Works Cited

DICKEY, JAMES. 1968. *Babel to Byzantium*. New York: Grosset and Dunlap.

ELBOW, PETER. 1999. *Writing Without Teachers*. 2d ed. New York: Oxford University Press.

MACRORIE, KEN. 1984. *Writing to Be Read*. Portsmouth, NH: Boynton/Cook.

MURRAY, DONALD. 1979. Workshop on Writing at Georgia State University, Atlanta, GA.

PIRSIG, ROBERT M. 2000. *Zen and the Art of Motorcycle Maintenance: An Inquiry into Values*. New York: HarperCollins.

10

Revision: The Student as Editor

*The writer of any work . . . must decide two crucial points:
what to put in and what to leave out.*

ANNIE DILLARD, "To Fashion a Text"

Revision. It may be the most frustrating part of writing to teach, and to learn. Your kids have been writing for a long time in their journals; their entries have grown from only a sentence or two to a page and more of writing each day. Good things are happening in there. Their writing in the journal and in class is spontaneous, alive, creative, self-revealing, often entertaining, sometimes very good—*but* their writing is also sloppy, plagued with spelling errors, punctuated indifferently if creatively, often one rambling paragraph, usually too fat, and in dire need of cutting. Verb endings have evaporated, sentences run into each other, verb tenses and pronouns are erratic, conclusions don't conclude, introductions don't introduce, descriptions don't describe— in short, the writings are first drafts and need to be *revised.*

Okay, you say to yourself, it's time to get *serious* about this writing stuff. The fun and games are over; it's time to bear down and get to work. These kids can obviously write—they're just lazy.

So you return that last batch of papers, give your students a little speech about cleaning up their act and maybe even getting ready for college English. You tell them to go back to their computers and correct their errors. You even generously offer to help them make corrections, not wanting to be too much of an ogre.

The students groan but get to work readily enough and rewrite the papers in a suspiciously short time. They ask only two questions while they work—one about how to open the spell checker on the computer, the other about whether you want their first drafts, too. When you face the batch of "revisions" after school that day, the results confirm your worst suspicions. Most of the papers are very neatly retyped, carefully preserving every error in the original draft. A few kids have made a halfhearted attempt at correcting misspellings and punctuation. By and large, however, their papers get worse about as often as they get better. Only two kids seem to have done any effective revision of their papers, and they always do the best writing in the class anyway.

You wonder where you can go from here and think maybe your students are just too irresponsible to do any really good writing and maybe you'll take that job at Wal-Mart and forget the whole business. Or that's how it looks right now, late in the day, fatigued, frustrated, and feeling dead-ended.

But keep in mind that revision in writing is more than eliminating surface errors in spelling, punctuation, and usage. Before you sigh and reach for the grammar book and those *serious* writing exercises, remember that revision does not have to be drudgery either. Revision is just that—*re*-vision, "seeing" it again. When we revise our writing and do a good job of it, we see it anew, and from a different perspective. We become our own reader, and we become critical and questioning, at least as much as we are able. We also read with appreciation and enjoyment. But we have *learned* to ask such questions and read with such a stance. When students don't revise in detail a paper that has been given back to them with the impatient command to redo it and make it better, it's not because they are lazy. They simply haven't been taught *how* to revise yet.

Learning to revise writing is part of the larger developmental process of learning to write. Because learning to revise is a growth process, it needs to be approached systematically and with some knowledge of how it's likely to take place. Our job is to help students become competent *revisers*, and therefore better writers, rather than to turn them into error-correctors. In this chapter, we suggest some good places to start the process of revision with students once you have them writing, and we point out some ideas about revision that will help you teach this potentially frustrating part of writing more systematically and with more success.

Thoughts on Revision

IDEA #1 *The revision process is really a series of closely related activities.* A term describing writing, and especially revision, that you will often hear is *recursive*. Writing is recursive because the writer keeps circling back on the writing, tinkering, changing things, rethinking, rearranging mentally and on paper, and anticipating what is coming up. This act of recursiveness complicates writing wonderfully, making the actual act of writing practically impossible to describe with complete accuracy. To set aside the theorists and researchers for a moment and say it another way, when we write we also read and fix. We read in chunks the stuff we've just written, checking spelling, adding a word, moving a sentence, putting in details, and crossing words out, all in an effort to get it to sound right. We run ahead of ourselves down the page, already thinking of what we will say next. We write, pause, reread, reflect, and write some more. Fluent writers complete these recursive activities very quickly as they write; it's part of what we do to make meaning and to keep the flow of ideas and of meaning going. Without this recursive capacity, writing would be virtually impossible, as would talking, thinking, and even reading.

So writers do many activities all at the same time, and they should. So how do we teach revision? Knowing students are going to be all over the place at once in a piece of writing does not mean that we cannot point out to them parts of the process that will most help them make their writing better. The teacher's job is to simplify the complexity of activities associated with revising and to chop it up into pieces so students can handle the process of revising in manageable chunks. Because writers are doing a lot of things at once does not mean that writers can't be taught. Fly-fishing is a pretty complicated activity too, but Dan can teach you how to do it. You see what we mean? When we teach writing as *craftsmanship*, and not as a body of knowledge to master, the job becomes doable.

It helps us to think of revising writing in four steps, knowing they overlap and can happen at the same time. The four steps are *in-process revision, re-vision, editing,* and *proofreading.* At some point in our work with writers and in our teaching, we focus attention on each revision step separately, coaching young writers in the tricks of the trade, demonstrating to them how revision works for us as writers.

Four Steps of Revision

STEP #1: IN-PROCESS REVISION In-process revision takes place as the writing is going on, and it is part of what makes writing such a complicated business. Writers ask themselves as they go along questions such as, "Is this what I really want to say?" or "Is this part clear?" or "How can I say this part better?" and then they make adjustments to try to get closer to their intended purposes. They add words and phrases and sometimes sentences; they delete and cross out; they change and reorder and alter. They listen to the *voice* of the writing and make adjustments so it will sound right. They become their own *readers* even as they write, often stopping to reread part of the paper from the beginning. They look back to see what has already been done, and they look ahead, anticipating what will be said next.

In-process revision is hard to observe, probably impossible to measure, and is certainly as individual as the writer; but we do know that it grows with practice. As writers reach maturity, they probably interrupt the writing more and more and spend more time as readers and in-process revisers than they actually spend writing. They tinker more with the finer points of expression as they write, getting that first draft closer to what they want to say than they were able to do as novice writers.

Reading out loud is one way to enhance in-process revision in the classroom, but reading aloud has so many benefits for growing writers that it's difficult to isolate its effects on revision. We try to teach students to "read with a pencil" as we do. In a reading session, we always have a pencil in hand, marking our pieces of writing as we read from them. We try to make our thoughts visible to student writers, interrupting to tell them what we're doing to the writing as we read it. We talk about our struggles, writer to writer, and our efforts to "make it sound right."

STEP #2: RE-VISIONING *Re-vision:* We write the word like this to remind us and our students that a good bit of revision is seeing the writing again in a different way.

There is value in trying a piece or a subject from several different perspectives, of literally writing whole drafts from scratch. Most teachers, anxious that the writing job be done by Friday, have never encouraged enough of this in their classrooms. Deadlines are necessary. All writers have them. But we also need to teach our students the option—and even the necessity—of trying the writing in a different way.

Students tend to balk at the idea of rewriting a whole draft over again from scratch, so we often begin reinforcing this notion of re-seeing the writing by working on writing leads. Students can have better papers instantly if they will just do something about how they start them. You grab a reader or lose that reader in the first paragraph or half page. It's a simple matter to write three or four leads for a piece of writing that is off to a rough start. No, we're not talking about topic sentences. We're talking about working on the device and on crafting the writing that is the opening of the paper. Is the piece of writing improved if it begins with a scenario? A rhetorical question? A startling statement? How can the writer best draw the reader into the piece?

Our job as teachers of re-vision often is simply to be alert to possibilities that student writers might have missed and to ask a lot of questions. Have you thought about doing it this way? Are you satisfied with this order? How will you end the piece? Where does your writing gain momentum? What are you really trying to say? Does this piece of writing do what you want it to do?

STEP #3: EDITING Editing, to us, involves at least two people, writer and editor, working on the piece of writing. The relationship is a special one, supportive, helpful, nonthreatening, probing, and sometimes challenging. We work as editors with our students, but we prefer to teach them how to be editors for each other in writers' groups.

This task takes time early in the class, but it saves time later. Plus, the rewards go far beyond teaching writing. We often model response groups after the techniques used in the National Writing Project. Each group has a leader, responsible mainly for seeing that each member reads and participates. When Dan leads a group, the first question he asks before each member reads is, "What help do you need from this group for this piece of writing?" Dan wants the writer to put into words specifically how the group can help her before she reads. Doing so keeps the group from shotgunning, and it keeps the group from making vague comments like "That was nice." To enhance this part of the responding and editing process, Dawn has the writer prepare in advance three to five specific questions about the piece of writing the group is to consider. These questions ask for specific advice and cannot be answered with a simple "yes" or "no." Instead of asking, "Do I have an effective introduction?" a better question is "How can I make the opening scene more action-filled?"

After the reading, we make sure each person around the table responds to the writer/reader's request for help. We at least want those in the group to speak to the writer/reader's stated problems or questions with the piece, but these are usually the catalyst for discussing the writing, not the sole points of the discussion. At first, addressing the writing in this manner is not always easy; but the members of the group keep at it, and it doesn't take the response group members long to become pretty good editors—not merely error-hunters—for each other. Because everyone in the group takes part as responder and as writer/reader, all have ownership in the group.

At the same time, as the teacher, we rotate from group to group, concentrating mainly on modeling responses after members read. We use a fishbowl approach to teach response groups how to be true editors and responders. In this approach, we pull a group of experienced student writers into the center of the room, their five desks facing each other in a tight circle. The other students circle close behind them. Then, we simply lead the group in reading and responding, pausing now and then to point out to the audience at their backs why and how they are doing certain things. It looks weird at first, and the first time in the center of the fishbowl sure feels funny, but it works.

STEP #4: PROOFREADING Proofreading sometimes takes place with editing. It's the job of cleaning up the paper and eliminating surface errors. It's the least important activity of revision, until the final stages of the paper. Traditionally, some writing teachers have taught only this kind of revision, leaving their students with the impression that learning to be a good writer is learning to avoid or correct errors. It's a narrow and narrow-minded approach to teaching writing, and alone it produces properly correct and uniformly dull prose since it teaches students to edit out the risks in their writing in favor of correctness.

IDEA #2 *Revision should be taught in terms of what we know about the processes of writing and in terms of what we know about the growth of young writers.* We don't get frustrated and angry when the novice violinist saws out squawks and screeches. We encourage the novice to practice, and we endure the assault on our ears with patience, knowing this racket will grow into sweet music with time, regular effort, and proper direction.

A lot of our problem is solved when we quit thinking of revision as correcting mistakes and start to *teach* student writers how to revise. When we do that, we discard the old prejudice that students are lazy and have to be forced to make their writing better, and we become able to see just what they do when they write and revise—if we are willing to take the time to watch them. We also start to see how they develop as writers and how revision fits into that development.

Kids are not lazy. They want to write good papers, and they work hard at it. We have done a lot of formal and informal research on students' writing. We've watched a lot of kids writing and revising papers. We're amazed at how hard they work. Tom watched and documented one high-school senior who planned, drafted, revised, and rewrote a paper in one class period, after instructions, and made fifty-three effective changes from the original to a revised draft! Her work is not unusual.

We have seen students do a wonderful job revising and editing their writing when it has been clearly demonstrated to them what they are to do and when they work in an atmosphere that is not threatening. We have seen them grow from halting, damaged writers barely able to fill part of a page with unreadable prose into good writers with style and sometimes brilliance, and always with excitement and joy, in one semester of work with a well-trained editing group.

Forget the notion that student writers can't revise, and take some time to watch them. Then, structure your class to help them do a better job. Show them how and plan ways for them to help each other. Make sure that what you ask them to do is appropriate, for them and for the writing job at hand.

IDEA #3 *Revision cannot be successful until students are practiced in a particular mode of writing.* Students cannot be confident enough to tinker with a piece of writing until they have practiced enough and know they will not destroy what they have worked so hard to get on the page. If you're getting resistance from normally willing students when you try to get them to work on revision, then you may need to go back to writing assignments such as those in Chapter 4 for more practice before pushing revision too hard.

Remember, when your students begin a new mode or form of writing, they need time to practice this new experience before they can be expected to be able to revise it with any success. Students who happily write and revise personal narratives into flawless form cannot be expected to write and revise well a movie review the first few times they try, although both are legitimate kinds of writing for your class. Let them get comfortable with the new kind of writing first. Let them get the feel of it and find out what they have to say before you expect them to do a good job revising it.

IDEA #4 *The piece of writing to be revised needs to be important to the student.* The usual situation in the classroom is that students want to finish papers as quickly as possible and turn them in so they'll not have to fool with them anymore. This is especially true when your students feel that their writing is not good enough. School has encouraged this get-it-done-fast approach to writing with days neatly divided into hour-long class periods and teachers insisting, "Turn it in at the end of the period." Because we're not willing to take extended time with a piece of writing, we get hastily done and shoddily produced two-draft papers (one class period for the assignment, prewriting, and first draft; then one more class period for the rewrite; and too often, older kids get to do *both* drafts in one period!). We teach our students to write fast, and we teach mediocrity. There is no reason why we can't spend more time teaching revision on fewer papers. Often, less really is more.

One of our jobs is to recognize promising pieces and encourage our students to keep them going. Dennis was a big, lumbering boy in Tom's second-period class.[1] He was state champion and an All-National wrestler, and he had trouble with his writing all semester. Tom trotted out his best, most creative, and strangest assignment, and watched as Dennis sweated and suffered and wrestled the pencil across the page. Early one week, Tom assigned one of his more bizarre flights of fancy. The class buzzed with prewriting talk for a few minutes and fell to work writing. Dennis chewed his pencil.

The class was working on writing about personal experiences. "Just write me a *memory*, Dennis. Tell me about it." By the end of the period, he was writing. He stopped precisely five minutes before the bell rang with that uncanny sense of timing students seem to have.

"Here. This is about my uncle. It ain't too good." He grinned as if he was glad the ordeal was over. Dennis was right. It ain't too good.

> I'm going to tell you about a man that lives in Chicago. He has a 6th grade education and is an elevator repairman. He quit school and went to work because his parents were very poor and he stopped caring about education. He lived in the ghetto and was in a street gang. When he was about 18 or 20 he was learning a lot about mechanics. Finally he started working on elevators and he was doing great. One of his biggest jobs was working on the elevators in the Sears building. He is the best man in the business. They want to move him up higher, but he refuses to take the written test. He could take an oral test, but he is too proud to tell them the reason for an oral test. So he hasn't moved up in a long time. He now has a 10 year old son that reads as good as him.

Dennis was reluctant to go back to work on the paper the next day. Like most students, he figured that one period and one page ought to be enough to satisfy any English teacher. Tom and Dennis talked for a while about his uncle. Tom wanted to read more about the uncle, Tom thought that possibly a good piece of writing was lurking within that first draft, and Dennis was certainly interested in *talking* about him. Then Tom and Dennis talked about the writing. Tom told Dennis to concentrate on *seeing* his uncle in the writing and to "tell me about him." Dennis added this part quickly on the back of the first paper.

> he is a short stocky man about 30, he is Italian always has hair greased back, he is always dirty, he is considered a dago, he lived in the mid western part of the city, I'm not sure what the neighborhood was called, except for don't go through there all the dagos will kill you.

Tom said that he liked the details. Tom and Dennis talked some more about the uncle. Dennis' ideas were really cooking. "Okay, Dennis, now put it together, and how about some paragraphs this time?" So Dennis wrote a third draft.

> I'm going to tell you about a dago from Chicago. He has acquired a 6th grade education and he is a elevator repairman. He quit school to get a job because his parents were poor and life was hard.
>
> He lived in the ghetto in an all Italian neighborhood. He belonged to a street gang. He was now about 18 or 20 and learning about mechanics. He got a break and started working on elevators in the Sears Tower. They want to move him up in the business, but he refuses to take the written test. He is too proud to tell them he can't read to take an oral test. You can still picture him sort of short, stocky build, hair greased back, dago t-shirt, tatoo of a heart and an old girl friend's name, he is always dirty. His house is filled with comic books of his sons that he reads for practice.

His 10 year old son now reads and writes better than him. He is now about 35 and makes the same pay as when he was 30, and he does a better job.

Well, the paragraphs almost got in. Dennis knew that it still didn't say what he wanted it to say, but now there was a piece of writing with which to work. Most importantly, Dennis was willing to work at the writing to get what he wanted. Tom and Dennis went over the draft carefully together, talking about what was good, how to use particular details to say some things better, where paragraphs might go, how to punctuate it, and some points about spelling. Tom and Dennis talked some more about the uncle, and Dennis wrote his fourth and final draft.

> I'm going to tell you about a dago from Chicago. He has a 6th grade education, and he is an elevator repairman. He quit school to get a job when he was a boy because his parents were poor and life was hard.
> He lived in the ghetto in an all Italian neighborhood. He belonged to a street gang. He was 18 and learning about mechanics. He got a break and went to work repairing elevators, and he was doing great at it. His biggest job was the elevators in the Sears Tower. They want to move him up in the business, but he refuses to take the written test. He is too proud to tell them he can't read.
> I can still picture him—sort of short, stocky build, hair greased back, dago t-shirt, tattoo on his arm. It is a heart with an old girl friend's name. During the day he is always covered with dirt and grease.
> His house is filled with his son's comic books, but he reads them too. His 10 year old son reads and writes better than he does. He is about 35 and makes the same pay as he did five years ago.

Dennis' paper still doesn't capture the feeling he has about his uncle when he talks; and in many ways, it's not a good piece of writing from a high-school junior. But it's much better than his first try, and he learned by working with it. He and Tom felt good about the paper when Dennis finished it. Dennis also recognized that most readers would deeply resent his using the word *dago*, even if it was a neutral term to him.

If the piece of writing is meaningful to them, most students are willing to revise extensively and will seek your help in making it better. Your interest in what they're writing and your encouragement of the good things you find in their writing are the most important factors in keeping students going through the work of several drafts, but there are a few other simple ways that you can encourage revision.

Choosing from several pieces to edit is one way of getting something the student is willing to work on longer. After all, *selecting* is an important form of editing. If we expect our students to take a paper through more than one draft, we always try to make sure they can choose from at least three things they have written.

Better yet, Dan and Dawn work from within a framework of writing, such as memoir. Within the memoir framework, we have students write several short pieces such as a name piece, a map piece, a neighborhood piece, a parent piece, a piece about an artifact from childhood, and several others. Then, students choose several pieces to weave together for inclusion in their final memoirs. This type of revising is effective for student writers for several reasons. First, it allows the writer to select pieces for revision with a theme or focus in mind: What is it that the writer wants the reader to understand about him or her as a result of having read the memoir piece? Second, it allows the writer to work from within a sound knowledge of a genre of writing since we have read thirty or more excerpts from published memoirs as we wrote our own pieces. Third, it allows the student writer to work on meaningful transitions and other devices to weave the separate pieces together into one final product in an effective manner. Finally, the writer is completely in charge of choosing what goes into the memoir, so that the writer cares about the writing and is the authority on the writing. These factors encourage student writers to work on revision following processes used by real writers. This approach to selecting and crafting writing also allows the student to choose for revision only those pieces that are personally significant and important to the writer. Then, of course, we move into deciding how to publish the students' memoirs.

When a piece is revised to be published, the writing takes on new importance and the student is more interested in getting it right. Publishing makes the writing real to your students, no longer only an exercise to turn in to the teacher. In-class publishing is essential to any meaningful work on revision because it gives students a valid reason to revise their writing.

Working together in groups to revise papers is another way to give students an audience for their writing and, therefore, a reason to revise. Reading aloud the papers on which they are working is an important tool in revision work, but you'll have to structure opportunities for it in your classroom carefully. Students need to hear their writing, and the immediate response of a group of classmates can be very valuable in editing a paper.

Tom doesn't hesitate to use the grade to get students to revise their writing. Part of Dennis' willingness to work so hard on his paper instead of turning in the first draft and forgetting it was that Tom promised him a good grade if he would improve it. Notice, we say *improve* it, rather than correct its errors. Tom wanted Dennis to do more than merely proofread it. We have found that our students do a better job and work harder when we point out the good things in their writing and ask them to expand on those, rather than telling them, "This is what you did wrong." There are times when Tom withholds the grade for poorly done papers from capable students until they try again—whatever works. But our best successes with revision in the classroom have always come when we've emphasized what the student writers are doing right.

IDEA #5 *A short, focused conference can be very effective in teaching revision.* Conferences don't have to last twenty or thirty minutes per student in order to be effective. A short conference of three to five minutes, conducted by a teacher skilled and practiced at asking pointed questions to help focus the conference and the student's ongoing writing, can let you confer with most of your student writers each time that you conduct conferences.

Just like in the response group, we ask the student writer, "How can I help you?" The writing belongs to the writer, not to us. We do not take papers out of their hands and show them how to fix them. We do not talk first, unless it is to ask students to tell us about their pieces of writing and the help they might need as writers and as revisers.

If students draw a blank and don't know what help they need, then we ask them to read the piece to us quietly. We tell them what we hear and ask them again, "What help do you need?" Usually that gets us going. Sometimes we send the student writers back to their response groups, and in some classes we will not conference with students if they haven't tried their pieces out on their groups.

During revision, we continue to stress the fact that students own their writing. We don't want our student writers to be overly dependent on us. Students' questions such as, "Is this good?" or "Read this and tell me what you think," or "Can you fix this for me?" get merely a look from us. Students soon learn that they are to go *first* to their groups for responses, that they need to work on elaborating and crafting and otherwise revising their papers based on the in-class activities we have explored together as writers, and that *then* they might come to us for a more extended conference on what the paper needs. We are not in the business of reading most first drafts, other than for a general impression, and we are not in the business of being the only responder in the classroom. We *are* in the business of offering meaningful writing opportunities to students, of teaching them how to write and revise effectively and how to respond to each others' writings, and of using short, focused conferences with our student writers *at the point of need*.

We frequently use conferences in our teaching of writing and revising, and we see some real growth in students' writings as a result of that technique. We enjoy conferences because they let us work as writers, one-on-one with our students. What we like best about this technique, however, is that it is directed by the students according to what each one needs for a particular piece of writing at a particular time and within a particular context.

IDEA #6 *You're the first model for your students. We advise you to both write and revise with them.* Let your student writers see you struggle with writing. Talk to them about what you're doing as you revise. Go through the whole process with them, talking about your problems and the way you try to solve them with each step. Show them the different drafts of your work and the way your writing changes from one draft to the next.

IDEA #7 *Remember that there are individual differences in the way students revise.* Revising is one of the many processes of writing; therefore, it is as unique as each writer who undertakes it. When you teach revision, allow enough flexibility for these differences among the student writers who are in your classroom.

You've seen the drafts of the paper Dennis produced, each time getting a little closer to what he was trying to say. Look at this original and revised paper by Lynn, from the same class.

Original Draft

The jumps are coming and the horse breaks into a dead run. Low again the rider prepares for the jump. Up and over, the horse's legs stretch outward and down for the ground making a huge arch.

Revised Paper

The jumps are nearing and my horse breaks into a dead run. Staying low on its back I prepare for the jump. Up and over. My horse's legs extend. Stretching and reaching for the ground on the other side. Making a huge arch in the air.

—Lynn[1]

It's a very different kind of writing, of course. Lynn is also a very different type of reviser from Dennis, as this paper illustrates. Two drafts usually do it for her, but she does a great deal of in-process revising. She does little editing (she changed the point of view on Tom's suggestion), but she's a near-perfect proofreader.

Being able to do a good job in two drafts is rare in the high-school classroom, but you'll have a few students who work well in a short time. Cary, a senior, did this remarkable job of editing a creative response to a song from only a series of impressionistic notes.[1] He did the whole job from listening to the song for the first time to the final essay in less than an hour.

Original Draft

There Only Was One Choice

"Strum your guitar, Sing it kid"
"Just write about your feelings, not the things you never did"
You can hear your footsteps shuffling in the dust
Rustling of shadows tells you secrets you can trust.

—Harry Chapin (Dance Band on the Titanic)

An attempt at a modern American ballad, but also a stream of consciousness, dreams and subconscious thoughts. The story of his life? yes but also a returning cycle. He begins as a young boy playing a guitar on the street corner, and as he grows learns the secrets of life through his music, that he can use his music to make other people happy and to give his own life meaning that he might otherwise have missed, "Strum your guitar, Sing it kid/Just write about your feelings, not the things you never did." An expression of individuality, a stab at being different and getting the most out of life. He, through music, discovers the little secrets that life offers, "You can hear your footsteps shuffling in the dust/Rustling of shadows tells you secrets you can trust." He has been happy with his work and his accomplishments, that "his journey has been worthwhile." And he passes on his knowledge to his son, "Just write about your feelings, not the things you never did." But the one question is whether he is singing about himself, his son, or maybe the two are actually one and inseparable. Maybe he and his son, and his son, and his son, etc. will always continue, throughout eternity, mortal, yet immortal through time, synonymous with his/their music.

Revised Paper
There Only Was One Choice
HARRY CHAPIN

Chapin makes an attempt at a modern American ballad, creating a folk hero in the music field, but the song is also a stream of flowing dreams, aspirations, and conscious and subconscious thoughts. Maybe the story of *his* life, but also a recurring cycle of generations past and yet to come.

He begins his story as a young boy playing a guitar on the street corner, and as he grows, he learns the secrets of the trade as well as some idea of what life is about through his music, travel, and dedication to his calling. He learns to live in reality, "Strum your guitar, Sing it, kid/Just write about your feelings, not the things you never did."

The song is an expression of a young man's individuality, a stab at being different, in a search for the most living life has to give. Music is the young man's form of self-expression, but also a close friend and advisor, "You can hear your footsteps shuffling in the dust/Rustling of the shadows tells you secrets you can trust."

Chapin also makes a point about his age, and the fears of growing old without some great accomplishment, but he wants to pass his knowledge on to his son, to start him on the same road he passed as a growing boy. And so the story ends, and so the story begins again. He sings of the mortality of his self, but his dreams and hopes, through each preceding and each following generation, each revolution of the wheel, starts an old journey all anew. Each individual is not really separate, but each entity is only one being, striving as a whole toward perfection. The only problem is that there are so many footsteps to take, and each foot is unaware what the other is doing until the results can be analyzed and the next move made. Only experience counts, and to gain this, inexperience must be overcome, only to reveal more inexperience to be overcome again.

"Strum your guitar, Sing it, kid/Just write about your feelings, not the things you never did."

—*Cary*

Certainly, this is a fine effort for so short a time.

To illustrate further the point that we are all different as writers and as revisers, look at how we three—Dan, Dawn, and Tom—write. Tom is usually a two-draft writer, or he may do three drafts sometimes if the piece is for publication. Dan is a reflective writer, thinking about and planning for a long time what he will write, organizing it in his head. Then, he writes a first draft, usually on the computer. Dan needs to see a printed copy of his writing in order to work on it further, so he prints his draft, seeks feedback on it, writes another draft by editing and revising with a pen on the printed copy of his first draft, and seeks more feedback. Then, he finishes it all up in one or two more drafts. Dawn composes only on the computer now, waiting to do a first draft until she can be on the computer. She writes a first draft straight through with lots of in-process revision. She has some general idea about what she wants to write before sitting down at the computer, but she shapes her writing more at the point of utterance rather than in advance in her head. She's not the careful advance planner that Dan is, nor is she the nearly one-draft writer that Tom is. Like Dan, Dawn prints her draft, revises it with pen in hand, and then returns to the computer for more drafts, seeking feedback from a partner after her second or third draft.

Dawn is a meticulous proofreader as she writes. Dan worries about proofreading only at the end of his writing, and he'd prefer that an editor take care of most of the pickier details for him. Tom uses lots of in-process revising as he goes slowly through his writing, proofreading along the way. We also write at different speeds. Dawn likes chunks of writing time in front of the computer and pushes through to the end of the draft before quitting. Tom writes a little each day; it took him over nineteen days to draft his part of this chapter. Dan, on the other hand, wrote a draft of the whole chapter on the journal in two hours; he revised it extensively after that, and finished the whole chapter in less than three days. Despite our differences, we all go through the *agonies* of prewriting. We think that is universal for writers.

The point is that there will be all kinds of writer/revisers in any writing class you teach, and all of them need your suggestions and encouragement to get better at writing.

IDEA #8 *Students should have the choice not to revise.* Remember that students can't really do a good job of revising unless the piece is important to them. If they are not ready for revising, or not really involved in the writing, then pushing them to edit in depth and proofread in detail will be a frustrating experience for them and an exasperating one for you. As you work on revision, be sensitive to when students have had enough. Dennis and Tom could have continued with Dennis' paper, but both of them were tired of it after four drafts. They may return to it later, but they had done enough for the moment.

Remember, also, that sometimes the piece of writing itself is not worth the trouble. Sometimes, filing the writing in the Writer's Notebook is enough.

Keeping It Going

Most students we teach come to us knowing nothing of revision beyond hunting for errors in a first draft, and they're not very good at that. What we have to do first is get them to work on a paper for a longer period of time than a class period. Sometimes more than fifteen minutes.

Students want to finish the thing and turn it in. We want them to write something real for them and for us and turn it into a quality piece of work. How do we keep them working, writing, revising, and editing?

First, the writing must be important *to the student* because *their writing belongs to them*. You will save yourself and your students a lot of grief—and your students will write better—if you can accept that idea.

Working in response groups in an inviting and encouraging atmosphere shows students possibilities and lets them know that their writing is appreciated and is taken seriously. For most students, their peers' approval makes the difference between writing that is merely a class exercise, something to get done and turn in, and writing that is an expression of who they are.

We push our student writers. Nancie Atwell "nudges" her students. We shove ours. "Tell me more. Tell me more." They hear that more than anything else from us. We tell them frankly, "You are used to finishing it and turning it in. I want you to try to stretch it. There's something here you haven't said yet," and we tell them, "Write more. Tell it all. Take the reader with you."

Our students write lots of short, exploratory pieces, looking for important writings that will grab them. Then, we have them work on what Dan has termed *elaboration* and *crafting*. These are two types of revision for which Dan has devised specific activities suited to the type of writing that students are doing. Take a look at his notes on the personal narrative, the kind of writing done in the "Anatomy" suggested on page 20 of Chapter 2. The following are brief samples of these types of revisions as devised by Dan for the memoir framework.

Elaboration: First Revision Options for Personal Narrative

Read your piece aloud to a partner. Listen for places where you can add more stuff. Mark these places as you read it.

Try at least two elaborations. More is better.

1. *Character.* Flesh out a person in your story. Describe the character in more detail. Select one or two things about the character and develop them like a cartoonist would. How do his hands look? How does her mouth work when she smiles or talks? What about hair, eyes, clothes? Favorite sayings? Where do you see the character when you close your eyes?

2. *Dialogue.* Let them talk. Don't tell us what they say. Let's hear it from them. Don't worry about how you punctuate it now. Just use real voices.

3. *Scene Setting.* Develop scenes in your piece in more detail. Look for parts where you mention a place but don't give us a picture of it.

4. *Looping.* Find the best parts in your piece and take off on another freewriting from there. See what else you know about this memory. Run the movie in your head again.

5. *Write More.* Finish it. Tell it all. Pick up the story right where you left off and ride it to the end.

Remember, the key is to write more.

After students have worked with another draft that includes their elaborations and with their response partners, they're ready for further revisions called *crafting*.

Crafting: Second-Revision Options for Personal Narrative

This is the tough part. You have to work alone, and you won't always know what you're doing. You can try these revisions out on somebody later, but right now you have to hack it out alone.

Begin first with chunks, pieces of text that are several sentences long. Choose at least one of these to work with.

Beginnings (Try at Least Two)

1. The Hook: "I should have known Mrs. Swartz hated kids."
2. Scene setting: "It was a dark and stormy night."
3. Telling detail: "There on the pavement was a small child's tennis shoe."
4. Character throwing: "Teddy Howland was the skinniest, ugliest kid in Eureka."
5. Walking: "Giving credit where credit is due, if it hadn't been for my mother, I never would have gotten him in the first place, mainly because my father didn't like dogs" (Goldman 2001).
6. Dialogue: "I'm not even sure I like you."

Endings (Try at Least Two)

1. Circle: End where you began.
2. Aha!: Sadder but wiser, or gee look what I learned.
3. A feeling: Stuck in Mobile with the Memphis blues again.
4. Drawstring: "And that's how it happened."
5. Surprise: The strange twist at the end.

Moving Chunks (No Limit; Cut and Paste)

1. Movement: Pacing readers, making them play your game.
2. Paragraphs: Have some. Keep them short unless they have pictures.
3. Scenes: Shuffling the story.

Deleting Chunks (No Limit; Follow Rules)

1. Nice but doesn't fit. Save it.
2. Not nice and doesn't fit either. Cut it.

3. Eradicate chaff words: *-ly* words, *being* words.
4. Compact and compress. Cut the "telling."

Now that the hard part is done, turn to some relaxing sentence-level revisions. Make at least ten specific changes.

Sentence Level

1. Concrete detail. Add sensory stuff.
2. Specificity. Name stuff.
3. Strong verbs. Get rid of those adverb props.
4. Search and destroy the *is*'s and *was*'s.
5. Cure a serious case of the *would*'s.

Notice that whether you teach revision strategies like these in two formal steps coupled with response groups and conferences the way Dan and Dawn do or informally in conferences and editing groups the way Tom does, your students are still writing and you haven't gotten to proofreading yet. Do it last, as we suggest, and you will find it is less of a problem than it once was. Try it. It may surprise you.

A Word About the Computer and Revision

Years ago while Tom was working on his dissertation, he spent a lot of time in Dan's home. While Tom was laboriously writing chapters out in longhand and typing them on a typewriter—and retyping and retyping and retyping—Dan was happily working on a couple of books in front of his computer. Tom was tearing his hair out over every revision and every correction in a draft. Dan was pecking away at the computer, easily moving things around in his chapters, cutting and pasting, throwing stuff out, putting things in, fixing things—and *smiling*! By watching Dan, Tom began to think that there might be a better way to revise than the laborious one he was using. Yep.

As we have mentioned in this book, when revision is technically easy, students are more likely to do it. Rather than just retype the piece and fix the commas, students can move chunks of text with ease with the computer. They can save one opening paragraph and write two more to see which one works best. They see how the piece sounds when it starts in the middle or even with the last paragraph of the piece, all with cut-and-paste options that they can undo if the writing isn't enhanced. With the computer, students can re-see their papers each time they drop text in or out of the draft, helping them understand real revision, not just minor correcting. They can track their changes as they write draft to draft, they can chat with student writers in Sweden, and they can use a split screen to see the same portion of their text written in two different ways to help them judge which one is more effective.

Kids learn computing at an early age. Dan and Dawn's seven-year-old daughter can point and click, load software, use painting and drawing programs, play games on the computer, compose simple word-processed texts, use the Internet to get to favorite websites, and type with more than just her two index fingers. Who knows the extent to which computers will assist her as a writer, reviser, and editor? (We'll take careful notes and send you an email.) But it's clear that today's students know lots about useful computing that can enhance their writing and academic lives—not just their knowledge of games—with the right encouragement.

Help students explore PowerPoint® presentations instead of just making the same old dreary speech. Help them add clip art and charts and graphs and spreadsheet data to their action research papers. Encourage them to work with digital photographs and streaming video as part of the multimedia presentations of their writing. We know that computers enhance writing, but we don't yet know many of the inherent limits and liabilities for writers. For now, the limits may be only our own lack of resources and confidence. Explore and experiment. Encourage and turn your students loose to research and write and revise on the computer. Show students your writing and revising processes by working on the computer in front of them.

As with most else that we do when we teach writing, we use computers and word processing with our students because that's how we write, and we want our students to see real writers at work. Modeling, discussing, and working on all phases of writing together—that's what works best for us as writers and as teachers.

Note

1. Dennis Turner, Lynn Aaron, and Cary Quinn were students at Gainesville High School, Gainesville, GA.

Works Cited

DILLARD, ANNE. 1998. "To Fashion a Text." In *Inventing the Truth, the Art and Craft of Memoir*, edited by William Zinsser. Boston: Houghton Mifflin.

GOLDMAN, WILLIAM. *The Temple of Gold*. New York: Ballantine.

11

Writing Poetry

*Poetry helped make me the person I am today, awakening creative
elements that had long lain dormant in me, opening my mind to ideas,
and enabling my intellect to nourish itself on alternative ways of being.
Poetry enhanced my self-respect. It provided me with a path for
exploring possibilities for my life's enrichment that I follow to this day.*

—Jimmy Santiago Baca, *A Place to Stand*

"Can I write a poem instead?"

Tom looked up at him from his carefully made plans for that Monday morning
class, plans he had sweated over the night before. What he was really thinking about
before Johnny broke into his assignment-giving routine was how badly he wanted
another cup of coffee.

"Do you think you can handle it?" Tom asked with only a slight edge of sarcasm
in his voice. Tom was looking for something to get these kids going. It was a large
Basic English class for juniors, loud and often defiant. He had lost some sleep over
them already. Besides, it was too early in the course to be fooling around with poetry.

Johnny's big hands fumbled with the anthology of too-hard and too-dull stories,
and worse poems—but cheap and on the state's approved list.

Tom stalled him. "Look, what about one of those other writings? How about an
interview with one of the characters in the story?" Tom wondered if Johnny was trying to duck the assignment. Johnny hadn't done much so far with writing.

"Naw," Johnny said, "I got an idea, but it's a *poem*. I don't feel like doing none of
that other stuff." So much for planning. But he did look as if he was interested.

"Do it," Tom said. Johnny smiled and went back to his seat in the back of the
room. At the end of the period he turned in this:

A Kiss

A kiss is short and sweet, but
after that it is gone forever just

> a soft quiet touch in your memory.
> Showing your love and
> care for her and letting her know
> she's yours. Just a touch of the lips
> is now forever gone, but soon
> another one will be coming on.[1]

Tom was disappointed. That was *all* Johnny had written in response to a story on which the class had spent so much time? We suspect that your reaction now is similar to Tom's thoughts then. The poem is inchoate and rather silly. Nothing very profound is said in those fifty-five words. Besides, it doesn't *look* like a poem. By any adult standard, it's just not very good stuff.

But Johnny's eager and proud expression when he turned in the piece kept Tom from saying anything right then. It seemed to be important to Johnny somehow, so Tom reserved judgment and took it home with the other papers. Tom put it aside until he read the others. He really didn't know what to do with it.

When Tom reread the poem, he was thinking about *Johnny*, not about the *assignment*. It was the first thing he had written in which he was personally involved. It was *real* writing, not just writing for the teacher. Of course, it was adolescent. He was using his own experience to respond to a reading assignment in which he saw some of his own feelings reflected. Although the piece may not be profound, it does work as a poem. It has movement and rhythm, alliteration and rhyme, figurative language, and a gentle sort of irony. And it has a striking image in the third line—"a soft quiet touch in your memory." Johnny used the techniques of the poet, not because Tom had labored over rhyme and meter and metaphor in class, but because Johnny had something to say and intuitively used those language resources, automatically fitting the form to what he was saying.

In poetry, as in all writing, the technical aspects of the poem are really of secondary importance; good writing is *honest* writing. The writer risks feelings with us, and we respond to the words because they touch our feelings through shared human experiences. The subtleties of form, the intricacies of vocabulary, the erudition of allusion may contribute to the experience and to our pleasure in the work, but without that risk-taking and sharing of feeling, they are an empty shell. For an adolescent boy in a large and rowdy high-school class to write about kissing a girl this way, he has to take quite a chance with his reader.

This raises an important point about Johnny's poem. One of the best ways to encourage immature writers and to help them control their writing, without crushing them with the weight of unreasonable adult expectations, is to use the natural audience in the classroom. Johnny's adolescent poem was written for adolescents; adolescents read and responded to it, and they liked it so much that they put it in the school literary magazine. That did more for Johnny's writing than anything any teacher could have done.

Writing Poetry: Things to Remember

1. *The growth process in writing poetry is the same growth process operating in all forms of writing.* Most teachers are intimidated about writing poetry, although they teach it effectively as literature. Usually students are not given an opportunity to write poetry or, worse, they are expected to start generating Petrarchan sonnets or haiku (the more difficult of the two forms to write!) the first time poetry writing is assigned. The results are predictably dismal, and teachers are further convinced that students cannot, and should not, write poetry.

Poetry grows the same way prose does. It's not a mysterious process. When Johnny wrote "A Kiss," he was just becoming fluent as a writer. He needed a lot of practice. Strong criticism would have been of little help, and would have done considerable damage, until he reached a point at which he was more comfortable with writing. You can already see at this early stage in his writing that poetic form was beginning to emerge.

Especially in poetry, content controls form. The natural spoken rhythms of the language help form lines and even stanzas as the student writes more. You may want to suggest alternate forms for a particular verse, but such crafting of writing happens in later drafts and revisions of a piece of writing. The best thing you can do at the beginning is to *let* form be controlled by content.

2. *If there had not been a plan for writing in the classroom, with many options and with personal writing encouraged and supported, then the poem would never have been written.* Writing must be planned, but there must also be freedom for the students to explore their own forms of expression. When students are ready to try new forms of writing, especially those first few times, support their efforts fully.

In other words, students must have the freedom to start some place. Whenever possible, remove the restrictions, give them their heads, and be receptive to their efforts. Class environment is crucial, and you set the tone.

3. *The important thing is that Johnny wrote what he wanted to write.* That's the whole point of a writing class. As long as the student is writing about what's important to him, then his writing is real, it's motivated, and it's likely to improve.

When poetry is first written, it is almost always personal, as is all real writing. As immature writers grow, their writing will naturally become less egocentric. They will strive to reach their peers, and perhaps eventually a wider audience, and that growth will move them gradually away from what is sometimes painfully personal writing. The intimate nature of these early efforts, however, puts a heavy burden on the teacher. Tact and sensitivity are required when a student writes about that first kiss.

4. *At this point in the writing, quality is not the most important consideration.* Expectations of Wordsworthian or even Brautiganesque prosody will only stop the student from writing. Lower your standards a little. At first, the emphases should be on hon-

est writing and honest responding. Understanding and recognition are what students are seeking. Save the criticism for when they are more accomplished and confident.

Encourage them to practice. Take a risk yourself. Respond with a poem of your own. Give them lots of opportunities to write and share their poetry.

5. *Gently push students to widen their audience.* Display poetry in your room. Publishing student poetry in the classroom is easily done and is the best possible way to encourage more poetry writing. When others are regularly reading and responding to their writing, students work hard at shaping and fine-tuning their poems. Student readers are always the best audience for student poets.

6. *Kids like poetry.* There's a kind of freedom in writing poetry that appeals to many students. They feel less threatened by poetry than by prose writing. Johnny is a good case in point.

Because poetry is usually an intense and brief writing experience, students are often able to write and rewrite a complete draft in a class period and get immediate satisfaction from the finished job. They also can receive an immediate response to what they have written, which is especially important for those students for whom writing is an ordeal, threatening failure. Positive responses encourage writers and make them believe that they *can* write something that others want to read.

7. *When poetry writing is taught, prose should also be an option.* Just as Johnny had the choice of writing poetry when the assignment was prose, the student should have the choice of *not* writing poetry in any given situation. Understandably enough, some students are afraid of poetry. Johnny may be an exception, but there is evidence that most writers must write prose before they can write poetry. It's not unusual even for an accomplished poet to begin a poem with a prose sketch.

The writing teacher can be alert for prose pieces from the students that are rich in images and wordplay that might easily be turned into poetry (the reverse is also true, of course—poetry can become prose sometimes). Students can learn a great deal about their language by switching forms with a piece of writing, that is by turning a piece of poetry into prose or a piece of prose into poetry. There's also the option of prose-poetry, a form of writing popular with modern writers and one that has many possibilities for the classroom. The best way to encourage reluctant poets, however, is sharing with them and the class the writing of their peers. They see that it's not so hard after all and will often try it themselves on the next assignment.

8. *Understanding poetry follows most naturally from fooling around with poetry.* To teach poetry by parsing lines, unstringing iambs, and calculating rhyme schemes is a barren exercise unless students have done a lot of writing, sharing, and talking about poetry previously. Reading is important, of course, to the poet. Put off the classic poets until later. Instead, get out poets like Jimmy Baca, Jorey Graham, Gary Snider, Nikki Giovanni, Billy Collins, and even the pop songwriters to whom your students listen all the time. Popular singer Jewel, for instance, has published a book of poetry (*not*

song lyrics) that is popular with young adults. It's a bit steamy in places, so use it with caution. It's time we declared a moratorium on the Great Symbol Hunt in poetry teaching and, instead, allow students to create their own symbols. Even if students never write very good poetry in your class, they will learn about poetry by playing with it. Then, they will enjoy reading poetry more.

9. *Writing poetry is one of the best ways to study language*. As students write and share and write again, they begin with their knowledge of words from spoken language. They expand on that knowledge very quickly, however. Every time they grapple with a different image, a subtle emotion, or an elusive rhyme or line ending and have to hunt for a word that fits, their language grows. Every time they ask you, "What's the word for this?" or say, "This word doesn't sound right here," they're growing as users and writers of language. (They may also come to appreciate a thesaurus!)

10. *Grade poetry very carefully and very gently*, just like all writing in your class. Many teachers don't give students the opportunity to write poetry because they don't feel they know enough about how to grade it. However, the approaches to writing we are suggesting will revise your grading strategies and make the question unimportant. We suggest some alternative methods to red-pencil grading that we have found particularly useful when students in our classes write poetry.

Early poetry from the student is *not graded at all*. It is read and responded to; it is shared and published in some form. It may be displayed in the room, or photocopied and passed around, or read aloud. The student is given credit for doing the assignment. Tom uses a point-based grading system for early poetry efforts by students. A portfolio or folder may be used in which the writing can be kept to be examined in a private conference to decide on a grade later. Or, selected pieces can be revised for careful (and perhaps gentle) grading after the student has more practice with writing poetry.

Once a student is a practiced poet and begins to demonstrate control of poetic form, Tom usually insists on certain types of revisions of the draft poetry in order to encourage the student poet to attempt new techniques with poetry. The student picks the specific works to be revised. Tom responds as a *reader* to the student as a *writer*. The grade is negotiable, depending on the extent and kind of revision done, but the grade is not given until the revising is done.

Every once in a while Tom has had a class in which most of the students write poetry with ease. They control form and content, are sensitive to audience, and seem to be able to write poetry at will in addition to revising it effectively. Developing as a poet takes time, and students will have to write a lot of poetry and struggle with a lot of revisions, getting it right, before they reach this stage. Most high-school students never get there and should not be expected to do so. When Tom senses poetry control in a class, however, he pushes students beyond their comfort zones to try new poetry forms and techniques. He also encourages them to publish outside of class and outside of school.

Do not try to push advanced writing and publishing too soon. Even the best student poets react at first with fear. It's a big step to move from the safe approval of their friends to the harsh scrutiny of the marketplace. *Students must be well prepared for such a step and know what to expect.* A rejection slip is hard to take for any writer, much less one inexperienced in the ways of publishers. Once students are prepared, we get down to work. In conference, in groups, and as a class, we pick their very best stuff. We fine-tune those poems, reading them again and again for flaws. We prepare them for publication, working together as editors, and we search for places to send them, including appropriate websites and e-zines. Tom always sends some of his own poetry off when the students do. Then we watch the mail together and wait anxiously for notice about the fate of our work.

These days of feverish activity are the best possible in a writing class, and they don't come very often. But that look in a kid's eye when he bursts into your room waving an acceptance letter from a little magazine in Podunk will keep you working hard at teaching poetry for years!

11. *If the poem is just plain* bad, *look hard for something* good *in it*—especially if it is an early poem from the student. Search for an interesting image, a well-done metaphor or simile, a phrase, a *word*! If there is nothing in that poem you can *honestly* applaud (but there almost always is), then you are reduced to merely offering encouragement, which also helps immature writers.

If the poem is from a student you know is practiced enough to exercise some control, and if you are asked for a response, be gentle but *be honest*. Your judgment as an informed reader is important. Don't be afraid to exercise it when the time is right.

The important thing with poetry is that students need immediate response to their writing. Because poetry is a short, intense experience, it lends itself to the kinds of pieces that can be done in a single class period, yielding fast results. Look for ways to celebrate and *publish* students' poetry in order to keep spirits and efforts high.

Remember that developing techniques and trying out new forms and ideas are important for developing student poets. Here are some ideas for ways to help students produce accessible poetry.

Name Poetry

This simple kind of poetry—name poetry—works with the poetic line from the most natural of starting places—the student. You will need a supply of butcher paper or newsprint, felt-tipped pens, and masking tape.

Students write their names down the page, one letter per line. Each letter becomes the first letter in the line. We suggest they begin with one-word descriptions, asking students to be honest about themselves. We put our name poetry on the board first, making it up on the spot.

Sometimes the kids get in on the act and yell out suggestions as we write it. Several students helped Tom write this one.

> Teacher
> Odd
> Moustache
> Laughing
> Intense
> Nutty
> Easy going
> Riter [sic]

(You may want to cheat and write yours the night before class.)

The second poem is written with lines, and we ask students to tell a ministory about themselves or simply write about themselves. Teresa had school on her mind.

> Toward the
> End of the day
> Restless in class
> Encouraging my
> Silly self to go on
> Alone.[1]

Winford is more religious than most, and he rhymed his name in this way:

> We walk along the dim shore
> In the light that shows the way
> Not the light that brings the day
> For He is the Way
> One man that leads the way
> Reads the words that he had to say
> Death carry me away[1]

But Gene just likes to be strange:

> Go to the moon
> Eliminate the sunshine
> North of the south star
> East of the western hemisphere
>
> Sit on all the cheese
> Mirage of purple creatures
> In and out of the shadowing light
> To the far side where it's dark
> Holes and mountains disappear[1]

After several tries, we work together choosing the best poem, cleaning up spelling, and thinking of better words to use in places. The finished poem is copied onto the butcher paper and displayed in the room.

If your students are interested, name poetry has other possibilities. Writing a name poem about another person in the class is a way to share personalities. If you want to push the students to be a little more sophisticated, you can try having them rhyme the lines or you can have them write lines with a specific number of words or syllables per line. (Five words or ten syllables usually work well.) Or, you can branch out into more abstract subjects for name poems—love, hate, beauty, death, life, friendship—the list is endless. Finally, consider having students respond to a piece of literature by having them write a name poem about a character.

Prose into Poetry

Have your students freewrite several times while listening to different kinds of music, or have them freewrite on such potentially symbolic or abstract topics as rain, snow, wind, the tread of a cat, or fear. Help them pick the piece that is most "poetic." Encourage them to throw away every spare word or sentence in the piece that they possibly can. Then, chop what is left into lines, making it a poem.

Happy's poem started as a journal entry about daydreaming. We cut it into lines first.

Daydream (Original Prose Draft)

Where have you gone, so many times I wonder/And I turn around, there you are/ but it's only a dream./Thinking of old times when you walked down the hall/You're on my mind all the time,/on the road, and everywhere./Where did you go when it ended?/Somewhere far off./When I think of you, it's a sad expression in my mind./It was talking with you all those crazy lines./I dream of a dream with you in it and I am lonely./It was only a daydream with you/as only a vision in my head./It was only crazy to dream that daydream everyday./Yes, you were the one in my life./Trying to get you back into this world of mine is only a dream I once had./The nights are dark/ and filled of many things I wish I had said./I let you go into the clouds/and now you're nothing but a dream/and I'm the dreamer/wanting to see/this dream of you come true, someday.[1]

Then we marked off stanzas where the natural breaks in ideas seem to fall, and Tom suggested what might be cut out to tighten the poem a little. Suddenly, Happy had made a poem.

Daydream
Where have you gone, so many times I wonder,
And when I turn around, there you are,
But it's only a dream.

155

Thinking of old times when you walked down the hall.
You're on my mind all the time.
On the road,
Where did you go when it ended?

When I think of you, it's a sad feeling in my mind.
It was talking with you all those crazy lines.
I dream of a dream with you in it.

And I am lonely.
It was only a daydream with you.
As only a vision of the past in my head.
Trying to get you back into this world of mine,
Only a daydream I once had.
The nights are dark
And filled with many things I wish I had said.[1]

It is also interesting to have students turn poems into prose.

Dawn has had good success with having students turn professionally published pieces of prose into poetry. This activity works well with descriptive, evocative, or lyrical writing, and it teaches students to capture the essence of the piece. Dawn uses nonfiction essays, such as those by nature writers, most often for this activity. Try excerpts from the writings of Annie Dillard, Loren Eiseley, or Barry Lopez for openers; then, discover your own favorites. After students have switched the published prose to their own poetry, Dawn and her students discuss the merits of each piece— published prose and the genre-switched poem—noting similarities and differences. Students come away from this activity with a better understanding of the essay because they had to read and reread it carefully in order to create a poem from it. They also better understand the format and precision of poetry. Finally, Dawn likes this activity because students take from it the knowledge that they can write poetry.

Don't Forget the Good Old Paraphrase

Paraphrasing a poem is a good exercise in dealing with language. With immature writers, you'll need to pick the poems carefully, however. Keep them short. Narrative poetry works well, as do song lyrics. Remember, the purpose is to play with language and meaning, not study classic poetry.

Sometimes an assignment to paraphrase a song can turn into considerably more than that, as in this response to the Jefferson Airplane's "White Rabbit" by Cindy.

The drumsticks, gently tapping
    Are vibrating my eardrums.
The music, gradually louder
        waves crashing against my brain.
        Slick's voice; uncaring, evil/telling the truth

> The pills slowly falling
>   thousands from the sky
> The trip is really freaky
>   with white rabbits and all
> Grace singing in the corner/telling them all
>   Go ask Alice/She thinks I'll know . . .[1]

The following fine but disturbing poem by Jimmy began as a paraphrase of Leo Kottke's song "Morning Is the Long Way Home," but it soon became its own work, far removed from the original song/poem.

Bleed Silver

> The streets unfold.
> a town. It throws.
> a straight. It hits.
> But warm, wet blood/burns cold, wrenched steel.
>
> And light bathes
> A cool green glow moves
> Softness is the real dream
> Real dream.
> How can you ask why?
>
> Wet glows fade to
> Glowing realities
> So bright as to seem vision.
> But beyond the point is the only/Living Silver.
>
> Your silver spoon bleeds
> a fatal wound
> From my steel
> That always unfolds the street.[1]

Personal Poetry Anthology

An anthology of personal poetry takes time, and we suggest that you allow at least a week for it. Bring in several poetry anthologies with themes that will appeal to your students. Classic favorites of Tom are *On City Streets, The Poetry of Rock, The Poetry of the Blues, Reflections on a Gift of Watermelon Pickle, Some Haystacks Don't Even Have Any Needle,* and *Two Ways of Seeing.* Talk about the titles of the collections and the way each one is organized, using the table of contents. Talk about the kinds of poems in the collections and why they were chosen for each book. Talk about the illustrations. Read what the editors say in the prefaces and introductions.

    Students may work in pairs to make their own anthologies. We suggest that each anthology contain about twenty short poems chosen because the students like them and because they go together thematically. The anthology should have a brief preface or introduction, in which students explain why the poems were chosen and how they are related and organized, and a table of contents. We encourage students to illustrate their anthologies with magazine photos or with their own drawings and to make fancy covers for them with original titles. We also encourage students to include some of their own poetry or the poetry of their classmates in their collections, but we don't always require that students do so.

Dawn has had great success with a themed anthology modeled after Edgar Lee Masters' *Spoon River Anthology*. Creating characters, interweaving plots, and depicting settings all through soliloquies spoken from the grave appeal to many students. After character and subplots are established in the poetry, students illustrate gravestones, the town, or the living relatives of the characters found in their poetry on a bulletin board or on butcher paper for display in the class alongside their anthologies. This multimedia work helps students delve into the literature, write their own poetry, and work on presentational options. The displays are also impressive for Parent Night.

The students' finished personal poetry anthologies are fun to share. We have colored paper, a box of magazines for pictures, markers and pens, and other materials on hand to help students make the booklets attractive. Of course, the computer is a great tool for creating borders, finding clip art, using fonts to enhance the poetry, and for creating color displays.

Found Poetry, Dada Poetry

Have the students search for quotations they like from any source and on any subject. Suggest that they look for quotations in songs, posters, advertisements, street signs, movies, TV programs, news broadcasts, and websites. We make available in class as many sources as we can find—newspapers, magazines (the ads are good for this activity), copies of CD inserts, favorite short books, and posters. We also provide computer time so that students can explore interesting websites.

Have the students share with the class particular favorites they have found, and put the best ones on the board. Talk about the *words* and *phrases* that are most effective, that hit the hardest, and that sound the best.

The students may work individually, with a partner, or in groups of three. (We suggest no more than three students per group for this activity.) Brainstorm with them subjects for their found poems. Subjects should be fairly general—school, things I like, things I hate, favorite sports, life in my neighborhood, love, children, working, my friends, happy things, bad things, weather, seasons. With a general topic, students are less likely to become frustrated in looking for fitting quotations. Emphasize that they are to look for quotations that get at the feeling of the topic chosen, not necessarily ones that describe the topic exactly.

After a subject is chosen, have students find and copy the chosen quotations, in no particular order, that they like for it. At this point, it is helpful to show them examples of found poems on topics similar to the one they have chosen, preferably poems made by other students. If no student examples are handy, you may want to share found poems of your own. This one is from the local newspaper on a normal day.

Classified

APARTMENT FURNISHED
Bachelor
unique duplex
carpet, icemaker, micro oven
bar and fireplace
TV and AC
lakefront.
883–1401

FIREWOOD
all oak
cut, split, delivered
after 7 pm

MAID WANTED
no ref. light work
nights

MONEY TO LEND

Then you work with the students choosing the best order of parts for their found poems, deleting words and phrases not needed, and cleaning up the final copy.

A refinement of this kind of assignment is the modified *Dada poem* (nonsense poem). We use the term to refer to a poem fabricated from pieces of other writing, not for the literary and artistic movement attributed to Tristan Tzara. To make a Dada poem, the student takes words, phrases, sentences, or lines from other writings (from a daily newspaper, for example) and combines them like a puzzle to make a poem, usually absurdly funny. This Dada poem was pieced together from country and rock music oldies.

Mamas don't let your babies
grow up to be cowboys with
four hungry children and a
crop in the field.
My mama's got a squeeze box
she wears on her chest and
my daddy don't rock-n-roll.
Love me tender or do you
just want to fool around?

. . .

Baby, come back! Any kind
of fool can see—you're sixteen,
you're beautiful, and you're mine.
I see a bad moon rising,
so take it on home.

—*Teresa and Heidi*[1]

As a further refinement, have students make Dada poems by combining lines, parts of lines, and single words from other poems, either poems dealing with a single subject or well-known poems from one poet.

The Good Old Reliable Cinquain

We suggest that you teach the cinquain in three stages, moving from a loose word cinquain form to the rigidly structured formal cinquain based on syllable count.

THE SIMPLE WORD CINQUAIN The first time your students write cinquains, have them write a simple five-line poem following this pattern:

1. The first line contains one word, usually but not necessarily the subject of the poem.
2. The second line contains two words.
3. The third line contains three words.
4. The fourth line contains four words.
5. The last line again is only one word, which may be repeated from line one.

Frog
Funky warts
Making foggy sounds
Lovely, Madly, Slimy, Green
Frog

—*Terrill*[1]

Rain
Damp grass
Lonely, Misty Trees.
Lost in thoughts of you.
Empty.

—*Dan Kirby*

THE REGULATED WORD CINQUAIN This poem is like the first, except the content of each line is prescribed. It's harder to write.

160

1. The first line contains one word that names a thing.
2. The second line contains two words that describe the thing in line one.
3. The third line contains three words that describe an action related to the thing.
4. The fourth line contains four words that express a feeling about the thing.
5. The fifth line contains one word that sums up the entire poem.

> bass
> dark silver
> ambush from silence
> shattering the pond's stillness
> predator

THE FORMAL CINQUAIN This is the form invented by Adelaide Crapsey and is based on the syllable count of two, four, six, eight, and two syllables per line. Students who are already experienced with poetry should have no trouble with the formal cinquain.

> moon up
> over the trees
> shadows dance in cold light
> something moving down the darkness
> silence
>
> —*Tom Liner*

The cinquain is a friendly kind of writing to do. Reluctant poets, younger kids, even those students who are accomplished poets already—all of them like the cinquain. Like all poetry written in your class, it should be shared, copied, and passed around or, better yet, put up for display.

I Remember *Poetry*

The instructions for *I Remember* poetry (Grossman 1991) are simple. It works best when you write with students and show them how you do it first.

Open your journal and make a list, starting each line with "I remember. . . ." The memories can be important or trivial. Make the list quickly. It will serve as a type of jot list. Here's a sample list from Tom's journal written with a ninth-grade class at Albany High School in Georgia.

> I remember slamming Tommy's hand in the car door
> I remember Anna's birth
> I remember Terri's death—the phone call

I remember a '58 Edsel
I remember a shotgun in the car window
I remember Panther Creek
I remember W. Gordon Street, Rossville
I remember seeing little Thomas the first time
I remember skydiving
I remember Roundhouse Shoal on the White River
I remember Doc Anderson
I remember flying a kite with my brother Steve.

Next, share the lists, but don't talk them to death. Then, choose the lines from your list that will become part of your poem, adding others as needed and editing as you go.

Matt is quite an outdoorsman, and his poem is about his first South Georgia duck hunt.

The Duck Hunt

I remember my first duck hunt
paddling out to the blind
into the long tall sawgrass
the ducks feeding
in the back of the pond.

Too dark to see,
yet the tale-tell sound
of beating wings
is all too tempting.
I peer over the tall sawgrass
to see many dancing shadows.

As I stand in the blind
I see a lone duck
winging for my stand nestled in the tall grass.
I ready my gun and slowly
shoulder the weapon.

All is silent
as I carefully watch the form wing overhead
as the boom of my shotgun
awakens the early morning dawn.

—Matt[2]

Class Poetry

The class poem or collaborative poem is a good place to start your most reluctant student poets. Each student contributes one line of the poem anonymously. You collect the lines and put the poem on the board. A student can claim ownership if the other kids in the class like the line.

The form and something of the content of the line should be given in your instructions. A popular line-starter is the phrase "I wish. . . ." Students include in the line a cartoon character, a color, and the name of a place. The kids, of course, often break the rules, but that's not important. What is important is imaginative combinations and the repetition that holds the poem together. Here's a sample collaborative poem from one class:

> I wish that I was Superman so that I could fly to Florida,
>   spend the night at the Palms Hotel and go to the blue beach.
> I wish I could see Donald Duck standing on his hands eating an
>   orange and drinking water.
> I wish that I lived in the country so that I could have some
>   horses and a red and black house with a bulldog.
> I wish I was Bugs Bunny so the kids will think I am funny.
> I wish I was Shazam because when I hit the ground everything will
>   say, "Bam!"
> I wish I was in a spaceship going to the moon.
> I wish I was like Spiderman and could spray people with my web.
> I wish I was in Florida where I could kill Mr. Jaws.
> I wish I had a go-cart so I could jump the Grand Canyon with
>   Evel Knievel.
> I wish I was in the city to meet Flip Wilson.
> I wish I was Superman and could fly all over New York City.
> I wish I was Ultraman for I could fight all the monsters.
> I wish I was in the country where I could have beautiful flowers
>   all around and grass growing everywhere.
> I wish I was Fat Albert because I want to be fat and have a lot
>   of friends to play with everyday.
> I wish I was a blue jay so I could play in the sky and live in
>   a tree in my own little nest.
> I wish I was a red car and could drive away to Atlanta forever.
> I wish I was Popeye eating spinach so I could beat you up.
> I wish I lived in Atlanta so I could be close to Six Flags.
> I wish I had a dog that had his tail on his face and his name
>   was Pluto.

I wish I had a farm that had horses, cows, chickens, and Porky,
    Pluto, Daffy, and Mickey Mouse working on it.
I wish I had a date with Mickey Mouse, and everything went goofy
    because Minny Mouse showed up.
I wish I would turn bright red so you could go to bed.
I wish I could turn my back and count to thirty and see Grapeape
    dirty.
I wish I saw Superman in color on TV on Halloween and then I
    would grab him out of the TV.[3]

This same form, of course, can also be used for individual poems.

Being the Thing

The technicalities of poetic terminology can be deadly dull for all but the most so-phisticated consumers of poetry, but writing activities can prompt the use of figura-tive language and other poetic techniques even if you don't formally teach the terminology. Try asking students to write prose-poems that begin with "If I were . . ." *wind* or *rain* or *sun*, or whatever the weather outside the room might suggest. Many students enjoy being the thing, and metaphors come naturally from their active imaginations.

Look at these students' "Being the Thing" prose-poems[3]:

If I was wind, I would make people's hair go up and down.

—Emma

If I was the rain I could hear the children splash me.

—Patricia

If I was snow when the sun comes out, I would hide in a very little corner.

—Mary

Sometimes a student will come up with something more sophisticated, and you have to be sensitive to possibilities. When thinking about how to "be the wind," Gary turned in this piece:

The wind blows freely across the sky and I just sit and look at the clouds
go by and I think of a way to be part of the wind.

Then, Gary added this part:

The wind blows across the sky making birds free and high.
The wind cools the sun blows the trees and gives me a breeze.

But Gary wasn't through yet. After looking through some books of modern poetry for models, he edited the appearance of his poem. Gary worked on line breaks and spacing techniques particularly appropriate to this poem about wind and freedom.

> The wind blows freely across the sky and I
>   just sit and look at the clouds go by,
> And I think of a way to be part of the wind.
>
> The wind blows across the sky making birds
>   free and high.
> The wind cools the sun, blows the trees and gives me
>   a breeze.
>
>   —Gary[3]

As with most writing, work, reflection, and revision paid off.

Sometimes You Get One Like That: Teaching the Exceptional Student Poet[4]

Late in an afternoon in early autumn, Tom was still in his classroom reading student journals, trying to finish that final stack to return to a class of juniors the next day. No one was around but Tom and the custodian working down the hall. It was a good, quiet time to work and think. Tom was reading Jimmy's journal.

Jimmy was a tall, lonely kid, a quiet and sometimes intense student who sat in the back of the room. He was a competitive swimmer and a good student. He and Tom had talked a little about canoeing, a shared interest. He liked to write, and Tom always looked forward to reading his journal each week. Tom knew he wrote poetry sometimes, but Tom had seen little of it. In a large class with a lot of work to do, the good and quiet student is lost in the daily uproar. But the writing in his journal this particular week seemed particularly sensitive to the details of his surroundings and to the subtle changes in them at this time of the year.

Tom can't remember exactly what it was that struck his attention. Perhaps it was the fragment of a poem Jimmy had started but abandoned for other things. It was only five or six lines long and stopped in midline. But it was good. Outside the classroom windows, the wind played with sunlight in the trees. In Jimmy's journal, Tom wrote a note praising the fragment, and quickly Tom wrote this in response to Jimmy's poem:

> **Perspective**
> maple leaves:
> each one holds
> a piece of sky

and the earth
in its place—

from this window.

The next morning, Tom returned the journals in the usual buzz of excitement that's typical when a class gets involved in the journal—some laughter and smiles at what was written in response to them, some groans at Tom's bad jokes, some arguments over points for credit, some "Hey, look at this" to neighbors across the aisle. Tom gave Jimmy his journal.

"You going to finish that poem? It's real good."

"No, sir, that one doesn't feel right."

He smiled when he read Tom's poem but said nothing. Tom was disappointed. "Well, so much for that," he thought.

But two days later, Jimmy came into the room beaming and thrust his journal into Tom's hands.

"I wrote a good one this time. Want to read it?"

Peep Show

creakcreak   slam
    as the door opens   m swallows
Howdy Pete   so Pete ducks under the senile no-pest strip
    m pulls up a cokecase
Whazat Pete cause Pete's bin stackin wheat but still says he
    feels *good* as he spies the flask stickin outta Pete's
    overhauls
he smiles   standin   neath n old Marlboro sign thatzall faded
    face dirty m hard as Pete's calloused palms

Tom knew that, at sixteen years, Jimmy had the fine touch for detail of a full-fledged poet. But he refused to share his poetry with the class. For all his skill, he was always shy about his poetry and never willing to read it aloud in the classroom. Only much later was he even willing to share it in print. So what do you do when you've got a good young poet on your hands? Tom wrote him a poem back. Tom says that his poem wasn't as good as Jimmy's, but it was still the right response. Jimmy and Tom started a dialogue in poetry that continued for the rest of the year with a "conversation" almost every week.

A week or so after his "Peep Show" poem, Jimmy had been deer hunting.

Burlesque

rehearsing the sight, the squeeze, the kick and fall
oceans beating my brains to dust inside my stand alone but
surrounded

by years-old images of other hunters here before me
    my gun illuminated by a single shaft of filtered light
rests against a tree bole
and also rests inside the cavity in my shoulder
    worn away by years of constant contact with the stock
(the firm steady wooden support)
it is a part of me but remains a useless amputated limb
because it is separated separated and dead
in my mind it also tracks the deer
    tracks the deer and kicks and kicks and kicks and conquers
and time the ever-present harlequin knows this and more

the deer so cautious sniffing the breeze
fool he does not know his danger
    now now the sight rehearsed
    my gun raised from the dust and given life by me
hard, steel-grey still, silent waiting
long-rehearsed the sight
    oceans beating my brains to dust
    the squeeze the kick the fall and
and   and dust

Tom responded with this one about backpacking and a favorite place in the Georgia mountains.

Jacks River
Cohutta Wilderness

the fire-watcher
my boots hanging over my head
wet from the river
that gives and takes
pulling the life from your legs
cold as night and death
and beautiful and strong
my bare feet warm at the fire
but the river talks to me
over the rocks
with laughing promises of another life
and rest
the trees are changing in layers
up the hollow
and high there is sun
very high over the ridge
just touching the tree crown

167

red and yellow, bright
and the river laughs beside me
over the rocks
the trees are changing
and I warm my feet
and stare at my boots hanging over my head
and listen

To which Jimmy, in turn, responded with this magnificently complex poem from his experience canoeing the Chattahoochee River.

The Nexus

the river/here/below the bridge
    it never changes—
    new faces and water and habits/but
    /always the same river
the fighter/the fulcrum
that cannot/give without/taking
or take without giving
it is/its own slave/and/it
pulls us in
onto the treadmill/the sluice/the canoe as it settles
breaks/through the leaves—
    a pasquinade of success
    /reflected from the water/again—sliding forward
and hearing a roar
the bend in the river can't quite contain/develop
    into a frothing fist/looking quickly—
    then in—

a drawstroke to/the right
we miss one/rock but hit another/and another
sending to safety/us in our canoe—
made by/so many different/hands . . .
    /molded into a shell/an animal/a spirit
    vengeful/and/treacherous—
"Goddamnit" from the stern
when we/swirl back/into the current
to be taken away
/and see trees flash by like saviors/
we pull and pull/and pull
but are taken on
down into the rapids/that build into a
white/forest of hands/grasping hands

> and/
> the river/soaks our/safety in contempt
> /sprays it back/in our/faces
> at the entrance to its soul/and fire spurts out
> then rushes us/further
> and/
> capsizes our canoe/swamps
> us and/leeches/into our clothes
> /hair and skin and/boots
> and closes over us like night
> /and contaminating/germs
> we're coughed up on the bank
> and left to dry/while/the river keeps/changing
> but we've taken back part of the river
> and when it dries out of our clothes
> it
> will be dead to us forever

Tom thinks that poem was the best thing Jimmy wrote that year. Jimmy wrote several very fine pieces, but perhaps the most important result from the experience of sharing poetry was his growing confidence in himself as a writer. He was always too shy to read his poetry aloud in class, but he and a few other student writers started a literary magazine later in the year. (They let some of the teachers help.) They actively sought out and published other writers in the school. That magazine, student-generated and student-supported, remains a going concern in the school. Jimmy has since gone on to be a published poet and a serious writer, in addition to being a doctor.

Whenever possible, write, share, and revise your own poetry with your student poets. If you are sensitive about someone else seeing what you write, think how vulnerable your students must feel. There's no substitute for sharing your writing with your students. Grow a tougher hide if you have to, but *write and share your poetry with them.*

Student poets can and should be encouraged to use models from the best poetry in their literary heritage. They need to read widely, especially in the modern poets, and they need to try those forms that appeal to them. Give them room to experiment. The journal, of course, is invaluable. Encourage them to play with the intricacies of meter and rhyme scheme, the complexities of free verse forms, the subtleties of metaphor and imagery. Originality is often not as important as exploration, and an interesting failure is more valuable than a dull, polished draft. Also insist that student poets regularly choose their best work, revise it, and publish it.

Knowing what to do about a skillful student poet like Jimmy is one kind of joyful problem you'll have now and then. Enjoy.

Final Thoughts: More About Poetry

There really is a magic to poetry. It will capture some students if you give it a chance. We either make it harder than it is, or ought to be; or we teach it with gimmicks. Of course, we'll use a gimmick in a heartbeat if it will interest a student and get her writing; we just become concerned when the writing doesn't grow beyond the gimmicks. We've found, however, that students become poets if they're around poetry a lot. It's catching.

Here are a few final suggestions for beginning poetry in your classroom.

1. *Read poetry* aloud *a lot*. Somebody in the room will get the idea and write some of their own. Pretty soon everybody will be writing poetry. This works better if the poetry you read to them is your own.

2. *Search out your own favorite resources for poetry.* Lots of classic and contemporary books have been written about how to teach poetry. See which ones you like the best and try out the ideas in them in your teaching and writing.

3. *Don't overlook the simple List Poem.* A favorite formula lists the senses about any subject you pick.

A frog, for example.

> It looks like—*a baggy suitcase.*
> It sounds like—*sandpaper.*
> It feels like—*a wiggle.*
> It smells like—*green.*
> It tastes like—*yuck!*

Or you can use colors for a quick and enjoyable poem.

> Red sounds like—
> Dark blue tastes like—
> Black feels like—
> Purple smells like—

And there are many, many other kinds of List Poems. In his book, *Writing with Passion*, Tom Romano (1995) has some examples of interesting and sophisticated List Poems. Students can also try out their own ideas, such as Musical Metaphors, Lies, Wish Lists, 10 Interesting Things, 10 Boring Things, Ugly Things, Lovely Things—and catalogues of flowers, birds, animals, cities, countries, friends, and the pleasure of playing with the names of things. Remember that what you are looking for are unusual combinations, unique twists, and surprises. See also the very fine book of ideas for writing poetry by Steve Dunning and Bill Stafford entitled *Getting the Knack* (1992).

4. *You can even cluster a poem*, as Gabriele Rico demonstrates in *Writing the Natural Way* (1999). The object is to write a poem to someone you know well, beginning with a bold statement like "This is a poem about . . ." or "This is my poem for. . . ." Perhaps a jot list would work just as well about the subject of your poem, although Rico's clustering technique is useful to know.

In this poem to his daughter, Tom tried to put it all into one long sentence. It really is a kind of formula poem with the opening and then *who* and *whose* clauses followed by a series of *ands*.

Anna

This is my poem to Anna, whom I hear talking and playing somewhere in my happy house

whose gap-toothed laughing is pure body-joy and sunlight to her daddy, dancing dark eyes and third grade jokes, and open-mouthed singing

who is sitting in the green yard with a cat nobody can touch or even get close to curled purringly in her lap in the sun

and who is running across the afternoon, knees and elbows and boyish strength and little girl skinniness and the fun of just running for no reason

whose watching can be heron-still but never quiet, looking at woodpeckers, frogs, shiners, lizards, baby squirrels, bugs, and looking a long time at turtles and at the living day growing around her

and who does her homework on the floor, books open and scattered like fallen birds around her, intent on the hard mysteries of math, the jokes of spelling, the games of social studies and stringing questions across my evening

and because I listen in this house for your talking and I dance inside at your laughing and because you're almost NINE and this spring is greening toward summer

and to tell you a daddy's love is one thing but I really like you, too, Daughter

When teaching poetry writing to your students, being a poet helps, but having the right attitude and eye and wonder with the world is more important.

Notes

1. Johnny Sheridan, Teresa Lott, Winford Butler, Gene Smith, Happy Smith, Cindy Strickland, Jimmy French, Terrill Brawner, Teresa Lyle, and Heidi Falls were students at Gainesville High School, Gainesville, GA.

2. Matt Rushton was a student at Albany High School, Albany, GA.

3. These examples were composed by students at Clark Middle School, Athens, GA.

4. This section of the chapter is reprinted, with some changes, from *Connecticut English Journal*, Vol. 10, No. 2 (Spring, 1979). Jimmy Barfield is from Gainesville, GA.

Work Cited

BACA, JIMMY SANTIAGO. 2001. *A Place to Stand*. New York: Grove Press.

DUNNING, STEPHEN, AND WILLIAM STAFFORD. 1992. *Getting the Knack, 20 Poetry Writing Exercises*. Urbana, IL: NCTE.

GROSSMAN, FLORENCE. 1991. *Listening to the Bells*. Portsmouth, NH: Heinemann.

RICO, GABRIELE. 1999. *Writing the Natural Way: Turn the Task of Writing into the Joy of Writing*. New York: Putnam.

ROMANO, TOM. 1995. *Writing with Passion*. Portsmouth, NH: Heinemann.

12

Writing About Literature

[R]eading, like writing, should be seen as inventive, constructive activity. . . . They are symbiotic . . . they mutually reinforce, enhance, and shape each other. Reading helps writers discover structures and forms and voices just as writing helps readers uncover meanings and strategies.

—ELEANOR KUTZ AND HEPHZIBAH ROSKELLY, *An Unquiet Pedagogy*

Writing and literature just naturally go together. English teachers become English teachers because they love literature—reading it, discussing it, responding to it, and maybe even writing about it. Many times, English teachers' favorite courses to take as students and to teach to students are literature courses. Many of us would happily teach literature, and only literature, for our entire careers. That's fine, but we find that the longer we teach, the more we look—not for *separate* literature and composition units or classes—but for ways to *combine* literature and composition. After all, both are active meaning-making processes. Good writers write with their readers in mind ("What will my audience need in order to understand what I'm trying to say here?"), and good readers read with the writer in mind ("Why did the author use *that* image and *that* word? What does she want me to think here?). The two processes are reciprocal. We use writing to extend our reading of literary texts and to help us as readers to make sense of text. We use writing about literature as a way to support our analyses and close readings of literary texts. These are techniques that we have learned as students of literature and of writing ourselves, and we want to pass them on to our students. We want to grow lifetime readers and writers and thinkers in our classes. We want to share and enjoy good literature and good writing experiences with our students.

This chapter is not going to tell you *how* to teach literature. (See Chapter 16 for some good ideas on that topic.) What we do discuss in this chapter are techniques and ideas for writing about literature. We begin by giving you some ideas to think about; then, we suggest a few experiences with literature and writing for you to try with your students.

Things to Think About When Your Students Write About Literature

1. *Our job as English teachers is to help our students* experience *literature through writing, as well as reading.* We use writing in the literature class to help our students discover *what* they know about the literature they read. Writing is a way of exploring ideas, of organizing perceptions, of expanding intuitions about experience—including *reading* experience. We encourage our students to explore, clarify, understand, and relate to what they read *in writing.* Writing is a way of approaching meaning in literature backwards or sideways, for more understanding and more enjoyment.

2. *One of the best ways for students to experience literature through writing is the now classic "creative response (CR)."* (See the CR sequence in the activities listed later in this chapter.) There's something almost magical about encouraging students to react personally and honestly in writing to a piece of writing that moves them. The creative response helps students grow as writers and grow as readers at the same time.

Like freewriting, your students may need some time to become accustomed to the types of writing indicated by creative response. It's a type of writing that they may associate with only creative writing, not with insightful literary study. We think that the analogical thinking required by the creative response, however, works well as a tool for close reading of text, for writing well about literature, and for focusing on a *response* to literature—not just a critique of it. Creative responses are one of the many tools that we use to further our goal of having our students become more perceptive and willing readers of literature.

3. *Students of literature should write every day, just like students of composition.* Okay, most of us no longer teach literature classes separately from composition classes, but the point is that writing about literature requires practice in order for students' acumen as readers and writers to increase. Perhaps one reason that you like to teach literature is so that you won't have all those stacks of papers to grade, but both literary study and writing are enhanced when they are integrated. Daily responses in writing to what students read are essential for their growth as writers and readers.

The *journal* is a good way to encourage daily written responses, and we've had success using the first ten minutes of the class for a quick journal response to the literature we're talking about that day. It's better than the threat of the dreaded pop quiz to keep students up with assignments. They look forward to the writing, for one thing, and it has the extra advantage of giving us a daily monitor of their understandings, or confusions, about the material the class is studying.

You might even consider substituting a variety of responsive writings about the literature your students are reading instead of giving fact-recall tests with maybe a discussion question thrown in. Tom has taught very successful American literature classes in which students read a great deal and wrote every day, and in which there were no formal tests at all. Yet, Tom felt his students were rigorously examined on their reading and performed better than those in classes in which he gave weekly tests, unit tests, and a final exam.

The fact that the syllabus for the class we teach has the word *literature* instead of *composition* in its title does not release us from our responsibility for the growth of our students as writers.

4. *It is important that you model writing for your literature students just as you do for your composition students.* Use student examples for responsive writing about literature, but remember that *your* example is the most important one to your students. After all, you're the literary expert in that room. As often as you can, write with them about the same literary works—and share your writing with them.

5. *Writing in the literature classroom and sharing writings with one another allows students to compare insights, perceptions, attitudes, and even problems about what they read.* Instead of only the teacher's interpretation of a difficult poem or obscure passage in a story, there are many interpretations to consider. Also, because we give our students many choices of what they read for class, we share through our writings the things we particularly like to read. The students experience a variety of stories by Poe or Hawthorne or Hemingway, for example, instead of just one read by the entire class. If someone in the class likes a book, a story, or a poem, others are more likely to read it than if just the teacher recommends it.

6. *Variety is essential in any class, but especially in the literature class.* We don't want students to get in the rut of looking at a piece of writing from only one perspective. Given the limitations of literature anthologies and the school library, we give them as many choices in *what* they will read as possible; and once they are used to writing responsively to literature, we also give them lots of freedom in *how* they will respond to it in writing.

We give students concrete suggestions for their writing and show them examples, but we still give them lots of choices and encourage their own suggestions for writing. See what the students themselves want to say about what they're reading in class.

Other Things to Think About When Your Students Write About Literature

If you want students to write interestingly and well about literature:

- Let some of the reading be done for sheer joy and pleasure. Not every reading assignment needs a writing assignment.
- Allow for some writing before reading or during a reading of a literary selection. While written responses *after* the reading are standard practice, this kind of in-progress writing is helpful for sorting out ideas and responses to literature, for making inferences, and for making predictions.
- Encourage creative expression about the piece of literature, not just critical essays as the only writing choice.

- Realize that what students have to say in response to a piece of literature won't be as sophisticated as what the professional critic might say about the selection. Student writers are *students*, not professional critics.
- Grade less; *respond* more to their writing about literature. When you do grade what they write about literature, don't grade their writing as if you were trying to decide whether they should go to hell or heaven.
- Offer options. Students have unique preferences in literature and in writing. Not everyone in the class has to complete the same assignment.
- Let the response or writing assignment grow out of the conversations you and your students have had about the literature. Writing grows naturally out of talk, and that includes writing about literature.
- Offer students the option of modifying an assignment based on their understandings of the literature, their writing preferences, and their strengths as learners.
- Let students know clearly what you expect from their writing about literature—formal or informal, response or critique, essay or poem or drawing, for example.
- Read and respond to the students' writings as you do to the writing of established authors—somewhat humbly, somewhat tentatively.
- Make writing about literature a pleasurable experience that students will want to repeat, not avoid.

Tracking Literature Selections

When students are avidly reading and writing in your class, you will sometimes need a method for tracking the selections that students are reading independently, not just the selections that you are all reading in common. In fact, because *the literature class* and *the writing class* are most often artificial distinctions—most English teachers now teach both literature and writing in an English class with a name like English 9, meaning ninth-grade English class—you may find that students have several simultaneous reading and writing projects underway, so tracking who is doing what and when can quickly become an issue.

One method that Tom and JoAnn Lane, a colleague of Tom, devised is called Close Out Questions. Students complete Close Out Questions when they finish a book. Figure 12–1 is a sample of the Close Out Questions that Tom and JoAnn used, but adapt the questions to your own tastes and students.

We like using Close Out Questions because it's a quick method for determining how well students have comprehended what they have read.

Close Out Questions

Name _____ Date _____

Bibliography _____

_____

1. Situation. What is the book about?

2. What is the narrative point of view? Who is the narrator?

3. Setting.

4. Why is the setting important to the plot?

5. Characters. Identify the main ones, including name, age, features, and quirks.

   a.

   b.

   c.

   d.

6. Plot. What is unique about the plot (i.e. the way the action develops)?

7. Ideas. State in one or two sentences the theme of the book.

8. Quotable quotes. Give us two. (This is not dialogue.)

9. Vocabulary. Three words you learned here, and a sentence from the book using each.

   a.

   b.

   c.

10. Your turn. What is really unusual, gripping, awe inspiring, weird, funny, heroic, moving, disgusting, or comic about the book (anything but boring!). Or what about the character(s) or situations in the book do you identify with? (100 words, please)

Figure 12–1. *Close Out Questions*

May be copied for classroom use. © 2004 by Dan Kirby, Dawn Latta Kirby, and Tom Liner from *Inside Out, Third Edition*. Heinemann: Portsmouth, NH.

Writing Responsively About Literature

The activities we suggest draw on students' responses—their insights, feelings, perceptions, even negative reactions—to what they read. These activities begin with the student and his or her response to the piece of literature rather than with a traditional interpretation of the literary selection. You probably have already noticed that we haven't had anything to say in this chapter about writing themes about literature, or about the new criticism, or about any kind of literary criticism for that matter. We left that kind of stuff out on purpose. Although writing critical essays about literature may be all well and good for Advanced Placement classes—and later for graduate seminars and such places—there are many more profitable (and less painful) ways to stimulate and nourish students' written responses to literature. The following activities give you some ideas to start your own thinking of how to have students respond to writing as a means of thinking and as a means of expressing their insights about what they read rather than making writing about literature deadly dull and woefully serious. For most activities, we have indicated some specific literary selections from American literature that we have found work well.

CR *Sequence*

We use the Creative Response (CR) with our students in our literature classes the same way that we use freewriting in writing classes. We usually begin the class with this kind of writing, and we return to it often, especially when we're working with difficult and unfamiliar material—or whenever the students seem to be having trouble finding things to say about what they're reading.

The class begins with the Free Response, and from there we lead them into Guided Responses of various kinds (some of the most successful are listed). It's a good thing to do in the journal, but we recommend that the first responses be taken up and responded to individually to give students the immediate feedback they need to get a good start with writing in the class.

PHASE #1 OF THE CR: FREE RESPONSE Tom begins his literature class with a short selection. He likes to use a song that is related thematically to the other reading the class will be doing, but a poem or short story works just as well. He plays the chosen song for the class, supplies them with copies of the lyrics, and gives them these instructions: "You're to write a creative response to this selection. You may write anything about it that you wish—except you may not say 'I like it' or 'I don't like it' or anything like that. It's a *creative* response, which means I'd like you to *create* something of your own. Write a poem, write a short sketch, draw a picture, tell me how it makes you feel, write the daydream you had while listening to it, freewrite while I play it again—respond to it any way you wish, but try to get something on paper this period."

Be patient with students at this point. They will be confused at first by the freedom of the assignment. Reading to them examples of creative responses to the same selection done by another class will help, and read them your own creative response.

Tom takes the first few sets of free responses and "mines the slag heap," just as he does with freewritings, looking for the good things to praise and ignoring their errors in usage and mechanics. When he thinks they're comfortable doing free responses, he starts them on Guided Responses.

When choosing songs to play for students, Tom doesn't necessarily try to use songs popular with his students, although he sometimes uses those, too. He shares what *he* likes with them. He has found that using songsters/writers such as Bob Dylan, Bruce Springstein, and others who are storytellers in their songs works well to promote creative responses about literary and thematic connections.

PHASE #2 OF THE CR: GUIDED RESPONSES We use a plethora of guided responses to literature as writing options in our classes. We like to offer several of these activities at a time as choices to students for pieces that they can write in response to the literary selections they've read. Add your favorite activities to our ideas.

Quotable Quotes

After his students finish reading and talking about a piece, Tom puts several quotations from the work on the board, choosing ones that are especially evocative. He then tells students to write a creative response to the piece, starting with one of the quotes, and to use it in their writing in any way they wish. Often the papers that grow out of this activity are interpretive. It's a good approach to use with literature with which the students are having some difficulty.

A variation of this activity is to have students pick their own quotations, swap them with one another, and then write creative responses to them.

Literature by such writers as Hemingway, Tennessee Williams, Faulkner, Longfellow, Thoreau, Welty, McCullers, Kesey, and Tom Wolfe is good for this activity. Any clearly stated theme works well. We've also used this device successfully with movies.

Author Letter

"This is your chance to ask writers questions, to complain about their writing, to talk back to them, to tell them what you like," Tom tells his students. He and his students write a letter to the author of the story or whatever it is they've read. Tom likes to use living authors for this one because students can mail the letters when they finish them—or make up one class letter from all the things they want to say, and send it. This activity stimulates *real* writing and revision activities, and it stimulates a great deal of thinking about writers and how they work. Any living author is fair game for this one. Many authors have websites, so you can send an email instead of a letter to the author. Some may even graciously take the time to reply.

When Tom's students wrote real letters to living authors, the authors were generally contacted through their publishers. All letters were carefully proofread and mailed; Tom mailed them himself.

Here's an author letter from Byung,[1] who is, as you might guess from his letter to Thomas Dygard, an athlete and sports fan.

February 24

Thomas J. Dygard
c/o Puffin Books
375 Hudson St.
New York, NY 10014

Dear Sir:

I'm one of those many people who fell in love with your sports books. I have read *The Rookie Arrives, Running Scared, Quarterback Walk-on, Halfback Tough, Winning Kicker, Tournament Upstart, Outside Shooter,* and *Soccer Duel.*

I wish I could read more of your sports books, but these were all of the books my English teacher had which were written by you. I like your stories very much because they seem so realistic. You describe every action so realistically. Sometimes I feel like I'm in the book.

I have a question. Did you play any kind of sports? I really want to know the answer. I really appreciate you writing so many wonderful stories. Thank you.

Sincerely,

Byung Koo

Mr. Dygard is a gracious man. Byung burst into class three weeks later, waving his reply.

Students also received return letters from Caroline B. Cooney, Gary Paulsen, and John Grisham. Many students, of course, did not get a response to the letters that they wrote, but everyone was realistic about what to expect.

Writing the letters stimulated a lot of interest. Tom and JoAnn Lane, his co-teaching partner one year, found that most of their students did not really know how to write a business letter, so it was a good opportunity to teach letter form for real purposes, not merely as a classroom exercise from an English book. It was always fun when someone received a letter back.

Imitation in Kind (Vignettes)

We watch for pieces of literature that lend themselves to student imitation. Quite simply, the assignment is to do *the kind of* writing the author did, but *in each student's own way.* It should be a try-it-and-see kind of activity.

One imitation-in-kind exercise that has been successful in Tom's classes begins with Hemingway's vignettes from *In Our Time.* After reading and talking about them (and it takes a lot of talking—they're not easy reading for most students), Tom asks the students to try three or four vignettes of their own. He encourages them to draw on their *memories* and write about episodes that involve *action*. "I want you to put us in the action," Tom tells them, and he suggests car wrecks, sporting events, or fights as possibilities. He encourages students to *lie* when they write the vignettes. The results of this exercise are usually good enough to follow up with revisions.

The model here is from Hemingway, but brief, self-contained episodes from other writers work equally well: Brautigan, Lopez, or Flannery O'Connor. Try Sandra Cisneros, too. Kafka's riddles are good for advanced classes.

Narrators

Lots of literature features a narrator with a strong voice. This type of literature is ideal for generating a focused CR. Tom and his students frequently read and discuss young adult novels with memorable narrators in books like *Lizard*; *The Pigman*; *Fast Sam, Cool Clyde, and Stuff*; and *Foxman*. They talk about why some stories have narrators and some do not.

After students have read several literary pieces with strong narrators, have them respond to this literary technique by trying their own narrative skills and role-taking perspectives when writing a story using a narrator who is not themselves. If students get stuck while attempting this activity, tell them to look back at one of their favorite books or excerpts with a narrator and try doing it like that. Sometimes, you may need to read the first few paragraphs of a book with the students who are having difficulty and discuss with them the author's use of the narrative voice. Here is Sadiqa's moving and emotional story in which she uses a narrative voice that is not her own:

> my mama said its cause im a BAD GIRL. i don't much care. she can beet me all she want to. long as she dont beet Sweetie. that what i call my Brother. i luv Him and He love me. its my duty to keep Him safe. sometime he pee in His clothes. mama get real mad and say she gone beet Him. i tell her she better not cause He just a lil baby. He dont no better. she dont take no time to potty train Him anyway. when i tell her she slap my mouth and say i be dissrespectfull cause i talk back to her. she hit me hard. i taste the saltyness of the blood coming from my lip. but i just be happy its me and not Sweetie. mama say i aint nobody. i know i aint but Sweetie gon be somebody. He gon be prezadent or somethin won day.
>
> won day i came home from school and saw that mama had left Sweetie home alone. i hate when she do that cause He dont no how to care for Hisself. He only two. well Sweetie had got sick on Hisself and He had spilled some milk on the floor. i tried to hurry up and clean it up fore mama got home but i couldnt. i could tell by the way she slammed the dorr that she was pissed about somethin. another one of her mens probly left her.
>
> so i picked up Sweetie to leave so wed be safe from mama. cause she get in a beatin mood when she pissed. when i was walking out of the room she called to me in that mean voice, Bitch i thought i tol you to clean up when you got home from school! come in hear so i can learn you a lesson! well i knowed what that meant so i put Sweetie on my bed hopin He would fall asleep or somethin so He wouldnt hear the sound.

when i got in the room mama had the strap in her hands. she looked mad as hell. i seen that look and i started shakin cause i was scared shed beet me bad this time and then who would protect Sweetie? well mama took that strap to me and she beet me all over till i couldnt hardly hold my head up. i was hurtin everywhere. i felt the tickle of blood running down my face. i got up to check on Sweetie. i hurt bad but i just be glad its me and not Sweetie. cause He aint did nothin to nobody and mama just hit me cause im a BAD GIRL.

—Sadiqa[1]

Once students can manipulate narrative selves and voices with such skill, they begin to fully understand the distinctions between the narrator and the author.

Tall Tale Telling

Tom uses this activity when his students are reading Mark Twain and other authors who write from a strong oral tradition. He points out that most families have their own legends—most of them exaggerated memories—that they like to tell when they're together. He illustrates briefly with his grandmother's stories of "panthers" in the North Georgia mountains when she was a girl, and the tale his dad liked to tell about Shine Peacock, a state trooper and friend of his, who lost control of his patrol car one night chasing a bootlegger and ran through a farmer's chicken house.

The student's assignment is to think of a family story (or make up a convincing lie), and tell it to a partner or a small group. Sometimes the students write them down afterward; usually Tom and his students just enjoy the telling.

In addition to Twain, Tom has also used the works of Irving, O'Connor, Faulkner, and Thomas Wolfe for this activity. It's worth noting that such stories are often culturally bound and culturally revealing. Branch out to writers who explore diverse cultures and discuss what in their tales seems mythic rather than literal. Look to Amy Tan, Maxine Hong Kingston, and Alice Walker for examples.

Spooky Tales

Everybody likes to tell, and listen to, ghost stories. When studying Gothic writers, one assignment that Tom always gives his students is to tell a real live ghost story— one they have actually heard themselves. Tom closes the blinds and turns off most of the lights, and he and his students share their stories as a class. Tom doesn't push kids who are shy and who don't want to talk, and he begins by telling a story himself. Then he asks them to write their stories: "Tell me about it just as you did now."

For this activity, Poe and Hawthorne are useful, of course, as well as Frost's "The Witch of Coös," Beagle, and Mary Shelley.

Shopping for Poetry

Once our students are used to writing creative responses, we like to use this activity to break the routine of a class when things seem to be dragging. We make copies of several very short poems and cut the pages so that each poem is on its own small square of paper. After you've done this activity a few times, you'll have a collection of these little poems. Then, spread about twenty of them out on display on desks or bookshelves or some other convenient place before the class comes in the room. As the students enter, invite them to shop in the poetry supermarket. They can take as long milling around and reading the poems and talking about them as they like. Finally, they must choose at least three for creative responses.

Tom likes poems by Brautigan, Cohen, and Plath for this activity, and Tom includes one or two of his own poems as well as some by students. Dawn also includes some poets who write specifically for young adults such as Mel Glenn; some contemporary poets such as Billy Collins; and some poets of color, such as Maya Angelou, Nikki Giovanni, and Jimmy Santiago Baca.

Strange Poetry

This is strictly a Friday kind of activity. Tom finds three of the *strangest* poems and/or songs that he can. He plays the songs and he and his students read the poems aloud. Then, Tom gives his students these instructions: "I want you to write something *really strange*. It can be a poem, a song, a sketch, or something else—but *it must be weird*." The results are always entertaining.

Some of Tom's classic favorite strange songs are Kottke's "Morning Is the Long Way Home"; Dylan's "Changing of the Guard"; Crosby, Stills, and Nash's "Winchester Cathedral"; and Carly Simon's "De Bat." Some of Tom's classic favorite strange poems include Francis' "Summons," Monro's "Overhead on a Saltmarsh," and selections by Corso, Ginsberg, and Ferlinghetti. As a variation, Dawn includes an excerpt from one of Francesca Lia Block's young adult novels about adolescents on the fringe of society and displays it as found poetry or as prose poetry. If you use an author like Block, do so with caution; her work has been frequently censored.

Alternatives to the Book Report

The time-honored and time-worn book report! Kids hate it, and teachers are bored reading it. But your students ought to read books, right? So what we suggest are some alternative activities to make the chore more tolerable for your students and for you. Whenever possible, of course, students should have several activities from which to choose. Many of these suggestions also work well with short stories or plays. Most are good activities to use with films.

Advertise the Book

Have students write advertising blurbs (like those on the back of paperback books) and put them up in the room. Encourage students to make them as racy as possible, just like the real thing.

This activity is quickly done and generates talk about books and reading. A variation that Tom has frequently used is to have students make advertising posters for the books they've read, with a drawing and a blurb, and display these around the room.

Continue the Story

One of the most successful writing exercises on novels we've found is to have students continue the story for a page or two. We encourage them to keep the writer's style and approach intact as much as possible when they do so, and to include some dialogue if they can. The point, of course, is not to get them to write like professional novelists, but to generate thinking about the writers' techniques and the whole business of storytelling. Many novels lend themselves to this activity. Favorite authors for this activity are Hemingway, Steinbeck, Robbins, and Potter.

Dawn has had great success using this technique with young adult authors' books that don't end happily-ever-after, such as Robert Cormier's classic young adult novel, *The Chocolate War*. Students rewrite the ending or extend it for a chapter and then discuss which ending is better—theirs or Cormier's—and why.

For students who are a bit younger, have them write either a future-based extension of the book—say, five or ten or even twenty years into the future of the characters—or an intervening chapter among the novel's existing chapters. This activity works particularly well with young adult novels such as Cushman's *Catherine Called Birdy*, which is told from the first-person point of view and is written as a journal. Dawn's students have written intervening chapters that take Catherine, the protagonist, on another adventure, or a future-based final chapter that features Catherine as a grandmother. Both types of chapters give students practice in maintaining the novel's unique journal format and protagonist's distinctive voice.

A Family Tree

You're probably familiar with the elaborate diagrams of family relationships among characters in Faulkner's novels. Cleanth Brooks' *Yoknapatawpha Country*, for example, has the most detailed and accurate examples. On a smaller scale, novels like *The Grapes of Wrath* lend themselves to this way of looking at characters. We have students construct a family tree with brief notes on each character. The graphic representation helps students to clarify characters' roles in a long novel.

A family tree of the Joad family in *The Grapes of Wrath* has worked well in Tom's classes, and he's also used this activity with novels by Leon Uris and Frank Yerby. Tom has even modified this activity to show relationships of military rank in Heller's *Catch 22*.

Authors such as Bobbie Ann Mason in her memoir *Cold Springs* begin with the family tree and a chronicle of where the family has lived throughout several generations. Then, she goes on to recount her own memoir by authoring stories of her extended family and her relationship to them. Students can do the same sort of thing by generating their family trees and then telling stories of their places within the family web.

Further, completing a family tree for the characters of color in novels with multicultural themes can help students to explore important issues of cultural dominance and interrelationships. When students look at the family tree of Sethe in Toni Morrison's *Beloved*, for instance, they will begin to explore the ways in which slavery violated family bonds. The family trees for many of the characters in the novels of Louise Erdrich and Barbara Kingsolver similarly will generate discussions and raise issues about Native American families.

The Newspaper Interview

We sometimes have students conduct an imaginary interview between a reporter for a specific publication or television program and a character from a novel. For example, have a student imagine herself to be a reporter for *Cosmopolitan Girl* and then interview Janie from Hurston's classic novel *Their Eyes Were Watching God*. To what questions would the readers of that particular magazine be interested in hearing Janie respond? How does Janie as a character fit the profile of the modern woman as defined by that magazine's perspective? How is Janie a role model for today's teenaged females—and how is she not? All of these questions, and more, will come into consideration as students consider how the imagined interview would go.

As additional examples, a reporter from *Sports Illustrated* could interview Ender from Orson Scott Card's young adult science fiction futuristic novel, *Ender's Game*; or a reporter for the school newspaper could interview Melinda, the main character in Laurie Halse Anderson's young adult novel *Speak*, after she again decides to speak.

A good approach with this activity is to have students who have read the same novel pair up, one acting as the reporter, one the character. They can make a taped interview, or merely write it. The results can be remarkably insightful, sometimes hilarious.

Tom has also used this activity with classics and young adult classics such as *The Great Gatsby*, *Go Tell It on the Mountain*, *The Pigman*, *The Outsiders*, and *Ordinary People*.

This activity, by the way, also works extremely well with nonfiction biographies, autobiographies, and memoirs.

Shifting Points of View

A simple but effective activity is to have students rewrite a brief version of a narrated novel from another character's point of view. It promotes a lot of talk and thinking about characters and values. For this activity, Tom's favorite point of view shift is to feature Catherine Barkley as the narrator of *A Farewell to Arms* instead of Frederic Henry. Other examples include a consideration of how *To Kill a Mockingbird* is altered if Atticus is the main narrator, or in young adult literature, consider how *The Chocolate War* changes if Brother Leon or Archie tells the story.

Obituaries

Tom often asks students to write obituaries for characters who are dead at the end of a novel. Tom brings the most sensational obituaries that have been written before to class as models, and tells the students to write their own obituaries for one of those scandal-mongering, yellow journalism papers. We get started by brainstorming together as many sensational headlines as we can recall. A variation of the assignment is to write an exposé news story for a tabloid. Some very funny ones have been done on *The Scarlet Letter*.

Suitable novels are almost endless. Authors frequently kill off characters at the end of their books. Some of Tom's favorite authors are Heinlein, Styron, Vonnegut, Kesey, Wambaugh, and Jones. Older students may be intrigued with writing an obituary for Susie, the main character in Alice Sebold's controversial novel *The Lovely Bones*; but if you teach this title, do so with caution since both death and rape are dominant in the story.

Don't Forget the Little Guy

We like to focus some of our discussion on the *minor characters* in novels. This activity requires students simply to forget main characters for a while and "tell me about the unimportant characters, the ones you usually don't remember or notice or discuss much." It's a good sideways assignment for getting students to look at a book from a different perspective.

Many, many books have interesting minor characters worthy of notice. Some of Tom's favorites appear in classic books such as *The Electric Kool-Aid Acid Test*, *The Starship and the Canoe*, *I See by My Outfit*, *Dune*, *Exodus*, *Sometimes a Great Notion*, *Wise Blood*, and *The Heart Is a Lonely Hunter*. We also enjoy the minor characters in the works of Amy Tan, Barbara Kingsolver, Maya Angelou, Mark Twain, Michael Ondaatje, Larry McMurtry, Cormac Macarthy, and Annie Proulx, to name a few.

Book Quotes

In this activity, students collect quotations from their literary selections. Students choose the quotes because they resonate with them in some way. The quotes just grab them as readers. Students wish they could have written those lines. The object is to make connections to our real lives by reacting and responding to the quotes. We like to use double-entry journal formats for the book quotes, with the quote on the left-hand side of the page and the response to the quote on the right-hand side. This activity provides lots of starting points for discussions of character and theme, symbols and metaphors, foreshadowing and irony. The responses also are often the beginnings of more detailed written critiques of the literature.

This activity works well for all sorts of literary selections, including fiction, essays, short stories, poetry, drama, and film.

Nonwritten Responses to Literature

Not all responses to literature need to be written. Drawing is also a valid form of nonwritten response to literature. The response to the Book of Genesis shown in Figure 12–2 is one such valid creative response. Encourage students with drawing ability to respond visually to what they read whenever it seems appropriate. Remember, too, that there are some artistic nonwritten responses that don't require much artistic

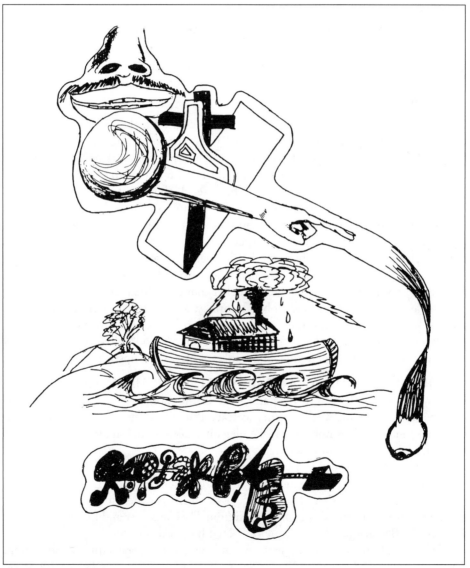

Figure 12–2. *Tracy Tate's Visualization*[1]

talent, especially if the computer—with its drawing and art programs and clip art files—is used as an artistic tool in your classroom by students for their creative responses. Visualizations help keep things interesting in the literature class. They stimulate talk about how we *see* the things we're reading. "That character doesn't look like *that*," someone in the class says about an illustration we put up. "I don't know," we might respond, defending the artist, "I kinda see the person like that." And the class is off, talking about their *perceptions* of the work.

Visualizations, like drawings, should always be only one choice of several that are available as responses to literature.

CHARACTER PORTRAITS/ILLUSTRATIONS We've always gotten good results with giving students the choice of responding to a story by drawing an illustration or a character's portrait from the story. This is an activity that allows the artists in your class to shine, even if they aren't gifted readers, and it works well for almost any literary selection.

THE CHARACTER LOCKER Have students create a locker out of a shoe box by covering it with construction paper or even with aluminum foil. Then, students select one character from a novel they have read and place real items into the locker in order to represent key events in the novel, items important in the character's life, and items symbolic of the values of the character. If the real item is too large to fit into the shoe box, students can create smaller versions of the real object.

Dawn's students love this activity and have created lockers for a wide range of characters in young adult literature, especially, but it works well for just about any literary selection with strong character development. It also works well for biographical and autobiographical selections. For example, one of Dawn's students who read a biography of Marilyn Monroe created a locker that contained an empty prescription pill bottle, pictures of John and Bobby Kennedy, a miniature poster created by the student for one of Marilyn's movies, pictures of her husbands, pictures of the young Marilyn in a swimsuit, the lyrics to Elton John's song "Goodbye, Norma Jean" rolled up as a scroll, a bottle of peroxide, and a tube of bright red lipstick.

THE ILLUSTRATED MAP AND DRAW THE NEIGHBORHOOD These activities are some of Tom's favorites and some of the most successful with his literature students. Students work in pairs to trace the action of a story by drawing an illustrated map (it does not have to be elegantly done—stick figures will work just fine) and labeling important actions.

Draw the Neighborhood is a variation of the *Illustrated Map* idea. Here, students draw the neighborhood where most of the action takes place in a novel or story.

Tom likes Steinbeck's and London's classic stories for the Illustrated Map activity, as well as Alfred Brooks' neighborhood from *The Contender* and Bumper Morgan's beat in *The Blue Knight* for the Draw the Neighborhood activity.

Dawn and Dan recommend the stories and memoir of Bobbie Ann Mason, Sandra Cisneros' novel *The House on Mango Street*, Bebe Moore Campbell's memoir *Sweet*

Summer, and Annie Dillard's memoir *An American Childhood* for these activities. You'll also find stories in your literature anthology with a strong sense of place in them that will work well for students who want to experiment with these activities.

BOOK JACKET DESIGN The idea of this activity is for students to design an original and, it is hoped, an attractive and interesting book jacket for a novel. We encourage them to stretch their imaginations and be as sensational and bizarre as any book designer. The finished products are put up for display around the room, and they stimulate a lot of book sharing.

CAST THE MOVIE For this activity, have students consider which actors they would cast in a movie made of the book or story they've just read. Many books have been made into movies, so we begin by discussing with students which castings were apt and which were woeful. Does it matter that in the book, the main character was short with blonde hair and in the movie, the actor is tall and a brunette? Consider classic books and movies, such as *To Kill a Mockingbird*, and which actors would have each role in a contemporary remake of the movie. Who, for example, is the contemporary Atticus/Gregory Peck? The discussions are always lively and sometimes choices are hotly defended.

Integrating Literature and Writing

The thing about teaching literature *and* writing is that we're looking for *connections*—points of contact between the writing and the reading, and between the student and the writing and the literature. When you look for ways to teach literature (and reading) with writing and writing with literature, you will have naturally integrated the language arts, which is what most district curriculum guides require. We've never thought that it made much sense to teach writing and literature separately anyway.

We want to develop lifelong readers, just as we want to develop lifelong writers and thinkers. To this end, go beyond the literature series and writing textbooks; do something real with your students. With every selection to be read, the question is, What's in it for the student? How can I put the student in touch with the literature? How can I bring the experience of an adolescent and the written word together? One way to do so is to give the student lots of choices, as we have indicated in this chapter.

Another way to develop lifelong readers is to talk about what *you're* reading with your students with enthusiasm and passion so that they see a real person doing real reading and loving it. We bring our reading into the classroom just as we bring in our writing. We read and share with our students what we like, and we encourage them to do the same. As appropriate, we give our students short excerpts from works we've read—from fiction to nonfiction to newspapers to book reviews—and we read aloud to our students because none of us outgrows the pleasure of being read to.

As you think about ways to blend reading and writing together in your classroom, think also about the objectives, standards, and goals that you want students to meet. One rich, meaty unit can help students to accomplish many reading and writing goals. The following is an example of such an integrated lesson.

A Literary Conversation: A Literature/Writing Lesson

This lesson is about blending literary experiences. It is about reading well and writing well and enjoying each more because of the other one. It comes from having fun with a favorite writer, Barry Lopez. (You can choose a favorite author of your own.) It's a favorite activity because it explores several possibilities with the selection, taking the reader back to the work again and again. It starts in the journal but will not stay there. It has removable parts, and it's simple. What more can you ask?

1. *Setting the scene.* Write about a favorite place. Jot-list or cluster details about the setting before you write. Try to visualize the place at a particular time, maybe when something special happened there.

2. *The pictorial display.* More scene setting. Put together a tray of slides or a collection of photographs or some streaming video with nature shots. For this particular literary selection, Lopez's *River Notes*, they can all more or less be shots of rivers. Then, select music to go with the visuals; for this particular literary work, consider using modern electronic jazz with no words.

3. *Reading aloud.* Next, choose short excerpts from Lopez's writings and make a copy of each excerpt. Give one excerpt to each student and have the students read the excerpts in a kind of unscripted conversation, each student reading when the spirit moves her to do so. This part of the activity takes a while. Let it. Listen for the interplay of voices and images.

4. *Short reading.* Then, give students a copy of "The Log Jam" section of *River Notes* to read silently; then read it out loud to them. (There are six vignettes in this section; there's one of them that you may want to censor for use in the classroom.) Read and talk, sharing what you each like about the selections. Don't push students too hard. The point is to make contact with the writing, not to explicate it or find the true interpretation. You don't need to feel compelled to point out the symbols or explain the elements of fiction or any of that stuff. Just enjoy Lopez's clever and beautiful prose as readers experiencing it together for the first time.

5. *Summary.* Have each student write a summary of one section, focusing on literal understanding—on comprehension. Look also for students having some problems understanding the piece. Usually, at least a few students will have a bit of difficulty comprehending all of what Lopez is saying. Lopez is not easy.

6. *Character*. Next, ask students to tell you about a character and briefly to "sketch" that person in their journals. It's always surprising how differently we see people.

7. *Mister Author*. Then, ask students to read the piece again and think about the kind of person who wrote it. After a five-minute freewrite about Lopez, share your collective insights of him.

8. *Creative response*. The point is to create something of your own suggested by or modeled after the piece. "The Log Jam" section from *River Notes* is particularly good for a CR.

9. *Wrapping up*. Share the drafts of the responses, looking over the other writings for other good things that have presented themselves; revise, edit, and publish the writings.

10. *Finally, circle up and read to each other*. Some will choose to read some more Lopez and to keep talking about him in their journals. Some will opt for other writers.

Consider the writing on as many different levels as possible. You can even get analytic if you want to, but do analysis last. It takes a good, interesting piece to sustain interest through all of these activities. That's a matter of feel, but push your students not to turn a piece loose too soon. There is always something else in there that the readers haven't seen yet.

Final Thoughts on Writing About Literature

The key to integrating reading and writing is to do so in a way that will enhance your students' understanding and thinking about both of these meaning-full processes. Doing so is based on relationship: the relationship of the teacher and the students, and that of the literature and the writing to each other and to you.

This chapter is full of our ideas about how writing and literature are reciprocal, meaning-making processes that fit naturally together and that are most suitably taught together. We can't imagine trying to teach writing without reading excerpts and books and plays and poems and essays by published authors. We can't image teaching literature without writing about it in a variety of ways. We've worked literally decades on devising strategies for incorporating the two, and we've shared pieces of those strategies in this chapter.

We encourage you to think about your own goals as literature and writing teachers and to reflect on how the strategies and activities and ideas presented here might work for you and your students. We also encourage you to devise your own activities suitable for your students' explorations of literature and writing. It's important, we think, to share your enthusiasm for reading and for writing with your students. Let them see you love what you read and write. Let them see you struggle with what you read and write. Let them see you reflect on what you read and write. That's how to grow lifelong readers, writers, thinkers, and learners.

Note

1. Sadiqa Edmonds and Byung Koo were students at Albany High School, Albany, GA. Tracy Tate was a student at Gainesville High School, Gainesville, GA.

Work Cited

KUTZ, ELEANOR, AND HEPHZIBAH ROSKELLY. 1991. *An Unquiet Pedagogy: Transforming Practice in the English Classroom*. Portsmouth, NH: Boynton/Cook.

13

Crafting Essays

Tell your daughter that she can learn a great deal about writing by reading and by studying books about grammar and the organization of ideas, but if she wishes to write well she will have to become someone. She will have to discover her beliefs, and then speak to us from within those beliefs. If her prose doesn't come out of her belief, . . . she will only be passing along information, of which we are in no great need.

BARRY LOPEZ, *About This Life*

Let's face it. Many of our students' essays come under the heading of "passing along information of which we are in no great need." More unsuccessful teaching of writing has been done in the name of essay writing than any other form. Sadly, teaching the traditional essay poorly does not just produce bad prose. Too often in our effort to teach the essay, we inadvertently teach kids to give up the very skills and instincts that have made them good writers of narrative and poetry. Worse, we miss a great opportunity to lead our students to discover their own beliefs and to become thoughtful and articulate spokespersons for those beliefs.

In earlier editions of this book, we called this chapter Expository Writing and we spent a good deal of time berating the five-paragraph theme in all of its manifestations. We know there are still unpleasant things going on in English classes in the name of teaching the essay, but we want this chapter in this new edition to focus on the vital and compelling literary form we are calling the *contemporary essay*.

The contemporary essay is alive and taking on new forms and finding new readers. Take a look at a fine piece of nonfiction by Lewis Thomas, a well-crafted essay by John McPhee, a memoir by a contemporary Southern writer like Janice Ray, or contemporary essays such as those by Cynthia Ozick or Barbara Kingsolver. Notice how these writers blur the sharp lines of form, putting all of the elements of good writing to work. Perhaps even more important, observe how the essay functions not as monologue, but rather as a conversation between the writer and the reader. As Kathleen Norris suggests in her introduction to *The Best American Essays of 2001*, a good essay causes the reader to conclude after reading the first paragraph, "[It] will tell me something about the world that I didn't know before, something I sensed but could not articulate" (2001). We encourage teachers and students alike to read and explore many examples of the modern essay to get a sense of how the form and its content have been reborn as a more artful literary *genre*.

Contemporary essays borrow heavily from narrative and descriptive writings. The contemporary essay as literary nonfiction is an easily accessible and popular form. It is, for us, the expositional form of choice in our teaching. Literary nonfiction blurs the lines among many genres of writing; it is highly literate, using the figurative language of fiction such as metaphor, foreshadowing, and character development; yet, it is nonfiction, essay writing. We see the popularity of contemporary essays in bestselling magazines and journals, and in collections of the best essays of each year.

Unlike traditional exposition, literary nonfiction deliberately employs description, narration, argumentation, persuasion, comparison, contrast—all of the traditional modes—but within the one essay or one memoir or whatever other *genre* the author is dubbing the writing. The modes and *genre* are identifiable, not as stand-alone pieces of writing, but as sections of the larger whole piece. In this way, the essay has become a much more sophisticated and literarily rich form. We therefore find ourselves expanding our definitions of exposition in our teaching and in our own writing to embrace memoir and other forms of contemporary essay far beyond formulas with names such as *accordion paragraph* and *five-paragraph theme*.

The good news is that this expanded view of exposition is working for us. We are energized when we teach it. We like reading the papers we get from it. Perhaps, even more important, it's working for our students, too. They like writing it. They learn about themselves as people, as writers, and as responsible beings in contemporary society. They see how description, comparison, and narration can work together to support an idea that they want their readers to get. They begin to understand the relevance and actual use of transitions and organization. Literary nonfiction—such as the memoir and nature writing frameworks that Dan and Dawn have worked on for the last decade or more to create—generates new possibilities for understanding the self and others via inquiry and reflective processes that both pose and attempt to answer questions. Our classrooms have become livelier places because inquiry lives in them. Our students' minds are engaged in making meanings, drawing conclusions from data, and in finding answers. Research no longer equals regurgitation.

Why have the traditional forms of the essay remained so difficult to teach, and why do they frustrate teachers and bore our students? First and foremost, the traditional essay is difficult to teach because of the way we have defined it in school curricula. Most of us remember a time when little writing other than the theme, the report, or the formal essay was taught. We use the word *taught* loosely. Most of us were simply told to write. The instructor set arbitrary standards that made the job of evaluating the paper easier—form, length, mechanics, spelling. But we knew that the teacher would give little attention to content, to voice, to style, or to the quality of our ideas.

Previously, the essay was to be written on a more formal, perhaps even esoteric, topic that the teacher had selected. It was to be tightly organized following a rigidly prescribed paragraph format, and the writer was to use an objective, third-person voice. In short, we were taught to write in a form that few could enjoy reading or writing.

It's time to reconsider our assumptions about the essay and to see it as a lively form in which a writer tries to create an authentic communication with a reader. It's time to see the essay, as Alan Lightman suggests, "not as an assignment to be dispatched efficiently and intelligently, but as an exploration, a questioning, an introspection" (2000). It's time to see the essay as an opportunity for our young writers to enter larger conversations with thoughtful, knowledgeable, and measured voices.

To redefine the essay for ourselves and for our students, we need to consider three myths about the traditional essay, myths that we must forsake. These myths concern topic, voice, and form.

Topic

Too often, essay topics have come from the teacher or worse yet from a composition textbook. One of our favorite examples of bad topics comes from that classic of grammar books, Warriner's tenth-grade book (1969). We hope these topics look pretty ridiculous to you now, but we subjected students to topics like these for many years.

1. the threat of Communism
2. the idea behind the United Nations
3. the balance of trade
4. voting
5. the tyranny of the automobile
6. air pollution
7. stream pollution
8. improving the schools
9. constant potential of war
10. fewer and fewer farm jobs

Some of these topics are clearly dated, but the topics offered in contemporary writing texts are often no better. Good essays will not come from topics that are thrust upon students. The problem with such canned topics—those in texts or those that teachers make up—is that they simply do not invite students to begin the thinking processes necessary to compose thoughtful essays. Imposing arbitrary topics on writers often results in a writing experience that is unpleasant for student writers who are offered too few opportunities to discover and create their own knowledge. It's deadly dull to write something about which you care little. That's when we get stilted language such as "Man in all times faces death," or "If one were to consider the role of George in Steinbeck's *Of Mice and Men*. . . ." That's when students press their automatic pilot buttons and slip into the writing robot mode.

Form

Somehow students get the notion that the form of what they have to say takes precedence over *what* they say—that is, over content. Teachers often talk too much about structure and form before students have a subject about which they understand enough to write in essay form. We need to spend more time noticing what students have to say. They hear us talk, talk, and talk about thesis statements, topic sentences, outlines, 500 words, and five paragraphs; but they hear little talk about collecting, percolating, and generating information, and they hear even less talk about more contemporary examples of the essay. Good essay writing can't be a cookie cutter operation. Subject matter cannot be rolled out, molded, and baked at 350 degrees.

As writers, we know that in our best writing the subject seeks its own form. Why is it so difficult to trust students to go through the messy processes of finding a significant idea upon which to write? Attempting to simplify the thinking task for students by reducing composing to a formula promotes bad writing and bad thinking habits. The six-trait paper and the five-paragraph theme, complete with topic sentence and the well-tuned outline, are too often artifacts of formula writing that diminish student options, hamper their development as quality writers, and stifle writing processes. The result is often form without meaning, correct language without power, and empty rhetoric that speaks to no one. Too often, we settle for idealess and voiceless papers with impeccable structure.

We think it's high time to declare the old expository essay and all of its derivatives as moribund. It's time to look around at the contemporary essay in the hands of scholars, artists, naturalists, critics, scientists, and even engineers as they create new forms to express both ideas and feelings. It's time to notice that they *never* write in five-paragraph themes.

Voice

Students who have found a voice in journals, in stories, or in poetry suddenly lose confidence when they undertake the dreaded essay. Their voices turn stiff and lifeless, and their writing turns timid and halting. When we ask even "smart" kids who can write well to compose an essay, we too often get stilted thesis statements, simplistic topic sentences that introduce new paragraphs, and surface-level transitions that use the right words, perhaps, but not the sense of meaningful transition.

We talk to students about the value of getting their voices back into their writing and of using their unique ways of seeing in the essay. We tell them that we know they can do it because we have heard their voices and experienced their perspectives in their stories and poems. They are reluctant to trust such advice. They know how essays are supposed to sound. Questions fly:

- But aren't essays supposed to give an objective voice of authority and straightforward information without any of the creative stuff?

- We were told you can't use "I," and now you tell us it's okay. What will next year's teacher say?
- I thought essays had to sound academic. Am I credible as a writer if I use my own voice?

We answer, "Well, yes and no."

What's to Be Done?

We've come to believe that when we teach the essay, we should employ the same strategies we use when we teach students to write poems, short stories, or chapters for a book. First, we get them excited about a subject and get them talking about it with peers. We encourage them to read numerous examples of the *genre*, and we look with writers' eyes at many models as we work on a particular essay. We encourage them to jot, to write notes to generate ideas for the essay, and to write exploratory drafts to think through their ideas. We create opportunities for them to read drafts aloud to other readers. We admonish them to read whatever they can get their hands on that helps them clarify their ideas. We ask them to check to see if what they've written represents their thoughts and ideas. Subject, language, and form work together when they get rolling. We show them how to move pieces of text around and try them out. As they work at the difficult task of making sense of the subject for themselves, the pieces start to fit together naturally. We encourage them to tinker with language and reflect on expression until it feels right. We remind them that writing processes take a long time and that their writing will get messy and frustrating, but that's the road all writers take toward shaping a meaningful essay. At the end of this process, if all goes well, they have found ideas worth communicating and a suitable form in which to express those ideas. What follows are ideas on how to engage students in these challenging processes.

Help Students Actively Explore Potential Topics

The most successful teachers of the essay expend a good deal of energy and time helping students find worthwhile subject matter about which to write. The essay assumes an audience out there somewhere, but writers must understand the topic for themselves first. We encourage our students to put away audience constraints initially. Conscious decisions about the effect of a piece on readers are important at some point, but those decisions require writers to be first interested in and knowledgeable about their subject. When writers worry about their audience before they know what they think, those concerns may interfere with thinking. The initial processes for essay writing must center on writers' personal synthesis of the topic as they make sense of the subject, wrestle with ideas, and construct texts that represent those ideas clearly.

Brainstorming frequently gets the juices flowing. The process generates enthusiasm and ideas. It engages the entire class in talking and thinking about approaches to the writing task. How do we brainstorm with a group? Matthew is thinking about the prom Saturday night; Lashandra is worried about the track meet; and Jorge worked until 2:00 AM at a local restaurant. You have to get their attention somehow. We often resort to controversies and ideas that we know will get kids fired up. We often begin by introducing our own uncertainties and a variety of ways of looking at an issue. Students take over and learn from one another's knowledge and experience as they discover ideas or concerns about which they genuinely want to find out more.

We offer the following ideas for engaging all students in topic exploration.

VIRTUAL EXPERIENCES For our inexperienced essay writers, topics cannot be too far removed from their knowledge and experience. Of course, since most of our students are terminally underexperienced, we must work to create virtual encounters with ideas that offset their limited knowledge of the stuff we're trying to teach them. As with all writing, previous experience as a reader, person, and thinker counts. Experience precedes effectiveness in essay writing.

We try to provide intellectual stimuli, to arrange problems and puzzles to which students can connect and extend their personal experiences. Film, photography, works of art, news sources, fiction, poetry, personal experience, artifacts, and experts in the field invite students to shift their perspectives and see their subjects through a variety of lenses.

What other strategies can we use to make ideas concrete enough to help students convert them to text? One way to engage reluctant essay writers is to create scenarios, happenings, problem situations, dilemmas, and writing/thinking tasks that stimulate students' curiosity and participation early on. Debates, role-playing, vignettes, improvisational problems, extemporaneous solutions, readings, field trips, and discussions can help.

HEURISTICS Guided thinking procedures can sometimes help students develop richer ideas, particularly if the teacher models this kind of thinking for the students. Often sequenced and guided questions, which cause students to think about a topic in an orderly progression, are helpful. The old journalistic heuristic of Who? What? When? Where? Why? and How? is a classic example of directing a writer by posing leading questions. Of course, the purpose of a heuristic is to stimulate and guide writers, not to create a stepwise formula for them to follow. This means that our questions should lead them deeper into their topics. Try questions such as, What are the key terms in your topic? and What are the two or three key ideas in your topic?

CLUSTERS AND WEBS Brainstorming of all kinds is helpful in generating a plethora of ideas. The genius of clusters (Cs) and webs (Ws) is that they make thinking *visual*. These techniques are not just for narrative writing. These strategies help writers get their thinking and ideas on the drawing board so that they can work with them more concretely. Taking the time to construct order from ideas that are represented visually is a real help to many writers, particularly those who have limited capacity both to generate ideas and to construct text models of them simultaneously.

STORYBOARDS In the same way that Cs and Ws work as visual representations of thinking, storyboards (SBs) help students think about arranging the elements of the message they want to deliver into a logical presentation. Have your students create PowerPoint®-style slides of their essay ideas to keep them focused as they create the supporting documentation for those ideas. The storyboard functions as an outline, but with far more flexibility and has the added advantage of its visual quality.

METAPHORS, ANALOGS, AND STORIES Many of our students construct meanings and build individual understandings based on their culture, ethnicity, and life experiences. The directness of essay thinking is aberrant to students whose cultural pattern is to approach ideas more indirectly through metaphor and story. Conventional essay strategies such as Aristotelian logic, a "cut to the chase" presentation of ideas, or the typical five-paragraph strategy of "tell 'em what you're gonna tell 'em, tell 'em, and tell 'em what you told 'em," may totally baffle some students. Encourage students to use a method of organizing ideas that seems natural to them. Beginning an essay piece with a quotation, an anecdote, a story, an example, a picture, a song, a poem, or a remembrance may ease the writer into more conventional prose.

TALK, TALK, TALK Most of your students would rather talk about a writing assignment than actually construct text. Why is that? Talk is cheap. Disposable. Difficult to assess. Easy to revise or redo. Writing is more difficult to disavow, more permanent, easier to critique, and riskier, revealing flaws of both logic and linguistic ability. Encourage students to talk extensively about their ideas before drafting them into text. Create opportunities for your students to rehearse their thesis, titles, opening sentences, and supporting details with peer partners. Encourage the partner to become an active audience, recording important ideas as the writer talks. Encourage partners to discuss problems and potential text structures or organizational schemes for the piece.

Help Students Write Their Way into Drafts

We have found that the pathway from brainstorming ideas about the topic to a successful draft is a tortuous journey for many of our writers. The energy and fun of thinking about and playing with a topic is difficult to sustain as the writer stares at a blank page or screen and contemplates how to begin. Students need to live with their topics awhile—a few days, a week—collecting and recording ideas, information, and opinions from many different sources. Finding an interesting topic and watching it grow and take shape in the mind is important groundwork for effective essay writing. Organization and structure grow naturally from such explorations because the exploration itself begins to suggest its own organizational scheme.

We encourage students to write exploratory pieces to extend their thinking about their topics and to begin to organize what they know about a topic. Writers gain control over their knowledge base when they write out what they are thinking, connecting, and questioning. The following are some of the exploratory pieces that we use with our students.

HERE AND NOW Here and Nows, as Dan has labeled them, give students a chance to practice and play with the subject. Students explore in short notes what they know and need to know. Tell students that Here and Nows are written right now and reflect what they are thinking today about their topics and what knowledge they currently have. These are in-the-present writings that can help students see what they already know, hear what they have to say, and discover interesting questions.

Here and Nows can be recorded in a Thinker's Log. Use these entries to nudge students along. Help them keep their topics lively by consistently bringing in new bits and pieces of information, contrasting viewpoints, or downright puzzling and confusing ideas related to their topics. By the time the students sit down in earnest to compose their essays, they will likely have ten or more pages in their Thinker's Log of resource material and of personal reflections recorded in their own voices. The Here and Nows have been the bait on which they nibble. They have thought through their subject in a variety of ways and become more expert and interested.

DISPATCHES AND BULLETINS We love the Annie Dillard quote from her book *The Writing Life:* "When you write . . . you go where the path leads. At the end of the path, you find a box canyon. You hammer out reports, dispatch bulletins" (1990). Ask students to write dispatches to you or to their writing response groups on where they are in their topic exploration. What are their big questions? What sources have they found that are especially helpful? About what contradictions and unresolved issues are they stewing? How do they think their essay might develop? What kinds of information and specific details do they yet need to find? How are their work habits? When will they be ready to go for a draft? What kind of specific help do they need right now? These dispatches confirm for student writers that they own the writing on which they are working, and it makes them accountable to other potential readers as well. Dispatches also inform the teacher as to where each student is in the essay-writing process and who needs what kind of coaching and encouragement.

SPECULATIVE PIECES Encourage your students to ask themselves questions and then try to answer them. What would this piece be about? What would be difficult about trying to write on this question? Where would a good place be to begin the piece? Are my ideas clear in my own mind? Would a title help me now? What else do I need to know about my topic? Can I create a map for this piece yet? What are the chunks of text I already have that I can use? What other chunks do I still need to write? These metapieces turn students inward to examine their own thought processes and direct them away from the need for constant coaching and advice from others. This writing problem is theirs to solve.

BLAST PIECES These are espresso pieces written with energy and drive. Tell your students not to wait until they have all their ducks in a row. Tell them to assemble as many pieces of the topic as they can and then to *blast* into a draft to assess where they are in its development. You might organize your class so that on a given day they all do a blast piece. Or tell them to practice at home by setting time limits and goals: "Tell yourself you're going to write for thirty minutes or two pages or until dinner time." Remind your student writers to write as hard and as fast as they can to see if they can push through their inertia and fear into a rough first draft. Tell them not to quit too soon, but to go as far as they can. Encourage them to find the flow, to let the writing energize them. Then put the piece away and return to it later for a scan and to mark good stuff and begin again.

SPIDER PIECES In Whitman's poem, "The Noiseless, Patient Spider," the spider begins to construct a web by spinning out single filaments, one after the other— filament, filament. Initially, the filaments just float in the air and fail to connect. But finally, one of those threads catches hold, creating a solid anchor around which the web can be spun. Students can compose short pieces in the same way, looking for their hook filament piece. Provide a series of in-class practice sessions for spider pieces in which your students try writing an opening or a conclusion, or they try writing in different voices and for different readers. Encourage them to shift tense from past to present. Suggest that they shift person from third to first or vice versa. Help them to see their topics from different angles and different vantage points. They don't need to try to link these spider pieces. As writers, they are looking for a hook or an anchor piece, some idea around which they can spin their essay.

OPPOSITION PIECES Some topics are not cut-and-dried. They may be ambiguous and lend themselves to contrasting viewpoints. Many solid ideas have an upside and a downside. Structure an opportunity for writers to explore the contrasts and oppositions in their topic: then and now, good for some and bad for others, sometimes but not always, "It was the worst of times and it was the best of times." After they have written on several sides of their topic, ask them to see if they can construct a consensus piece or at least find a balanced and measured approach to the topic.

TALKING PIECES Some student writers do their best writing when they relax and just engage in an internal monologue. Give them permission to write notes to themselves. Suggest that they talk to a partner about the problem they're having with the topic or with the drafting. Tell them to talk about the events of the moment. They might make excuses for their frustrations with the essay. They could blame others. Encourage them to talk to themselves as a way of breaking the tension and stress they are feeling about the writing task and to talk themselves into new understandings.

LIST PIECES Perhaps the ultimate stalling strategy is to make lists. We all kill time waiting for inspiration by jotting a list. Suggest to those students who appear to be really stuck that, at the very least, they can make lists of things they need to be doing and thinking about where to begin their essays. Initially, they may not make lists about the essay assignment; they may drift into "What do I have to get done before prom?" or "What is due in all of my other classes by the end of the semester?" Those are favorite stalling lists. Give them time to list anything; then, tell them to put away anything that isn't related to their topic. Admonish them to gather together as many viable writing ideas on their topics as they can and to stare at them. Provide opportunities for them to share those lists with someone else. Encourage them to set some goals and some deadlines. Challenge them to promise someone they'll have a draft to share by a specific date.

All of these written explorations help students discover what they don't know about their topics and the holes in their thinking. Such gaps are not only the stuff of literary deconstruction; they are also the catalyst for more reading, research, writing, thinking, and planning. Once students' thinking begins to gel, they are ready to write exploratory drafts of their essay.

Use the Draft as Discovery

Encourage students to carry all of their preliminary thinking from logs and jottings into the draft writing phase. Because students may find essay writing more complex than other types of writing, you may find they need considerable time for drafting their pieces. Try to keep them from committing to a final draft too early. Encourage discovery drafts, admonishing them to delay outlining or other formal organization structures until they have fully explored their topic. Outlines can enslave inexperienced writers, taking away the opportunity to discover spontaneously an organizational structure and an appropriate scheme for developing ideas. A discovery draft shows a student writer where the paper is light on content, where transitions are lacking, and where more thinking is needed. The draft forces students to re-see the topic they are exploring. These exploratory or discovery drafts, which may be written in a time frame of twenty to sixty minutes, serve as a commitment by students to get the ideas with which they have been working onto paper.

Even more important, the discovery draft is a place where new ideas are born and new information discovered. In a classic analogy, James Britton et al. likens the writing of a draft to a person "pushing the boat out from shore hoping it will land someplace" (1975). Confident writers push the boat out fearlessly because they have been out before and know it will not drift indefinitely. Unpracticed writers need more support and encouragement during the discovery draft because they may be less sure about where a piece is going. Many writers discover what they know by playing around with a topic, turning it over in their minds, jotting down ideas, and working them over in informal writings.

Introduce a Variety of Essay Forms

Sadly, the school-based essay has been stuck in a formulaic and predictable form. We have taught students formats like the five-paragraph essay or the accordion paragraph and then find them using them automatically, year after year. They click into those formulas at the mention of the words *essay* or *exposition* in school settings, even if such formats are not appropriate to the writing task at hand. Granted, such formulas can provide shortcuts for beginning or struggling writers who need extensive help with organizational patterns. Once such struggling writers learn a pattern, they can concentrate on content and on what they have to communicate to a reader. But writers must develop beyond such mindless overdependence on formula. Dan frequently asks ～～"When is the last time you went to your local bookstore and ～～aragraph essays?" They laugh, they get the joke, ～～se seriously questioning a form they have fretted and sweated to learn.

We have found it useful and refreshing to introduce students to new and alternative formats in which to couch their ideas: critiques, reviews, white papers, belief papers (Here I Stand), editorials, investigative reports (I-Search), anthropological pieces, case studies, college application essays, historical pieces, change pieces, performance essays, scientific treatises, problem/solution pieces, speculative pieces—all of these writings have been useful to us in our teaching and to our students as they work on writing insightful essays.

WHITE PAPERS Technically *official reports*, white papers present a position or an analysis of the state of things. This form requires writers to have a solid grasp of their facts and information and to document their writing with solid evidence. White papers usually either recommend a particular course of action or lay out plausible alternatives. The voice is measured and reasoned. Large corporations, city governments, environmental groups, and various federal agencies write such pieces. Try looking for models of them in government documents and environmental groups' publications. We have used white papers as outcomes for group inquiry and research during which students identify a pressing, problematic issue and then propose a solution or options for resolutions. In that case, various members of the group author sections of the paper.

CRITIQUES AND REVIEWS Critiques are the backbone of writing for the college English major, but we aren't born knowing how to do this type of analytic writing. In order to ease students into critiques, Dawn has her students write movie reviews. She begins by having students brainstorm a list of favorite movies, new and old. Once they have a good list of titles, they talk to a partner about what makes that particular movie a favorite. Is it the action in the movie? Is it the lead actor? Is it the cinematography? Is it the soundtrack? After that, Dawn shows students the opening segment of two radically different movies, say *When Harry Met Sally* and the James Bond movie *Tomorrow Never Dies*. Students then discuss the features of those two opening segments that are noteworthy. Next, students brainstorm potential features of a movie that they might critique: acting, direction, cinematography, special effects, writing, editing, music, casting, originality of storyline, and so on. After that, Dawn and her students go to the Internet and to current newspapers and magazines to read reviews of favorite movies written by a professional critic such as Roger Ebert or a local reviewer. They study the purpose and order of each paragraph in the review: plot summary, features of the movie, strengths and weaknesses of the movie, and the reviewer's professional analysis and personal opinion of the movie. Then, they write their own critiques.

HERE I STAND PAPERS This type of essay encourages students to clarify their own opinions and beliefs and then to go out on a limb and state publicly where they stand on a particular issue. The *I* voice is important in these papers, but the *I* must engage the *you*, so the writer has a real responsibility to anticipate the audience's needs for understanding this position. The writer needs to acknowledge that there may be other legitimate viewpoints. We want the writer to come to a strong statement of their position, but we try to encourage the student to avoid inflammatory rhetoric so as not to create a "My way or the highway" tone for these pieces.

I-SEARCH PAPERS Ken Macrorie developed this form as an alternative to the traditional term or research paper (1988). Here, the student writer investigates a topic to which she is personally connected in some way by past experience, avid interest, family circumstances, cultural connections, linguistic links, or in other ways. Then, the student finds unique data sources to plumb for information. Instead of using traditional research, the student conducts interviews with key informants such as family members or notable people in the community who are in the know about the topic. Perhaps the student writer devises a survey and then conducts it with the affected members of the culture or linguistic group. After the data are gathered, the student writer determines findings from the data and draws conclusions about the topic under consideration. The final I-Search paper includes information about *why* the student was personally compelled to the topic, about *the process* the student decided to use in order to gather data, about *what* the data are and what they revealed, and about the conclusions the student draws as a result. This type of *I-search*—not mere *re-search*—helps the student to find personally meaningful answers to inquiry rather than regurgitating information found in some Internet or traditional research source.

EDITORIALS We like editorials for several reasons: There are many examples of these around, topics have a broad range, and the form and voice are quite flexible. Like white papers, students need to have accurate facts and information in hand; and like the *Here I Stand* paper, they need to be aware of the audience out there as they write.

INVESTIGATIVE REPORTS Some caution should be offered here. There are no doubt many injustices and potential targets for investigation in your school. Before you send your students on this quest, however, be sure that your administrators want the harsh light of student investigation turned upon the school culture. We have, however, found many students energized by the opportunity to research an issue that bothers them about their school. Favorite topics include whether athletes receive preferential treatment in some classes, why our school has certain restrictions that the neighboring high school does not, and why we pay parking fees and they don't. An investigation requires strong interview skills and a well-designed plan for collecting information. We always require that students show us their plan for data collection before we give our blessing to their hunt for truth.

ANTHROPOLOGICAL AND CASE STUDIES In *Mind Matters*, Kirby and Kuykendal (1991) offer a variety of explorations that lead students to conduct anthropological inquiry. They lead students step by step through question-raising, fieldwork, the systematic collection of data, and the challenging aspects of the final essay about the inquiry. This kind of writing and thinking not only leads students to sharpen their powers of observation, but it also helps them to develop multiple perspectives on the world around them.

COLLEGE APPLICATION ESSAYS Most college entrance applications still require that the applicant engage in either a biographical essay or in some other writing that asks for personal disclosure. We frequently offer students an opportunity to develop a personal essay that is both measured in voice and well-documented in content. Such an essay also tests the writer's ability to speculate about the essay's audience and the hidden criteria that audience may bring to the reading of such an essay.

HISTORICAL PIECES Pieces in which students trace family histories or the history of a place or in which they chronicle a particular cultural tradition in which their family participates are always favorites in our classes. Histories of particular family members give students the opportunity to learn about their own family and to celebrate a relative. These pieces invite the use of narratives and of interview data as well as offering student writers the chance to do a little historical investigation.

CHANGE PIECE—EVOLUTION, REVOLUTION Change pieces engage students in looking at a phenomenon or a set of ideas over time. Our best students have written change pieces on such diverse topics as "The NFL Quarterback: From Johnny Unitas to Michael Vick," "Jazz Trumpeters: Dizzy Gillespie, Miles Davis, and Wynton Marsalis," and "The Evolution of the Racing Bicycle." This form particularly lends itself to the performance essay discussed next, with writers free to add photos, art, and music to supplement their essays.

PERFORMANCE ESSAYS One of the best ways for students to learn about how an audience will "read" their essays is to create a two-part essay assignment. First, students compose essays that they believe other students will find interesting and engaging. Then, you plan a time when students perform their essays for the class. We use some of the many essays that are read on National Public Radio as examples of how to perform the essay. Students are free to use props and visual aids to illustrate their points and entertain listeners. Some of our favorites are essays about music, art, and pop culture.

SCIENTIFIC TREATISES Essays that advance scientific ideas or explain scientific phenomena can be interesting and entertaining. Look at the work of Stephen J. Gould, Jane Goodall, Loren Eiseley, Stephen Hawking, and Annie Dillard, for example. Often science students are some of our most original and passionate thinkers. Encourage them to read and employ the techniques of the contemporary science writers found in journals and magazines such as *Discover*, *Audubon*, *The Sciences*, and *National Geographic*.

PROBLEM/SOLUTION PIECES Dawn has her students brainstorm problems that they see around them, either at school or in their neighborhoods. Students discuss their lists with a partner in order to hear themselves talk about the problem. The writer selects a problem, offers *one* best solution, and writes a paper in which she argues effectively for that solution. In the past, some of Dawn's students have chosen as problems the cost of extra fees included in college tuition, city bus routes that are inconveniently scheduled, the issue of putting a trash landfill near a particular neighborhood, or the high cost of car insurance for students. The solution must be realistic, cost effective, rational, and believable.

Statistics and data may help students support their arguments, so some research and documentation of sources may be necessary. Another strong factor is personal experience: How is the writer directly connected with the problem? Such personal experience lends the writer a voice of authority, which is an important feature for a proposal. Problem/solution pieces, or *proposals*, as they are sometimes called, are a type of writing that students may have to do in the "real" world of business, so we stress that connection to future writing on the job.

MULTIPLE SOLUTION PIECES A variation on the problem/solution piece Dawn describes is a piece that asks students to examine a complex problem and to propose more than one possible and plausible solution for ameliorating that problem. A notable model for these pieces is former President Jimmy Carter, who is often at work in several places around the globe authoring multiple solutions for intransigent problems in third-world countries. In the writers' papers, there is no one best solution, but rather the writers offer a costs and benefits analysis for several alternative solution scenarios that may be equally effective for solving the problem under consideration. Obviously, however, some groups will prefer one solution over another, but the idea is to become the think tank expert for the affected groups facing the problem. These papers challenge the writer to develop a thorough understanding of an impasse and to engage in a careful analysis of the various groups that are at odds. Multiple solution papers must speak with reason and persuasion to multiple audiences. These pieces offer good practice for entering the diplomatic service or for being a teacher.

PROPOSALS, MODEST OR OTHERWISE Dan has a slightly different twist on the problem/solution paper. He finds students are often quick to offer analysis and advice on complex problems with little thoughtful deliberation. He likes proposal writing because the process begins by requiring students to construct a careful analysis of a problem or a need. The analysis must make use of data and be submitted to a panel of peers for scrutiny. Frivolous or half-baked analyses are usually vigorously critiqued by other writers. Then as the problem analysis is reworked and writers begin to develop solution scenarios, they conduct feasibility studies and ultimately develop a budget and justify the economic and social viability of their proposal. That sounds pretty sophisticated—and it is—but we have had relatively average student writers author proposals on such diverse topics as altering the school's daily schedule, forming a more representative student government, financing school clubs for rock climbing and fly-fishing, taking field trips to exotic places, and initiating service learning projects in the community. Of course, we welcome satiric proposals if they are terribly clever and well done.

After students have worked with topics, drafts, and forms, it's time for them to work with voice and language choices in their essay.

Encourage Students to Use Their Own Language

We're not suggesting that student essays be couched in teenage slang, but neither should they be laden with adult jargon. The best language for essay writing is language the writer knows. To borrow the words of others or to falsify one's own language is to doom the individual voice in essay prose. The debate around the use of the *I* pronoun in essay writing still exists, but contemporary writers are very likely to use the personal pronoun in their published works. We try to blunt the argument about the use of *I* by teaching students that there is an *I* that means *me* and an *I* that really means *us* or *we*. Is that confusing? In the hands of a good essay writer, *I* is not an egocentric or arrogant pronoun, but rather it is an inclusive one that speaks not only for the writer, but also for the reader as well. Arguments about whether the *I* pronoun is appropriate are futile at this point. The piece itself and the writer's own language resources dictate appropriate pronoun and diction choices. Inexperienced writers lacking in intuitions about appropriateness may merely need suggestions and feedback from their audience.

We support and encourage a student's attempts to find a unique voice. Rather than lock students' voices out of the writing, we encourage students to tell us what they are trying to say. They usually can. After they have told us their ideas orally, we nod and say, "Yes. Now, go write that." Students have words. Maybe we'll help them reconsider the exact word choice later (that's part of revision, after all), but students need to get beyond the fear of formal language and into the making of meaning. If language interferes with meaning, we need to help, but we do not need to inflict our voice on their writing.

Encourage Students to Use Personal Allusions or Cite Personal Evidence

The contemporary essay is rarely impersonal, detached, and devoid of expressive detail. In the past, in our attempts to help our students distinguish between informal and formal writing, we have overstated these differences or even described the division as a dichotomy. Effective essays, the kind people actually read and enjoy, are impossible to dichotomize. That's what we're finding in contemporary literary nonfiction. The writer uses what works for the expression of meaning; the writer is not limited by format. In a classic explanation of the ways in which literary techniques apply to any type of writing, Nancy Martin suggests that

Much effective writing seems to be on a continuum somewhere between the expressive and the transactional. This applies to adult as well as children's writing. What is worrying is that in much school writing, the student is expected to exclude expressive features. . . . The demand for impersonal, unexpressive writing can actively inhibit learning because it isolates what is to be learned from the vital learning process—that of making links between what is already known and the new information. The [effective] essay writing task asks the student to reconcile what he/she already knows with new knowledge or experience. As a student develops as a writer, he/she should be more able to bring appropriate inner resources to bear on knowledge of the outside world. (1976)

Sadly, too many of us have continued to teach exposition as a nineteenth-century phenomenon, ignoring the new, more exciting directions essay writing has taken. We've been using the wrong models—models that do not represent the range of contemporary exposition. Writers such as Loren Eiseley, Tom Wolfe, Rick Bass, Annie Dillard, Maxine Hong Kingston, Joan Didion, and Alice Walker, to name a few, have certainly found new ways to enliven essay discourse.

Discover New Ways to Introduce Traditional Assignments

Let's look at some of the traditional assignments English teachers make. It isn't that they are bad. It's the way we have approached them. Good student writing in the essay mode can happen only infrequently if we use the old "throw out a topic and ask them to write on it" approach. We want to free constraints and anxiety, instead piquing curiosity and interest. Here are some suggestions for doing old stuff in new ways.

COMPARISON AND CONTRAST ASSIGNMENT The C and C assignment has always been an English teacher's favorite. Unfortunately, it's an easy assignment to formulate, and easy for students to produce shallow, saccharine analysis as they try to fulfill the assignment. Rather than writing a formula on the board and telling students to go to it, we use a more inductive approach, which also generates some good writing in the process. As part of the process of writing memoir, we ask student to do the following:

1. Think of a favorite place or artifact as it looked when you were a child. Be specific, not general. Remember a favorite room, part of the park near your house, a toy such as a bike or doll, a desk, a wall with pictures on it—whatever. Try to choose a place that you visited across a period of time or an artifact that you owned for a number of years. Now, jot some notes about this place or artifact. Be as concrete and specific as you can. Remember the details. See the place or artifact in your mind. For this part of the brainstorming, Dawn chose to recall her first desk, one that she and her father bought together when she entered middle school, which she kept with her in college, and that followed her into her first house as an adult.

2. Share the notes. Try ideas on one another. In large classes the sharing goes on in small groups. Take enough time for this step. New ideas and details occur to the students as they discuss the experience with each other.

3. Now, think of the same place or artifact in the present, or at least several years later. Again, jot notes. See the place or artifact. Be concrete. What feelings do you have about the place or artifact?

4. Share the notes again. Allow time for discussion.

5. Ask, "What have you learned about yourself that you didn't know before you began reflecting on this place or artifact?" Jot some notes in response to that question. Sometimes these insights come to students immediately; sometimes they get stuck. If they get stuck, tell them to relax and work on this later. They may need to write more before the insights grow.

6. Write out a discovery draft. Begin at the beginning; begin at the end; begin in the middle. Don't interrupt the writing-out process. Give students plenty of time. Let them shape the piece, using their own intuitions.

7. Share the discovery drafts, reading them aloud. Talk about beginnings and endings. Talk about transitions. Talk about concrete detail. Talk about language and diction. Talk about anything that concerns you or the students.

8. Talk to your students about the *genre* of comparison and contrast. Because they've just engaged in a mental process of comparing and contrasting something meaningful to them, they'll understand the point and see the possibilities of the *genre* for explication.

Students may elect to rewrite, revise, or file their individual pieces, depending on their involvement in the writing and their assessment of its worth. We find that our students often continue working on this piece and choose to include it in their memoir collection for their final product.

ACTION RESEARCH PROJECT Breathing life into the old research paper assignment is not easy. Almost no one enjoys it. Students hate research papers because they are complicated ventures that take planning and discipline. Teachers hate them because they have to read and grade the massive papers, and they're mostly dull reading. Librarians hate them because that means thirty kids in the library for two weeks, misfiling resource books. Parents hate them because it means driving their kids to the university or city library on weekends, or it means hours of time that the kids monopolize the family computer. There seems to be no way out of the dilemma, however. High-school English teachers think they fail their college-bound students if they don't assign the research paper. We think that the value of the research project is in the process rather than the product. Good research projects are problem-solving experiences that challenge students and leave them with a positive feeling when finished.

Students need a model of how to work through the conceptual framework of conducting research as a meaning-making process that can answer real questions, and they need reality-based techniques for being successful researchers. Students often think that research is dead and deadly dull. It's done by bent-over scholars in the bowels of a dusky library. The very term *action research* seems to be an oxymoron to most students. But it doesn't have to be.

As we work with students on conducting research, we focus on the quality of their questions that drive the research. Without good questions, students aren't motivated to find good answers. What issues or problems exist about which students want to know more and perhaps change the *status quo*? We also focus not just on what they find out, but on *how* they find it out. Books and the Internet are powerful tools, but so are surveys and interviews—sources that are rarely used by students in authentic situations. In order to focus less on product and more on inquiry as a meaning-full activity, we follow a process similar to the following.

1. *Generate a class topic of interest to most students.* You might bring in an editorial, lyrics from a contemporary song, a short story, or a poem to get students started. Pick something that will generate mixed and rather complicated reactions: mandatory education, pros and cons; the individual's responsibility to society; students' responsibilities to the school community or teachers' responsibilities to students. Or perhaps even try tough topics, in the right situation, such as school violence—if your students, administrators, and parents can handle it.

2. *Check out the topic in subjective and objective ways.* Use fact and fiction in Here and Nows. Have students write short reactions and keep a Research Log while they explore the topic.

3. *After several days of seeing the topic from a variety of viewpoints, each student or a group of students working together can formulate questions about the topic.* The questions should reflect the complexities of the subject and avoid yes/no responses. Spend time with students helping them formulate questions.

4. *Ask students to answer these questions using their Research Logs for preliminary responses.* Fill in information with further investigation—readings and interviews with classmates and people in the community.

5. *Explore resources on the Internet available through the many contemporary search engines.* Use permission slips so parents know students are on the Internet. Caution students about inappropriate websites and chat rooms.

6. *Explore interview options.* Who in the community might have some insights about the question being researched? Who in the community might be able to offer some historical perspective? Who is most affected by this issue? Help students to formulate questions that knowledgeable community members might be able to answer, teach them how to conduct an interview that is more informative conversation than rapid-fire Q and A, and then help them sort through the data they gather from their interview sources. What are the new insights? What are the surprises? What are the

conflicting viewpoints among those interviewed? These are all inquiries that will spark discussion, reflection, and more research, as well as some conclusions eventually.

7. *Expand the students' repertoire for tracking their information and notes.* We encourage students to track their notes and resources on the computer, but we also explain how note cards work as a procedural way for students to compile information. In our process, note cards are useful manipulatives during the stages of summarizing findings and drawing conclusions. Bibliography cards can be compiled for all sources to help students sort the highly reliable and informative from the not-so-useful sources. Students use their Research Log reflections, Here and Nows, interviews, and information shared with classmates. No slavish copying of ideas from books onto note cards. Students have thought through their ideas in their own language first. Cards are merely a way of separating out the pieces and can be a useful hands-on organizational tool that students can shuffle and manipulate to help them formulate the order of their thoughts.

8. *Begin discovery drafts in which students explore findings and sort through ideas.* Students work their way toward a more formal paper through a series of short papers.

One thing we've found in following this procedure—students learn the process and can apply it for individual research at some future time. They have learned a way of collecting information and transforming it into an opinion paper.

The same process can be used with individual topics if your students have previous experience. It's tough for students and teachers when thirty students, covering thirty different topics, spread their books and notes out over a huge library or hog all of the available computers and Internet venues. Students, who all need help at the same time, get frustrated. We like to have several students work on various facets of the same subject. Each provides expertise and helps the others. The collaborative effort helps them explore the topic more thoroughly and brings other viewpoints to individual ideas. They follow each other through the exploratory discovery drafts and serve as a response group through the final paper.

WRITING ABOUT AN AUTHOR The problem in this assignment is to generate enthusiasm for finding out more about an author and then to get students into the author's work. Try this process:

1. *Choose one of your favorite authors, one who is prolific and appealing to your students.* Compile a series of one-page handouts that contain short excerpts from the author's writing, notebooks, journals, interviews, and other forms. Include photographs, biographical accounts, reviews of the author's work, and criticisms. Give students one handout per day and have them read, talk, share their feelings, and speculate about the author. What new insights emerge each day?

2. *Ask students to find out more about the author.* Each student brings to class a fact about the author, a selection to read, or a review. Students share this information with the class.

3. *Keep an Author Log in which students write reactions to what they find, write favorite quotes, and write original pieces triggered by some idea or technique the author uses.* Ask them to react to content, style, or whatever strikes their fancy.

4. *Read longer selections by the author.* Ask students to present interpretive readings to the class.

5. *Bring artifacts and use the language that represents the author's life and work.* For a nature writer, for example, fill the room with animal bones, seed pods, bark, and flora. Begin to use the same types of technical terms that the author would use as you discuss the author and her work. That's not an indiscriminate bird; that's a great blue heron. That's not just a pretty purple flower; that's a sage plant in bloom.

6. *Encourage students to develop their logs into more finished products on the author.* Include a range of options that students might pursue. Dawn and Dan continue to add to their lists of options that students reference when producing their final products. One student who enjoyed scrapbooking created a scrapbook of quotes from the author's work, wrote her reflections on the meanings of those quotes, and then illustrated the quotes with her original photographs. Include options for response and reflections and original critiques. Encourage students to list questions yet to be answered about the author and his work and then to conclude with insights about the author. Encourage divergent thinking and diverse products.

THE MULTIGENRE PAPER The multigenre paper is exactly what it says it is—a form of exposition that employs many modes and *genre* of writing in one product. Tom Romano has popularized the form in his books, and Dawn teaches versions of the multigenre paper to students from high school to college. The concept is modeled after Michael Ondaatje's novel, *The Collected Works of Billy the Kid* (1996), which is itself a blending of fact, fiction, and supposition based on facts about the life and times of Billy the Kid.

When Dawn teaches the multigenre paper, she has students focus on one person or event about which they are passionate and about which they want to research and write for an entire semester. Careful selection of the subject matter is essential to the success of the final multigenre paper. Once the topic is chosen, students begin conducting research to find out the facts about their person or event. Once students have a factual core of knowledge from which to experiment and build, the writing begins. Students in Dawn's class are encouraged to stretch beyond their comfort zones as writers. They try unrhymed poetry, narrative, drama, obituaries, journalistic pieces, interviews, description, interior monologue, and other *genre* as a way of exploring their topic and explicating it to readers of their multigenre papers. They squirm with the Grammar B requirements—the deliberate breaking of some traditional grammatical rules in order to achieve impact in their papers—as Romano (1995) explains. But the most fun comes in the production and celebration of the final product.

Dawn encourages students to consider presentational format as an additional mode of expositional meaning. One student who chose to write her multigenre paper on a famous Scottish battle encased her final multigenre collection in a hand-made tartan cover complete with pin. Another student who chose to write about Georgia O'Keefe presented her final multigenre collection as an artist's portfolio that opened vertically and featured reprints of some of the art pieces alongside the student's original writings. Students also experiment with bindings, paper, and font color and style. Some creative students have hand-printed letters that were to have been written by the person who was the subject of their multigenre collection, and others have gone so far as to singe the edges of the pages that were to have been partially consumed by a fire. One industrious and talented student discovered that the person about whom she had written was an admirer of watercolor artwork, so she created an original watercolor on every page of her multigenre collection.

On the day that the final multigenre collections are due, Dawn asks all of the students to clear their desks of their belongings and place their multigenre collections on top. Then, we conduct a walkaround during which we all circulate among the desks, looking through the final products. After about twenty minutes, students return to their seats, and Dawn asks, "What did you see that you liked?" The compliments flow and the writers glow from the effects of praise.

Such writings and presentational considerations give students another lens through which to view exposition and research—not as deadly dull assignments—but as creative, meaningful expressions of self and of information. Students shape a message and deliver it to readers through a range of forms. When the writer's message is received by the readers, the inquiry process moves from the dusty, dusky library to the full light of celebratory achievement.

We began this chapter by talking about how often the teaching of the essay is drudgery for teachers and students alike. We end this chapter by sharing the fun we have and how much our students learn when they expand their range of expositional writing, blurring *genre*, conducting action research, and considering both the medium and the message. We've tried to explain our enthusiasm to you and give you some ideas for generating new essay forms for your students. Have we communicated our message? Have we answered some questions and raised others? If so, our exposition has been successful.

Works Cited

Britton, James, et al. 1975. *The Development of Writing Abilities (11–18)*. London: Macmillan Education.

Dillard, Annie. 1990. *The Writing Life*. New York: Harper Perennial.

Kirby, Dan, and Carol Kuykendall. 1991. *Mind Matters, Teaching for Thinking*. Portsmouth, NH: Boynton/Cook.

Lightman, Allen. 2000. *The Best American Essays of 2000*. Boston: Houghton Mifflin.

LOPEZ, BARRY. 1998. *About This Life, Journeys on the Threshold of Memory*. New York: Alfred A. Knopf.

MACRORIE, KEN. 1988. *The I-Search Paper, Revised Edition of Searching Writing*. Portsmouth, NH: Boynton/Cook.

MARTIN, NANCY, PAT D'ARCY, BRYAN NEWTON, AND ROBERT PARKER. 1976. *Writing and Learning Across the Curriculum, 11–16*. London: Ward Lock.

NORRIS, KATHLEEN. 2001. *The Best American Essays of 2001*. Boston: Houghton Mifflin.

ONDAATJE, MICHAEL. 1996. *The Collected Works of Billy the Kid*. New York: Knopf Publishing Group.

ROMANO, TOM. 1995. *Writing with Passion*. Portsmouth, NH: Heinemann.

WARRINER, JOHN. 1969. *English Grammar and Composition*. New York: Harcourt Brace Jovanovich.

14

Grading and Evaluating

Assessment should begin *conversations about performance, not* end *them.*
—GRANT WIGGINS, *Assessing Student Performance*

Grading students and evaluating their progress are the toughest jobs in teaching. After decades in the classroom, we still find the whole process tiresome, frustrating, and often in conflict with our objectives. Nowhere is that grading frustration more problematic than in the composition classroom. Not only does the paper-grading crunch take up too much of every teacher's time and energy, the grading process itself is often a futile and defeating experience.

The teachers to whom we talk are frustrated by composition grading because they often see little improvement in student writing even after hours of hard work. Even worse, their students feel negatively toward their writing classes because they find it difficult to accept the teacher's subjective criticism and critical marks on their papers. Some students view the whole process as a plot to make them feel inferior and inadequate.

Part of the problem is deciding just how evaluation and grading can help a writer. Do we evaluate to grade or grade to evaluate? Is the grade based on that final piece in front of us or on what we know about the work or lack of it that preceded what we have? Do we take into consideration the fact that Joe works until 2:00 AM every morning or that Wanda speaks English as a second language or that Renee is the first in her family to make it in school past the eighth grade? The issues don't sort out easily.

On top of all these perplexities, the teacher really represents only one reader of the text, one voice in the evaluation. We want to grade more than technical proficiency and form. We want to evaluate nebulous categories like quality of inquiry, risk taking, improvement through revisions, and control of language. Too many composition books ignore this subject altogether or dismiss it with a few simplistic suggestions, and the temptation to be glib or flippant is strong even now. But realistically, the grading of papers in composition classes will not go away. Also realistically, grading and evaluation will probably remain problematic for rookie and veteran teachers alike.

General Principles for Grading Writing

We don't have any surefire, simple answers. We wrestle with grading problems in every class we teach. A part of the problem is that our approach to teaching writing makes grading harder instead of easier. We have been encouraging you throughout this book to develop your responding skills. "Be a sensitive reader." "Look for the good." "Be positive." "Go to your papers with anticipation."

These attitudes and behaviors are absolutely essential to develop if you're going to get writers going. *But* it's difficult for teachers to make a smooth transition from reader to grader. Students who hear you say, "That's good. I like it," feel betrayed when they see the C in the grade book. Responding and evaluating are not mutually exclusive teaching activities, but it's not easy to work out the conflicts in those two roles.

First, let us suggest some general principles about grading in the composition class.

1. *Grading should be deemphasized.* Students have become very grade conscious, and they often bludgeon their teachers with the "Is this going to be graded?" question. If your answer to them is yes, that's the universal signal that the assignment is important, and they grudgingly set out to give you what you want. If your answer is no, they may decide that the assignment is not worth doing. At its worst, this grade-grubbing becomes a kind of "we won't work unless we're paid" statement.

Careful planning and deliberate strategies to deemphasize grading can do much to change the grade-grubbing syndrome. We begin all composition classes with the "not everything you do here will be graded" speech. We talk about the importance of practice and the establishment of a rigorous conditioning regimen. We tell them that practice pays off eventually in better grades because some major assignments will be graded, and the practice assignments lead up to and prepare them for the graded assignments. Some of you have given the same speech. Such a speech works, however, only if you actually deemphasize grades in your class by finding a set of strategies to put such rhetoric into practice.

2. *Drafts should not be graded.* The standard composition format—student writes paper, teacher takes papers home and grades them—teaches students very little about how writers work and how good writing grows from draft to draft. One of the surest ways to involve students in a viable composition process is to withhold grades until students complete a final draft. Comment and respond extensively to drafts without grading them. Don't use the grade as a threat or an ultimate weapon. Don't talk about grades much. Focus on the piece of writing itself. After a student has worked on several drafts of several pieces, ask her to pick one for careful evaluation.

3. *Develop grading criteria with students.* In Chapter 9 we talk at length about developing criteria for *good* writing. These criteria, when developed cooperatively with students, can become a grading scale that students can understand and accept. Furthermore, by using such cooperative criteria, students can see more clearly how to im-

prove and grow as writers. It's more than showing them what you want. It's developing their own critical sense and evaluative judgment.

4. *Students should be involved as graders and evaluators.* There's perhaps no more dramatic way to help students understand the pitfalls of grading than to ask them to participate by grading one another's papers. We're not suggesting, of course, that a teacher abdicate the role of grader. We are suggesting that students can and should *participate* in the evaluation process, not only to develop empathy for the grader, but also to become better readers of one another's papers. We don't necessarily count students' grades in our grade books, but we use that peer grade as a springboard for discussion and revision. If a peer partner grades a paper as a C, then the writer and the partner discuss what the paper needs in order to improve, thus indicating to the writer what revisions are still needed.

5. *Grade process as well as product.* We value both process and product. That letter grade on the paper carries meanings all out of proportion to its importance. We need to develop grading strategies that reward students for careful preparation, extensive revision, and practice. Dan and Dawn have students compile portfolios for each finished product in which the students put their jot lists, drafts, research notes, peer responses, revisions, experimentations with the writing, and anything else that indicates their processes as writers. These in-process products indicate the students' work as writers and show their efforts with writing prior to achieving a finished product. We grade these portfolios separately from the final products so that process receives an individual, and usually equally weighty, grade, as does the finished paper. The portfolio is evidence of effort as a writer. We know that a rich process can still result in a poor product (Have you ever worked long and hard on a paper and received a grade of C– on it?), and that a skimpy process can sometimes result in an A paper (Did you ever write a paper the night before it was due and get a good grade on it?). When we grade the portfolio separately, we are demonstrating to students that we value both product and process.

6. *Focus your grading.* Begin with a few criteria. Grade only the specific structures of writing you've been working on. If you have spent all week on concrete detail or strong verbs or beginnings or transitions, let your grading of that week's assignment reflect your teaching emphases. Don't try to grade everything all at once. Start small. Slowly add criteria to your grading scale, carefully demonstrating to students exactly what you're looking for.

7. *Give ideas, inventiveness, and content an important weight in your grading scale.* Most of us have tried the two-grades approach at least once. You know, A over C; A for content, C for mechanics. We've never found that very helpful. Students either average the two or see the A as a gift and the C as an insult. Instead, use a rubric that values both content and inventiveness.

If you follow our philosophy in this book, we propose that student writers experiment with ideas, explore options, and take chances. Remember, they are apprentices learning an art. They stretch further, try new tools, or follow an unlikely vision if they trust that we are their supporters. Our evaluations should reflect their increased confidence, their willingness to tackle difficult subjects, and their ability to analyze the strengths and weaknesses in their own writing. This approach may appear to de-emphasize correctness, but we want writers concentrating on shaping their subjects first. We honestly believe that the development of fluency through extensive writing practice brings with it growing control of the language.

The more students write and receive careful feedback, the better they become and the fewer problems they have with correctness. Not all things improve with practice. As any college composition teacher can tell you, some usage errors stubbornly persist even in the writings of college students. Subject/verb agreement and pronoun reference problems, for example, seem to persist in spite of practice. They're so much a part of the oral language process that students seem to have difficulty deleting them in written language. We'll certainly need to approach such usage problems directly. Yes, even with drills if necessary. But we make a serious mistake in the teaching of writing if we emphasize such surface considerations at the expense of real and powerful expression of ideas and feelings. Content and correctness are both important, but it makes a big difference to your success as a teacher of developing writers where you begin and where you put your emphasis.

There is a place for rigorous grading in the writing class. It is at the end of the process after practice, trials, and revisions.

A Little Self-Evaluation

A good place for any teacher of writing to begin thinking about grading is to engage in some self-evaluation. How do you grade your students' papers? What are your primary emphases? Have you worked out a grading scale? Does it overemphasize surface features? Do you respond to ideas as you grade the papers? What do you hope your grading methods will develop in your students?

Maybe you're not ready for an introspective look at your own grading procedures, but success in the teaching of writing demands that you have a grading system compatible with maximum student growth. Take a look at that stack of papers you've just finished grading and answer the following questions as honestly as you can. Write your answers down so that you can argue with yourself later.

1. Are they graded in the *deduct* manner? (You take off points for errors and sometimes the kids end up owing you points.)
2. Are there papers in that stack that make you feel uncomfortable (either good papers with bad grades or bad papers with good grades)?
3. What was your *primary* emphasis when you graded those papers? What were you looking for? Do the grades reflect that emphasis? Do your comments reflect the emphasis?

4. Is the grade *final*, or does the student have the option of improving the paper and thus the grade?

5. How have you responded to *what* the writers are saying? Do your comments question, confirm, and show interest in the content? What are the percentages of your markings that identify errors? How many positive comments, on average, have you written on each paper? Do only the *good* writers merit positive written comments from you?

6. What do you hope your grading will accomplish with these writers?

7. What type of follow-up teaching have you planned after the papers are returned?

Perhaps the most seriously damaging habit we get into as graders is mindlessness. The sheer volume of papers and their frequent drabness have a kind of hypnotic effect that can rob the evaluator not only of objectivity, but also of sensitive and insightful reading. If student papers are important enough to be graded, they deserve the best reading we can possibly give them. The rest of this chapter is dedicated to practical alternatives for making grading and evaluating a less loathsome activity.

Perhaps the most satisfactory answer to the grading headache is to present a number of grading alternatives and encourage you to take your pick. Our guess is that you'll end up using all of them at one time or another, perhaps arriving at some personal, eclectic system.

The Nongrading Approach

Some writing theorists (none of whom work in the public schools) recommend strongly against any kind of grading in the composition class. Several teachers we know have tried the nongrading approach, focusing exclusively on constructive responses to student papers, carefully keeping each of the students' papers in a folder or portfolio to serve as a record of progress. Several times during the grading term, the student and the teacher sit down in conference and discuss the student's progress in concrete and specific terms, referring to the collected writings. The advantages of such an approach are obvious. The teachers spend most of their time focusing on writing behavior rather than agonizing over grades. The students are weaned away from writing for the grade and are encouraged to practice and experiment with their writing. Progress is emphasized; evaluation is positive and helpful.

Unfortunately, the realities of the schools demand that even the teacher who deemphasizes grading in the composition class give some kind of grade for the permanent record when the course is over. This means, of course, that the teacher must grade something. We suggest that, at least with younger, less skilled, and less confident writers, you grade anything but their writings.

The disadvantages of the nongrading alternative are principally the hassles teachers face using such a system. Students exhibit withdrawal symptoms, parents think your course lacks rigor, and your principal thinks you're lazy. In the end you still face the difficult task of translating progress into a letter grade for the report card.

As a middle ground, we suggest that you have a number of assignments that are not graded. Call them *practice activities* or better yet *explorations* or *jottings*. Train your writing students to expect frequent practice activities and explorations. Culminate this practice by responding to, sharing, or publishing the writings rather than grading them.

A Performance System

The performance system is quick and simple for the teacher and clear and concrete for the student. If the student does the assignment, she gets the grade (or points); no value judgments are made about the quality of the work. You establish an acceptable level of performance in your class and students meet it. You may specify that you want five pages in the journal each week or two short writings each week with a revised piece every two weeks. Whatever your performance criteria, the student either does the work and receives credit or fails to do the work and receives no credit.

The advantages of such a system are its efficiency—it's easy to record who did what—and the psychological effect of transferring the responsibility of grading to the student. "You want to do well in my class? Do the work." Teachers can spend their time responding and commenting on student papers rather than counting errors or debating between a C+ and a B–.

The disadvantages are few but not unimportant. A performance system does not give the teacher the flexibility to recognize works of exceptional quality, bad or good. Such a system could lead to a lessening of incentive to do good work unless the teacher uses other things to motivate writing. Motivation comes through publishing class books that contain the best work on a particular assignment or by celebrating an outstanding piece through oral reading. Publishing excerpts on the bulletin board or class website gives credit for excellence. A performance system can lead to the complacency of just getting the job done unless we find ways to celebrate excellence and quality.

Holistic Grading Strategies

Charles Cooper and Lee Odell, with characteristic clarity, give a classic definition of holistic evaluation:

> a guided procedure for sorting or ranking written pieces. The rater takes a piece of writing and either (1) matches it with another piece in a graded series of pieces or (2) scores it for the prominence of certain features important to that kind of writing or (3) assigns it a letter grade or number. The placing, scoring, or grading occurs quickly, impressionistically, after the rater has practiced the procedure with other

raters. The rater does not make corrections or revisions in the paper. Holistic evaluation is usually guided by a holistic scoring guide which describes each feature and identifies high, middle, and low quality levels for each feature. (1977)

Holistic grading is a system compatible with our philosophy. It focuses on the piece of writing as a whole and on those features most important to the success of the piece. It helps the teacher to evaluate more quickly, more consistently, and more pointedly. The rating is quick because the rater does not take time to circle errors or make marginal notations.

The rating is consistent because the rater uses the same carefully developed criteria on all pieces of writing. This consistency is evident not only from piece to piece rated by the same rater, but also between different raters rating the same piece. This means, of course, that students can expect their English teachers to be more consistent in their grading, thus reducing the grading idiosyncrasies that so often frustrate student writers.

Roundtable Grading

Roundtable holistic grading can be a way of letting students into the evaluation process. Students read papers, establish criteria, and evaluate. Each student has a clearer idea of her own performance on a particular paper after the experience and is responsible, with the teacher's input and several markings by peers, to assign her own grade. If students take on this role of evaluator, the most useful part is that they become better judges of their own work. They have a clearer idea of what they can do to improve their own piece in light of the features they established as rubrics. Students come up with categories for evaluation:

- a coherent plan is evident behind the text
- the writer resists tangents or straying from the subject
- focus is maintained
- explanations give the reader what she needs to know to be satisfied
- errors do not distract attention from content
- natural transitions grow out of content discussed

We've found that writers are particularly sensitive to problem areas in an assignment while they are drafting. They have a healthy notion of the pitfalls and have good ideas about what might present problems or successes. We develop the scale at about the mid-stage of writing, prior to final drafting. After roundtable evaluation, students see what they need to revise and are more motivated to do so.

Many teachers accomplish many of these same goals through the use of peer conferences. The difference between roundtable grading and peer conferences, however, is the focus on grading, not responding, which has a tendency to increase the stakes a bit. Students tend to take it more seriously than a rather friendly peer conference.

The *roundtable grading model* comes from the procedures the Educational Testing Services uses to rate student writing samples. Tom has used this approach with his advanced placement students with good results, but we have learned the hard way that evaluation by peers must be thoroughly structured and patiently implemented. Even then, we have sometimes been forced to admit that in some classes it just doesn't work.

Impression Marking

Perhaps the simplest and quickest approach to the holistic grading of student papers is to read them quickly without circling errors or suggesting editorial changes. The reader scans the paper and marks it based on some general feelings about the paper's effectiveness. The system is efficient and surprisingly reliable, particularly if readers have a clear set of criteria in mind as they read the papers. This set of criteria must, of course, be in the writers' minds as well as the readers'. So impressionistic criteria must be shared and illustrated for writers as a part of the full range of writing processes.

The following is a list of criteria that we sometimes use as a guide to direct *readers'* thinking as they read student papers. We caution against using the guide as a grading scale by converting various items to point values. This guide gives the reader a focus and suggests specific features in the piece of writing to key on, but the reader must read quickly and carefully to arrive at a feel for the piece and a grade.

First, read student papers using the guide as a reminder. As you finish reading a paper, place it in one of three or four piles without marking it. When all papers are read, go back to the piles to argue with yourself a bit, perhaps moving papers from pile to pile. When you're satisfied with the relative value of the papers, assign grades by piles and reread each paper, writing some notes to the student about the paper.

We use the holistic approach sparingly during composition classes, preferring to focus more on developing fluency in first drafting and fine-tuning during revision stages. But like most of you, we must grade our students, and we feel they have a right to know where they stand long before the mysterious grade appears on the report card.

We also involve students in the grading process and train them in the impression system. A student's final grade in our writing classes usually consists of several holistic grades given by the teacher and at least some given by the student's peers. Our students seem comfortable with the fact that their grades are in such humane and understanding hands.

Holistic Guide for Evaluating Student Writings

(Do not make a scale of these criteria, but use the list as a reminder of important characteristics of good writing. When you are providing opportunities for students to respond to peer writings, help them recognize and value excellence and experimentation in any aspect of the writing.)

1. Impact

- The reader's interest is engaged.
- The writer has something to say and is imaginatively involved.
- The idea or experience is conveyed with fluency or intensity.
- The writing is convincing. It may have a sense of immediacy, a complete-ness, or a rightness of content and form that makes it effective.

2. Inventiveness

The reader is *surprised*—finds that the writer has not followed the usual or the trite but has introduced elements that are new and unexpected.

Evidences of the writer's inventiveness may include:

- Coined words (onomatopoeic, portmanteau, etc.)
- Tag names (allusive or symbolic)
- Unusual point of view (often to add humor or irony)
- Figurative use of language (to clarify meaning, not to adorn)
- Significant title—one that augments the meaning of the writing
- Original, surprising, and appropriate element in content or in arrangement
- Use of unconventional punctuation, spelling, or format to achieve desired effects

3. Individuality

The reader is aware of a distinctive speaking voice. This sense of persona, or indi-vidual flavor, seems to come from the writer's control of tone and point of view and/ or distinctiveness in the ordering of ideas or in using the resources of the language (figurative language, vocabulary, syntax, etc.).

The sense of a distinctive persona is usually strong in good monologues—expres-sive, expository, or dramatic.

In narration or dialogue the sense of control comes from the appropriate meshing of all parts into the whole.

Portfolios

One very popular means of gathering students' papers into one place and evaluating them is that of portfolios. In fact, it's become difficult to use the word *portfolio* with-out next using the word *assessment*. There are probably as many types of portfolios as there are teachers who use them. Many districts require student portfolios, so your district may have indicators in place for the types of portfolios that you will use and the ways in which you will evaluate them. If such requirements are not specified in your school or if you want to use additional versions of portfolios to enhance your own assessment plan, the following are some ideas for effective uses of portfolios.

Performance Portfolios

Performance portfolios indicate a student's point of mastery in a learning and/or writing process. The teacher establishes certain criteria that the students are to master, and the students compile products that indicate their level of mastery of those criteria.

For example, in one college where Dawn taught, all English majors were required to produce a senior portfolio. For those students in secondary English education, they included products in their portfolios that indicated that they had mastery of the areas of literature, composition, language, and communication, including the ways in which theory influences practice and the ways in which they will apply their knowledge to their future teaching. They may have included lesson plans, tests, finished papers, response log entries, or other products that show their mastery of these criteria.

The evaluation process for these portfolios was multitiered. The faculty members, two per portfolio, independently rated these portfolios as showing that students had met or failed to meet these criteria. Dawn held a follow-up miniconference with each student to discuss the student's areas of strength and weakness in content mastery, knowledge of theory, and ideas for future teaching. The faculty surveyed the overall results to see areas in the program that needed strengthening as they prepared students to become future teachers. These performance portfolios thus helped with program evaluation, students' self-assessment of their own work and knowledge, and with planning future instruction in specific courses. For the students, these particular performance portfolios were rated as pass or fail, and students were given a chance to revise and work to improve an area of knowledge that was weak or failing. By the end of the process, both students and faculty had a better understanding of individual achievement and of the link between instruction, student performance, and program assessment.

In the classroom, similar uses are possible. The teacher establishes criteria for mastery and the student compiles products showing such mastery. Then the teacher and perhaps other colleagues rate the portfolios for passing or failing achievement of the competencies. Given those ratings and comments by the rater, the teacher then discusses achievement and performance with each student, offering an opportunity for continuing to work on areas of weakness. Students see what areas they have mastered and on which areas they still need to work; teachers have indicators for future instruction; and the data can be used in departmental reports to parents and administrators about programmatic and curricular efficacy.

Showcase Portfolios

A showcase portfolio gathers together and highlights the student's best work for a period of time such as a unit of study, a type of writing completed, or a grading term.

Think of a model who is trying to land a job. He may go to the job interview with his portfolio in hand, one that shows various pictures of him in different manners of dress, with different lengths or colors of hair, and with or without a beard. He's trying to show prospective employers all of the many ways that he can look good and meet their needs.

The showcase portfolio generally features the completed, final draft products that the students feel are their best work. Process is not represented in this type of portfolio, so the reader doesn't see drafts, notes, or response logs—only finished, polished products. The showcase portfolio requires the students to cull through their finished products, select the best ones, and then arrange them effectively in the portfolio. Sometimes narratives or explications of how and why the student wrote and chose the particular work accompany the showcase portfolio.

Showcase portfolios are generally graded holistically. The best work indicates fluency, precision, and control; it represents a quality written product and polished writing; it fulfills the requirements of the type of writing included in the portfolio—or it doesn't.

A showcase portfolio frequently follows a student into the next grade. Next year's teacher receives the portfolio at the beginning of the year in order to be able to assess each student's competencies and weaknesses as a writer by examining what the student thought was her best work at the end of the previous year. Such portfolios can be informative to teachers and can help teachers determine peer groupings for workshops, initial minilessons on usage and mechanics with which to begin the year, or the types of writing that students have previously mastered.

Process Portfolios

Process portfolios are in some ways the opposite of showcase portfolios. Process portfolios include the full range of pieces, drafts to finished papers, produced during the process of writing a specific type of paper or produced during a specific grading term. The purpose of such portfolios is to profile the particular student writer at work. Perhaps during the course of completing an action research paper, the student worked as a writer, thinker, researcher, interviewer, and responder to peers' writings. Indicators of all of those roles should then appear in the process portfolio. The reader would therefore see drafts, thinker's logs, research reflections, interview questions and results, and evidence of having worked as an effective responder of others' writings in the portfolio, as well as the finished product. The student keeps "every scrap of paper," as Dawn terms it, composed during the process of producing a particular finished product, organizes the papers, and presents them as a portfolio at the time of product completion.

The difference between a process portfolio and a mere class notebook or some other comprehensive form of collecting papers is the element of reflection. Dan and Dawn both use a reflective writing guide developed by Dan for helping students to reflect on their processes and work as writers. This reflective piece opens the portfolio and is the first piece that we read when evaluating the finished products and accompanying process portfolios. We tailor the prompts in the guide to suit the specific body of work that the students have completed for their process portfolios, but the general nature of the questions remains the same. Here's an example of a reflective writing guide:

Reflective Writing Guide for Memoir Piece

Please respond fully to each prompt in an essay format. This is your opportunity to reflect fully on your work as a writer, thinker, and memoirist. Tell me what you've done, how hard you've worked, and what you think about your accomplishments. You may use an informal tone in your writing. Provide elaborated responses, not simplistic "yes/no/sometimes" ones.

- What were your work habits as you produced your memoir?
- How helpful were your peer response groups in helping you shape your final product?
- How helpful were our in-class activities in helping you brainstorm pieces for your paper and craft your finished product?
- What was the most difficult part of this process?
- Of what aspect of your finished product are you most proud? Why?
- If you had more time for this project, on what would you continue to work? Why?
- What other comments (not grade whining!) would you like to make about this product and process?

We like these reflections for a number of reasons. First, they cause students to think seriously about their work as writers, revisers, and compilers of finished products. They are asked to be honest in their assessments of their own efforts and to pinpoint areas of difficulty and pride in their work, adding both a metacognitive and self-assessment component to their process portfolios. As teachers, we like knowing what students thought was difficult in a writing process so that we can adjust future instruction; and we like knowing the area of pride that a student identifies in a piece of writing so that we can respond to that aspect of the writing with extra attention and sensitivity.

After students have completed several different types of finished products accompanied by process portfolios and reflective pieces, we ask students to survey their reflections. Are they consistently having the same problems in writing? What are their areas of growth as writers? What new skills have they mentioned in these reflections that they have learned? What new areas of achievement have they noticed in their writing? We have each student chart progress, difficulties, and accomplishments. In this way, learning becomes concrete for students and for us. We both, students and teacher, have a record of what has been accomplished and learned—not just, "I wrote three finished papers this grading period," but "I worked on the openings of my papers, on using more specific details, and on enlivening my writing with action verbs. I'm still working on conclusions and comma splices." Such awareness of the craft and techniques of writing helps to build more confident and effective writers.

Analytic Scales

Analytic scales are precise and carefully articulated grading scales that direct the reader's attention to specific features of the piece of writing and suggest relative point values for each feature. The grade for the piece is calculated by summing scores on the various subparts. Such a scoring tool is more pointed than impression marking because the rating guide defines and illustrates the grading criteria to writers and raters alike and keeps raters on track during the marking procedure. Such guides, when carefully shared and explained to students, can demystify the final grade and highlight strengths and weaknesses in their writings. The guides also ensure that certain surface features in the piece (handwriting, spelling, punctuation) do not influence the rating of the piece out of proportion to their importance to the piece's effectiveness.

An example of an analytic scale is the classic Diederich Scale (Diederich 1974); many English teachers will recognize it. Diederich and his colleagues at the Educational Testing Service developed the scale to use in scoring SAT essay examinations. Because the essay exams are read by several raters, Diederich needed a scoring tool that would provide a quick and reliable evaluation. The scale itself was developed primarily to be used for staff grading, but many teachers have adapted it to use with their students.

How to Interpret the Diederich Scale

1. This scale weighs content and organization at 50%, aspects of style at 30%, and mechanics at 20%. The multiplication translates the 40 point scale into a 100-point scale.

2. The ratings for each item range from 1 to 5. Regard 1 as the lowest grade, 3 as the average, and 5 as the highest. Use 2 to designate below-average performance but not marked deficiency and use 4 to designate above-average performance but not marked proficiency. *Reading five randomly selected papers from a set before you attempt to grade the set will help you to form a realistic notion of 1, 3, and 5 performance for that particular assignment.*

3. Observing the following guidelines will also help to assure more uniform and consistent grading.

   a. *Quality and development of ideas.* Grant the writer his choice of subject matter. He was, after all, offered choices dictated by the teacher and should *not* be penalized by the value you place on one choice as compared to another. Look for how well he has supported his subject and *his* point of view or attitude toward the subject.

   b. *Organization, relevance, movement.* A 5 paper will begin with a clear indication of its controlling idea, offer convincing relevant support, and come to a close. A 1 paper begins anywhere and goes nowhere. A 3 paper may be skimpily but relevantly developed or fully developed but including some irrelevant material.

Diederich Scale

1—Poor   2—Weak   3—Average   4—Good   5—Excellent

Reader_____

Quality and development of ideas	1 2 3 4 5	
Organization, relevance, movement	1 2 3 4 5	

_____×5=_____
Subtotal

Style, flavor, individuality	1 2 3 4 5	
Wording and phrasing	1 2 3 4 5	

_____×3=_____
Subtotal

Grammar, sentence structure	1 2 3 4 5	
Punctuation	1 2 3 4 5	
Spelling	1 2 3 4 5	
Manuscript form, legibility	1 2 3 4 5	

_____×1=_____
Subtotal

Total Grade: ____%

---

c. *Style, flavor, individuality.* Guard against the temptation to give a low score for the use of nonstandard English. Papers containing nonstandard English are often rich in flavor and individuality. Reserve 5 for the truly arresting paper. A single apt, precise, or arresting phrase can move a paper from a 3 to a 4.

d. *Wording and phrasing.* Here is the place to give a low score for an impoverished vocabulary and a high one for apt and precise diction and clear phrasing.

e. *Grammar, sentence structure.* Low scores should be given for frequent *and varied* nonstandard constructions like errors in agreement between pronoun and antecedent, dangling constructions, subject-verb agreement, and so on.

f. *Punctuation.* Again, frequent *and varied* abuses of standard punctuation marks deserve a low score; occasional varied errors in common punctuation marks receive a middle score; freedom from common errors, a high score. Errors in the use of the comma, the apostrophe, and end punctuation should be regarded as more serious than errors in the use of the semicolon, quotation marks (especially double quotes), parentheses, and brackets. Regard the mistaken presence or absence of the apostrophe as a punctuation error, not a spelling error.

g. *Spelling.* Give a score of 5 if the writer has misspelled no words; a 4 for one spelling error; a 3 for two spelling errors; a 2 for three spelling errors, and a 1 for four or more errors. This is the *only place* on the scale where you are to assess spelling. Misspelling the same word is only one error.

h. Adherence to *manuscript form* and *legibility* merits a 5. An unreadable paper without margins and without a proper heading merits a score of 1. Perhaps readers should attempt only a 1, 3, or 5 judgment on this item. Do *not* give a low score for neat cross-outs. (Remember that the students are writing their papers in class and that they have been encouraged not to waste time recopying.)

We primarily use this scale as a reference point in our overall knowledge of assessment and evaluation procedures; we have never used the scale more than once or twice during a writing class because it does not entirely reflect our own emphases in the teaching of writing. It is important, however, for students to be exposed to such a grading approach, and our students actually enjoy being graded by such a concrete and carefully articulated scale; they like to feel that their grades "add up." We also discuss this scale with students in order to explain to them the basis of how many college entrance essays might be evaluated and to show them the basis of other similar scales, such as the 6-Trait Scale, with which they may have more immediate experience.

6-Trait Scale

Now that you have seen the Diederich Scale, you will no doubt recognize it as the root of other similar analytic scales, including the 6-Trait Scale. The advantages of the 6-Trait Scale are similar to all such analytic scales: Students and parents become familiar with it; it's quick and efficient; and it allows the teacher at least the illusion of consistency in grading, a fact that may be important to teachers, students, parents, and administrators. Many districts with which we work have adapted the 6-Trait Scale to be the 6 + 1-Trait Scale. Such scales generally evaluate components such as ideas, word choice, conventions, sentence fluency, organization, voice, and presentation, considering the extent to which they are proficient or deficient in the written product being evaluated. Like the Diederich Scale, 6-trait scales use scores of 1, 3, and 5 to indicate deficiency or proficiency in each area.

The disadvantages of this particular scale, to us, outweigh its advantages. First, it has become institutionalized and industrialized. Dawn, who began teaching in the early 1970s, likens the advent of 6-trait scales to that of *writing process* in the 1980s. When the concept of writing process hit language arts pedagogy, it was the hot, new terminology. Every classroom displayed a chart featuring *the* steps—in precise order—of *The* Writing Process as though all writers compose every product in exactly the same way using the same steps in the same order—which is not the case in real, individual composing. Teachers even began referring to writing completed in this manner as *process writing* as though it were a *genre* of its own. Such is the current state of affairs with 6-trait scales. The notion has taken on a life of its own, evolving from just *one* method for evaluating students' papers into the preferred method for many districts. We hear teachers tell their students that they'll be "writing 6-trait papers in here" as though it were a *genre* of writing, not an evaluation scale. And we see charts in classrooms telling students the precise traits that all of their papers should contain and on which all of their papers will be evaluated.

That is the second disadvantage for us: 6-trait scales are used to evaluate all papers, regardless of form or *genre*, according to the exact same criteria. A poem is evaluated on the same scale as is a research paper. Although all forms of writing certainly share some of the same characteristics, and although we want all writing to be quality writing, we much prefer criteria that are established to reflect the uniqueness of each writing situation and the demands of each written product. Poetry and research papers, for example, seem to make different demands on the writer and seem to call for different considerations from the evaluator. Correct use of quotes, documentation of sources, and clarity of argument are all essential to the research paper, while use of figurative language, imagery, and precision of thought are all essential to poetry.

Yes, some of the criteria overlap for both types of writing, but we far prefer to tailor our evaluation rubrics to the particular demands of the specific written product, as you'll see in the next section on checkpoints. We also prefer that our evaluation rubrics be co-constructed with our students so that evaluation and instruction move toward becoming seamless activities in our classrooms. And finally, we prefer to be able to emphasize particular factors of each writing situation so that any one aspect of writing is not stressed to the detriment of others. For example, if we've already stressed a particular use of quotation marks in the last three assignments, which were research-based, we don't want to continue to stress only that feature of mechanics in upcoming assignments that are more expressive in nature, thus giving students the impression that quotation marks are the only important surface features of which they should gain mastery.

The third disadvantage of 6-trait scales, as we see it, relates to the current atmosphere of high-stakes testing in which schools' scores on proficiency tests are published in the local newspapers, administrators praise or condemn teachers based on their students' scores on such tests, and parents value or devalue a school based solely on its test scores. In some states, schools are even graded as *excellent* or as *failing* schools based on their test scores. Who wants to attend or work in a failing school, regardless of its other merits? Not many.

This situation is deplorable to us. It postulates that education and the learning process are easily quantified and containerized. It contends that simplistic tests are valuable indicators of the outcomes associated with the complexity of teaching and learning. It gives the illusion that the material tested is the ceiling, not the floor, of learning in our schools, that if students do well on *the test*, they have learned what they need to know in order to be successful students and productive citizens. Worst of all, such tests have become the proverbial tail wagging the instructional dog in that teachers spend inordinate amounts of time teaching students how to take the test and how to pass the test as though the test were all that mattered in learning. Content areas for which the tests have yet to be developed receive less curricular emphasis and cuts in funding.

To this volatile, intense, and politically charged situation, add the fact that 6-trait scales are the scoring devices of choice for the writing portion of such tests, and the associations become overwhelming. Writing is not a simplistic activity, easily and quickly learned, effortlessly and efficiently evaluated. Writing is complex, learned developmentally, and best evaluated with specific rubrics designed by knowledgeable professionals with the precise writing contexts in mind—none of which occurs with the use of 6-trait scales.

So, what's to be done?

Checkpoints

By far the most effective rating guides for student papers are the ones teachers themselves devise. These scales can be content-specific, focusing the evaluation on those aspects of writing that you've been trying to teach. Such guides should be used after you have demonstrated them, devised practice activities, and given students a chance to revise and improve their papers using the criteria in checklist form.

Figures 14–1a and 14–1b are two checkpoint guides that Dan developed for seventh graders, one for memoir and one for opinion papers (Olson, Kirby, Kuykendall, et al. 1981). Checkpoint 1 comes after two weeks of writing practice and is used on a student's revised writing. Notice that in addition to numbers, some specific suggestions are included for improving the paper. If students are rated low on vivid, concrete detail, they are encouraged to add more specific detail. The checkpoint scale focuses on specific aspects of writing instruction and also allows the teacher considerable latitude by including an Overall Impression section that makes up 30 percent of the rating.

A further advantage of the checkpoint idea is that teachers can standardize their grading and instruction at particular grade levels. Seventh-grade teachers could work to develop five or six checkpoints to use to focus composition instruction during the

Scoring Guide: Checkpoint 1 for Memoir

Your revised writing was rated as follows:

1. *Honest Writing*

1	2	3	4	5	×4=_____

   Try again. Write fast. Use the words in your own head. / You're moving. Keep working. / Yes! Fresh honest language. Good!

2. *Vivid, Concrete Detail*

1	2	3	4	5	×4=_____

   Try again. Your writing is bare. Add more specific detail. / Some good stuff in your writing. Add specifics. Stay away from generalizations. / Surprising words. Concrete word pictures. Good!

3. *Strong Verbs*

1	2	3	4	5	×4=_____

   Try again. Use verbs that paint a picture. / I see you've been working at it. / Good. I like those words!

4. *End Punctuation and First Word Capitalization*

1	2	3	4	5	×2=_____

   Many sentences do not begin with capitals. Many sentences do not end with appropriate punctuation. See me for help. / Several errors. Proofread carefully. / All sentences begin with capital letters and end with appropriate punctuation.

5. *Overall Impression*

1	2	3	4	5	×6=_____

   You really haven't given this assignment a fair shot. Spend more time developing ideas for writing. / Yes. I see potential. Keep working. / I was touched by your writing. You connected with your audience.

Total _____

Comments:

Figure 14–1a. *Scoring Guide: Checkpoint 1 for Memoir*

May be copied for classroom use. © 2004 by Dan Kirby, Dawn Latta Kirby, and Tom Liner from *Inside Out, Third Edition.* Heinemann: Portsmouth, NH.

232

Scoring Guide: Checkpoint 2 for Opinion Paper

Your revised writing was rated as follows:

1. *Evidence*

   1   2   3   4   5   ×4=_____

   Ideas unsupported. Rethink your reasons. Back to brainstorming.

   At least one of your pieces of evidence is strong. Support more completely.

   Yes! Good. Solid support. Fresh, convincing.

2. *Arrangement*

   1   2   3   4   5   ×4=_____

   Be sure you have each bit of evidence in a separate paragraph.

   Check your conclusion or beginning. You can find a stronger arrangement.

   Each paragraph fits with others. Your arguments build to your conclusions.

3. *Language*

   1   2   3   4   5   ×4=_____

   Weasel words. Use more forceful language.

   Better. Some words are strong.

   Good, strong, concrete words.

4. *Punctuation and Spelling*

   1   2   3   4   5   ×2=_____

   Proofread carefully. Too many errors. See me for help.

   Still have a few errors. Check and double-check.

   Good job. Careful proof-reading pays off!

5. *Effectiveness of Your Opinion Paper*

   1   2   3   4   5   ×6=_____

   I'm not convinced. Develop your paper more completely. Use good evidence.

   Yes. You're making progress. Keep working.

   I'm convinced. Good support. Solid paper!

   Total _____

Comments:

Figure 14–1b. *Scoring Guide: Checkpoint 2 for Opinion Paper*

year. Eighth-grade teachers could build on seventh-grade criteria, and so on, thereby developing a cooperative and compatible schoolwide curriculum and a consistent grading system.

The checkpoint scales are quick to use (averaging about three minutes per paper), self-teaching, and positive. Using these checkpoints decreases the number of papers that need detailed comments, and they free the teacher to work with students on first drafts and revisions. Use of specific comments under the ratings of 1, 3, and 5 on the checkpoint also reduces the number of repetitive comments that teachers must write on each student's paper.

For more technical discussions of holistic ratings, analytic scales, and primary trait scoring, read Cooper and Odell's *Evaluating Writing* (1998). The book is a good, long read, but it discusses clearly the theory and research practice behind several sophisticated evaluative strategies. Also see Chapter 16 for more ideas on sources on grading and evaluation.

Evaluation by Peers

Grading by peers is controversial and has even been the subject of court lawsuits. Many teachers feel that they abdicate their responsibility as evaluators when they ask students to grade one another's papers. Other teachers feel that students are not capable of careful judgment of the work of their peers. On the positive side, we involve our students in the evaluation process with quite favorable results. We teach students to evaluate one another's papers not to make our job easier or lessen the paper crunch (although both are side effects of peer grading), but because the process teaches them specifics about several aspects of writing better than we can.

First and foremost, grading by peers teaches students that grades belong to them. They come to realize that those letter grades do not flow out of the diseased mind of a cruel teacher. The grade represents a reader's estimate of the worth of the piece. A grade is simply a calibrated personal response. Second, careful reading of a number of student papers sensitizes them to problems in their own papers. As they offer editing and proofreading advice to peers, they are also learning. Perhaps even more encouraging is the fact that students use peer papers as creative sources for borrowing ideas, rhetorical and syntactic strategies, and even vocabulary. Taking students through the judgment process not only makes them better proofreaders; it also teaches them how to make critical judgments of written products.

We've found that students take the responsibility of peer evaluation very seriously and work as careful critics. Likewise, when they write pieces they know will be read and graded by their peers, they seem to take more care and work with real purpose on the assignment.

The key to the successful involvement of students as peer graders is the careful specification of evaluative criteria and careful modeling of the criteria so that all students recognize and understand them. It takes time to develop this kind of sophistication, but we think the results are worth the trouble. The following are some ways to structure peer grading.

Elbow's "Center of Gravity"

Peter Elbow suggested a method for giving writers group feedback on a piece of writing (1998). Although Elbow did not intend such a system to lead to grading, we've found that students can and do use Elbow's criteria for evaluative judgments. Groups of five work best for this process, but groups of anywhere from three to seven members can function effectively. The groups begin the process by *responding* to a student's paper. Elbow calls this *pointing* and suggests that readers point to words and phrases that work well or have a unique effect in the piece. Responders may draw lines under these words and phrases or simply note them on a separate response sheet. Likewise, student readers may point to weak or empty words or phrases. As students begin this process, suggest that they limit their negative pointings to only a few serious problems.

Second, Elbow asks readers to *summarize* the piece, using the following steps:

1. First tell quickly what you found to be the main points, main feelings, or centers of gravity.
2. Then summarize the piece into a single sentence.
3. Then choose *one word* from the writing that best summarizes it.
4. Then choose a word that isn't in the writing to summarize it.

Once the pointing and summarizing are complete, students are asked to evaluate the piece, giving it a 3, 2, or 1. A 3 piece has a readily understandable center of gravity and solid supporting detail. A 2 piece has a center of gravity, but it's not powerfully stated and is lost among the verbiage. A 1 piece starts anywhere and goes nowhere. It's not a centered piece.

The point of this kind of peer grading is to involve students in animated discussions about what works and doesn't work in their writings. The pointing and summarizing format keeps the discussions on track and helps students to become more specific in their responses to one another's papers. The 3, 2, 1 scale gives the paper a relative value in a low-threat and helpful manner. The emphasis of such an approach is clearly on discussing written products rather than assigning grades.

Cooperative Grading

The cooperative grading process involves the teacher and two students. Student readers are picked at random. Each reader reads and evaluates a paper, assigning it a letter grade. Specific criteria are discussed prior to the grading. Tom suggests that readers consider surface conventions, arrangement, illustrations and examples, and the care the writer took with the piece. A simplified version of the Diederich scale might serve

INSIDE OUT, THIRD EDITION

as a good guide. After each reader has assigned the paper a letter or numeric grade, the three grades are averaged for a final grade. The teacher's grade counts as a third of the final grade.

In her composition classes with English education students who are preparing to be teachers, Dawn uses a similar three-person grading system in which the teacher, the student writer, and a peer chosen at random grade the paper using the checkpoint devised cooperatively for the specific writing assignment. Each rater makes comments on the paper and completes the checkpoint; then, each rater's score is totaled and the average for the three ratings becomes the score for the finished product. Students report that this process gives them helpful information as writers and as prospective teachers who will be grading their own students' papers one day.

In both Tom and Dawn's use of cooperative grading, the student's paper receives a careful hearing by the three graders, and the weight of collective judgment is often more forceful as an evaluation tool than the teacher's grade alone would be.

Round Robins

Students sign up for or are assigned to round robin groups of three members. Each group member takes the responsibility for reading and responding in writing to the text written by the two other group members. We find that the procedure establishes a minicommunity that provides keen evaluation along with sensitive understanding.

Each responder writes evaluative comments and assigns the paper a grade. The group holds a conference, after each writer has had time to digest the comments, for each individual's paper. When the group reaches consensus about a grade, the papers are given to the teacher with comments and grade attached. We have found that the grades a group gives reflect honest and caring evaluation. Students receive the implicit message that their ability to evaluate is respected by the teacher. Students take these groups seriously and nurture one another's progress.

A Psychological Boost

Dan tells his students that an 87 on a paper represents how much they already have done with the paper. The 13 points they didn't get represents the tinkering and tuning that they could still do on this paper. Thinking about a grade as reflecting what is still to be done with 87 percent complete helps the writer tackle the fine-tuning with enthusiasm. For any of us, it's a boost to think that we've accomplished 87 percent of the task and that we still have a chance to get more of the task accomplished through future revisions of the product, provided we value it enough to work more on it. There's also a boost in letting students choose which papers to revise. Maybe a student will choose to revise a paper that is 76 percent complete, but is satisfied with the one that is 87 percent complete—or is just too exhausted with that particular paper to work more on it.

Dawn often allows students in her composition classes to choose up to two papers per semester to revise for a possible better grade, using the comments on the original paper, conferences, and peer responses to help the student target areas and techniques for improvement. Dan has conducted writing classes in which every student had the option of revising every paper at least once and sometimes even more frequently—a Herculean task for most teachers. Nonetheless, the psychological boost of such an attitude toward grading and evaluation of the writer's work is significant, and students seem to enjoy knowing that the focus is on degree of completion and on continued growth as a writer rather than on a deficit model of grading.

Self-Evaluation

One of the important goals of any writing class is to make the writer feel more responsible for the quality of the piece of writing. One of the more unfortunate side effects of having the teacher as the sole grader is that students either prostitute their own writing abilities to please the teacher or they rationalize the teacher's judgment with an "I wrote a great piece, but he didn't like it" attitude. Real growth toward precision as a writer comes only when students are willing to look openly at their own writing, judging, evaluating, reworking, and tuning the piece in the light of such examination.

Asking students to grade their own writings is difficult to do for most teachers and is a difficult task to accomplish for most students who want to get good grades, perhaps at all costs. There are many ways that students can be involved in making judgments about the effectiveness of a piece they have written. Donald Graves suggests that student writers look carefully at first drafts, asking themselves two questions (1979):

Question #1: What Is This Piece About?

At the end of a first draft, a writer needs to be able to formulate a clear and pointed answer to this question. If she has an answer, the piece probably has focus.

If she's not sure what the piece is about, the drafting is incomplete. Many times we've seen first drafts with real potential, either because of a strong personal voice or a patch of strong sensory description or a telling character sketch, but these good points have been submerged in circular verbiage. The writer has hit a few hot spots, but has not discovered exactly where the piece is going. By asking writers to answer question number one, you save yourself the trouble of telling them this point, and the lack of focus becomes clear as they stutter and stammer about the focus of the piece. We usually smile and the student says, "Looks like I need to write some more to find out where this piece is taking me." Sometimes just the act of talking through this question helps the students form the piece in their minds.

Question #2: What Am I Trying to Do?

Graves' second question is rhetorical and stylistic, and asks the writer to examine purpose and audience. For instance, the writer is trying to evoke sympathy in a reader but is actually alienating the reader by using overly dramatic or maudlin examples. Writers who can function as critical self-readers should be able to spot the problem as they answer question number two. Again, the discussion of this question helps the writer to clarify purpose and examine specific rhetorical strategies in the piece.

Steve Tchudi offers the following classic suggestions for engaging students directly in the process of assessing their own writings:

- Encourage the students to talk to you and to each other about problems while they are writing.
- Make it a standing invitation that any student can propose an alternative topic at any time in the class, thus reducing the number of lifeless papers.
- Let the students decide which of their writings is public and which is private. (In practice, most teachers find that the students are more willing to share their personal concerns with each other after initial phases of testing each other.)
- Describe the publication forms that are available. As the writing program develops and students catch on to the idea of publication, they should more often write with a specific audience and form of publication in mind.
- Encourage the students to serve as each other's editors. One doesn't need to be an expert in composition and rhetoric to make useful suggestions about the clarity and effectiveness of writing. Although students may not know terminology, they are certainly capable of spotting editorial problems and talking about them in their own language: "Hey, I don't know what you're talking about." (Translation for teachers: "Lacks clarity.") "That's crazy." (Translation: "Lacks logical structure.") "I don't believe it." (Translation: "Needs more supporting evidence.") Students are highly perceptive in these ways, and when their editing has real purpose, they can take over the process and make genuinely helpful suggestions to each other.
- Leave proofreading to the students. In every class there are some students who have mastered most of the proofreading skills. Often such students are simply good spellers or intuitive punctuators. Acknowledge their skill by setting them up as proofreading consultants to the class.
- Treat proofreading as something to be done quickly and efficiently, rather than as a climactic step in the process of composition. Only when proofreading is made a mysterious, complex part of the mastery of standard written English does it become intimidating and therefore difficult for students.
- Help the students learn to react to each other's work. Small- and large-group discussion of completed compositions should be a regular part of any English class. At first you may find that students are a bit hard on each other, no doubt imitating previous teachers. It may take some practice before the students can respond to the substance of each other's writing, but it will come with time and guidance.

- Encourage students to develop criteria of excellence, in advance, for the work they are doing by putting themselves in the position of the audience and asking questions it would raise.
- Encourage group and collaborative projects from time to time so that students can share both skills and critical knowledge.
- Read some of your own writing to the class, and share your own satisfactions and dissatisfactions with it.
- Encourage the students to develop lists of problems and pleasures that they associate with each project they do. (Tchudi and Tchudi 2000)

Editing Checklist

A more concrete and less sophisticated way to involve writers in self-evaluation is to provide them with an editing checklist that they can use as they rework first drafts. Although it's possible for students to use the checklist in a cursory and superficial manner, it does give them a tool and an opportunity to improve their writing before the final grade is determined.

Tom often uses the checklist for less motivated students, offering the potential for a better grade if the student wants to do a careful editing job. "The paper is about a C as it stands now. If you want to clean it up a bit, I could go a B. But if you're really willing to work on this thing, I'll consider an A. Get out your editing checklist and start working through the piece."

Editing checklists can be easily compiled by turning the checkpoint for the specific written product into a series of questions or bulleted items. Students then get an opportunity to interpret the rubric from a more personalized perspective. The rubric will seem familiar and right to them when they see it, and the important features of a particular writing assignment remain as the focal points of the students' writing processes.

Conferences

Throughout this chapter we've used examples of grading and evaluating that involve the reader and the writer in face-to-face discussion and negotiation. We honestly believe that the only consistently helpful and effective evaluation of student writings comes as the two of you—student and teacher—sit down with the piece of writing, focusing directly on what's on the page. Extraordinarily successful teachers of writing have one thing in common: They spend very little time in isolation, reading and marking papers, and a great deal of time responding and discussing student writings with the writers themselves.

There is some disagreement on the use of conferences, to be sure. Donald Murray uses the one-on-one conference almost exclusively in his teaching. Ken Macrorie prefers to work in a helping circle, using the writers themselves as a larger and more diverse audience. Macrorie feels that the one-on-one conference intimidates beginning writers. And Nancie Atwell has her own version of how conferences work in her classroom. We prefer to run the writing class more like a writing workshop, getting groups together whenever helpful and holding many thirty-second conferences with working writers as we walk around the room. All of us agree that looking at the writings and discussing strengths and weaknesses is a far more effective evaluation strategy than taking stacks of papers home on weekends to grow blind and bitter as we puzzle over grades that many students will ignore or rationalize away.

And perhaps it is fitting to end this chapter with a reminder that many researchers confirm our gut instincts about grading and evaluation: 1) It's nasty work, but schools are unlikely to abandon the practice of giving grades, so we need to find ways—such as those suggested in this chapter—to make grading an informative part of learning; and 2) Positive comments do more for building confidence and for promoting learning than all the red ink marks teachers can ever put on papers.

Works Cited

COOPER, CHARLES R., AND LEE ODELL. 1998. *Evaluating Writing: The Role of Teachers' Knowledge About Text, Learning, and Culture*. Urbana, IL: NCTE.

DIEDERICH, PAUL. 1974. *Measuring Growth in English*. Urbana, IL: NCTE.

ELBOW, PETER. 1998. *Writing Without Teachers*. New York: Oxford University Press.

GRAVES, DONALD. 1979. Workshop at Georgia State University.

OLSON, MILES, DAN KIRBY, CAROL KUYKENDALL, ET AL. 1981. *The Process of Writing: The Allyn and Bacon Composition and Applied Grammar Program*. Boston: Allyn and Bacon.

TCHUDI, SUSAN, AND STEPHEN N. TCHUDI. 2000. *The English Language Arts Handbook*. Portsmouth, NH: Heinemann.

WIGGINS, GRANT. 1999. *Assessing Student Performance: Exploring the Purpose and Limits of Testing*. New York: John Wiley and Sons.

15

Publishing Student Writing With and Without Computers

And for the first time I learned another lesson which every young writer has got to learn. And that lesson is the naked, blazing power of print.

—THOMAS WOLF, *The Story of a Novel*

It's almost impossible to talk about writing without talking about publishing and celebrating finished products. And it's almost impossible to talk about publishing in your classroom without talking about computers. This chapter discusses the uses of both publishing and computers in your classes to enhance writing.

Computers and Writing

Computers are ubiquitous. Many of our students have access to one at home. Most teachers have one somewhere. Almost every classroom has at least one. Almost every school has at least one computer lab with twenty-five to thirty computers in it. Walk into any business, any professional workplace, and there's a computer on every desk. Tom's daughter worked after school in a grocery store. She operated a computer. Her friends worked at Burger King and McDonald's where they also operated computers. The computer is the tool of American business, commerce, and education.

It is also the tool of the writer. Word processing makes writing processes so much more visible and stages of writing—like revision, editing, and proofreading—so much easier. Students love to write on the computer because making changes is easy, their printed work looks professional, and they can have fun adding color, clip art, and various fonts to enhance their pieces of writing. They also need the experience of working with computers for their smooth transition to the world of work and because they will work longer on products and projects completed in front of a computer screen. That, in itself, has a lot of benefit for teaching writing.

Getting Started

The fields of computing and of instructional technology (IT) are broad, complex, and fast-moving. Whatever we could tell you about hardware and software as we use them today is sure to be out of date by the time you read this chapter. For that reason, we're not going to name specific computers, printers, modems, software, programs, spreadsheets, and grade programs for you to investigate. All of that stuff is out there, and we use all of that stuff in our teaching, but you'll need to see what's available in your school, what works for you, and what meets your students' specific needs.

We will, however, make a few recommendations.

1. *To get started with computers, get to know the school's IT faculty members and resident computer wizards.* They know how to help you troubleshoot the glitches that are bound to occur. They know program shortcuts and features. They can help you surf the Web more efficiently and tell you the program best suited to help you construct your class' website. The computer wizards in your school might live in the computer labs, but they may also reside in the room next door, the chorus room, or the math classroom down the hall. Ask questions. Who uses the computer as more than just a fancy typewriter? Who's always in the school computer lab with her classes? Who do the students think knows stuff about computers? You'll find that most computer wizards are eager and willing to help you become a computer devotee.

2. *If your school has a computer writing lab or a general purpose lab, begin scheduling regular class meetings in the lab.* In the lab, you and your students will work on writing and on Internet research and, ultimately, on desktop publishing. You may not have enough computers in the lab for every student in your class and you may encounter some scheduling conflicts, so it's fine to have students start written pieces in their journals and get a zero draft or at least a good start on a draft going on paper before getting onto the computers. In fact, some students will prefer to draft the old-fashioned way with pen and paper and to reserve their computer time for revising and last-minute details. Whatever the individual preference about when computers are used during writing processes, get to the lab on a regular basis to make writing on the computer familiar and comfortable for your students.

You may work in a situation where there is no computer lab or where the lab is small. That situation creates the need for some careful planning and tolerant colleagues. Pat Bradley taught seventh grade at Albany Middle School in Georgia. Space was limited in the school, and there were not enough computers in any one place to accommodate her classes. As her students got to the point in their writing of needing to be on a computer, she sent them up and down the hall to work in other teachers' classes where there was one available computer here and two over there and six more in the library. It takes a lot of cooperation and good humor, but the teachers at the school made the situation work by planning together to meet their students' computing needs. It can be done even in the most challenging circumstances.

3. *Don't scrimp.* Whatever equipment and technological resources are available to you and your students, don't scrimp on computer disks for your students and paper for the printer. Tom once tried to use one floppy disk for an entire class and then dumped a week's worth of writing for five students one tired afternoon. He hit the wrong key and it just disappeared. Gone! He got that sick feeling that all computer users will experience sooner or later when a glitch surfaces, but it was worse than usual because the lost material was students' writing, not his own. We recommend that every student has a separate disk for her work—no sharing with friends—and we follow this policy even if we have to buy disks for some of our financially strapped students. We also keep some extra disks handy to "rent" to students for the day until they remember to bring theirs tomorrow, and we store the disks in our classes if necessary so that our most forgetful students always have their disks handy. Whatever it takes. We also would rather buy a case of computer paper than not be able to print our students' drafts as we work. Student writers consume a lot of paper. Try to plan for that fact.

4. *Keep asking.* Continue to research new programs and new hardware and new instructional uses for computers, and continue to ask for what you need to do the best job as a teacher of writing. In the meantime, do some planning, horse trading, and scrounging and use what is available to you and your students right now.

Word-Processing Programs

There's a plethora of word-processing programs on the market, with more arriving every day. Most schools must choose one or two programs since having more than that available in a school lab would be too expensive and cause too much chaos. So, what if you don't know the available word-processing program used in your school? Learn it. Learn to use whatever equipment and word-processing programs that are available for students in your school. Most programs are user-friendly, especially for the basic functions of the program. For the fancier, more elaborate tricks within the program, read the manual, experiment, and go back to that computer wizard friend of yours for help. Also, don't underestimate your students. Many of them are computer wizards who will be able to teach you and their classmates a technological trick or two. Even with the next Bill Gates sitting in our classes, however, we like to know the hardware and the software well enough to be competent and helpful to students on both.

Managing Instruction in the Computer Lab

Teaching in a computer lab with thirty kids and thirty machines—or worse, only twenty machines for thirty students—can be a daunting task for even the most avid computer aficionado. Many schools have elaborate computer use guidelines that students and parents must sign to assure that students are visiting only appropriate websites and using Internet resources in appropriate ways. Even if you have that type of support mechanism in place, managing your instructional time efficiently in the computer lab takes planning, organization, and practice.

Dawn finds it helpful to teach from the back of the room when in the computer lab. From the back of the room, she can see each student's computer screen to know if each student is keeping up with her instructions. Dawn also takes red plastic cups into the computer lab and places one at each computer. When a student has a question, he places the cup on top of the monitor, and Dawn gets to each cup as soon as she can to answer the student's question. In the meantime, students are to continue working, not just sit there and wait for their questions to be answered, wasting lots of valuable writing time. We also encourage the use of buddies in the computer lab to pair a skilled computer user with one or two less able users, but such pairings don't always turn out evenly in a class.

In order to track students' use of time in the computer lab, we suggest the use of an accountability sheet similar to to the one in Figure 15–1.

We collect the accountability logs daily and save them to help students track their time use, writing plans, and in-class instructional notes.

Cautions About Computers and Writing

Computers are powerful tools for writing and researching, but they are not panaceas to solve all writing woes. We keep the following cautions in mind as we use computers in our teaching:

1. *Not all students like computers.* Some students will be reluctant computer users. They may have little experience with computers or be afraid of breaking the machine. Some reluctance is understandable. Encourage them, praise them, and get them to do at least some work on the computer to help them incorporate computer use into their learning repertoires.

2. *Students need specific instructions about how to avoid plagiarizing from the Internet.* Cutting and pasting on the computer is easy—sometimes too easy. Plagiarism from Internet sources can be just a click away without the proper cautions and instruction. Teach students how to cite and quote sources they find on the Internet and how to avoid dropping others' work into their pieces and claiming it as their own.

3. *Students tend to view "printed" work as "finished" work.* Written products emerge from the printer looking so professional that students view it and think they're done writing and revising and editing. We encourage students to print frequently to avoid this printed-equals-finished mentality. We also encourage students and their response partners to take a pen and mark corrections, edits, responses, and minor rewrites on their printed drafts so that students have a new draft from which to work during their next computer session.

Computer Lab Time Log
Dr. Kirby's Third Period Class (55 minutes)

Student's Name: <u>A. Fine Student</u>   Date: <u>Today</u>

Today's In-Class Lesson: [We have students complete this section with their notes. We may present a ten-minute usage lesson, writing lesson, and/or computing lesson at the beginning of class to get everyone focused and to continue to enhance skills.]

Task Description	Time Spent on the Computer
1. Composing	11:00–11:15 AM
2. Revising, moving chunks of text	11:15–11:20 AM
3. Looking up my quote on the Internet	11:20–11:25 AM
4. Emailing draft to my computer partner	11:25–11:30 AM
5. Responding online to my partner's draft	11:30–11:35 AM
6. Running spellchecker	3 minutes at end of class
7. Saving work	2 minutes at end of class

8. During the last five minutes of class, plan what you'll do next as a writer and make notes to yourself here:

_____

_____

_____

_____

_____

Figure 15–1. *Computer Lab Time Log*

4. *Not all students will use computers at the same phase during their writing processes.* Some students will wait until they can get to a computer to write the first word of a paper; others will prefer just to type the finished product and print it; and still others will prefer to use the computer at other phases and in other ways as they write. Writing is still writing—whether it's done on the computer or with pen and paper. Individual writing processes vary with each student and with each writing situation. Respect and foster those differences in your writing classes.

Having endorsed computers and their usefulness for writing, we now turn to how to publish students' writing—with and without computers.

Publishing Students' Writing

Publishing and celebrating writing are essential phases of writing. Writing becomes real when it has an audience. Except in those isolated cases when we become our own audience in the diary or private journal, our purpose in writing anything from a note taped to the refrigerator to a Petrarchan sonnet is *contact* with other human beings. Responses guide the growth of our writing. We learn ways to make our writing more effective by seeing its *effect* on others.

We talked earlier in this book about the importance of publishing in the development of student writers. Our purpose in this chapter is not theoretical, but practical—to tell you some ways you can publish student writing in and out of the classroom. But first, a brief reminder of the reasons it is so important to publish student writing.

1. Publishing gives the writer an audience, and the writing task becomes authentic—a real effort at communication—not just writing to please the teacher.
2. Publishing is a primary reason for the writing to be important enough for the hard work of editing and proofreading.
3. Publishing involves the ego, which is the strongest incentive for the student writer to keep writing.

Ways to Publish in the Classroom

Provide *regular* opportunities for students to publish and celebrate their writing in class, and include all students. There are several relatively easy publishing and celebrating methods. We recommend that you use a variety of them.

READING ALOUD Sharing writing by reading aloud should be a frequent part of any writing class. It's the best way for students to get immediate reactions to their writing. It's a good tool for checking responses to a piece for editing, and writings simply need to be shared and enjoyed. Reading aloud grows writers.

Have students work daily with a reading partner with whom they feel comfortable and on whom they can try out their works in progress. They should also regularly form small groups for reading and responding. Tom likes groups of four or six students (two or three pairs of reading partners). Finally, there should be times when the entire class is the audience.

THE FAITHFUL PHOTOCOPY We have found that what our students look forward to most eagerly and read most carefully are the photocopied sheets we pass out at the beginning of class each Monday. Selecting and duplicating student writing should be done often. The selections from journals or in-class writings do not have to be long, but try to include as many students as possible. Select good writing, even if it's only a sentence or two with a vivid image, an unusual twist, the surprise of humor—writing with creative possibilities, not necessarily mechanically perfect writing. Talk about the selections to the class and tell why you picked them and why they're good.

Make sure, especially when duplicating selections from students' journals, that you have a clear understanding with your students about the things that will be published in class. Always get their permission before sharing their writing with the class. We recommend publishing journal selections anonymously (their authors will take credit when others respond positively in class). A system we have worked out with many of our classes for dealing with in-class writing selections is to identify them with the initials of the writers.

After you've selected and published excerpts from student writing for several weeks, turn that job over to the students themselves. Set up small groups as editorial boards (see Chapter 8) to pick writings and prepare copies each week. Rotate the responsibility from group to group so that all the students in the class have the regular job of editing during the course. Work closely with the editorial boards, but let them pick *what they like* to publish. Their selections, of course, will have to come from in-class writings and not from journals.

Word processing is an invaluable tool for classroom publishing. Printed text is easier to read and looks professional. And word processing makes editing easy. Chapter 10 discusses how the computer can help students become their own editors. Word processing also will make it possible for you to publish their writings more often and with less hassle.

MAKING BOOKS If you want to see your students' eyes light up with pride, have them prepare their best writings and bind them in their own books. All you need for bookbinding are some wallpaper samples, glue, construction paper, cloth tape, vinyl letters for the title if you want to be fancy—and patience. A simple soft cover for students' writings can be made by folding a piece of wallpaper over the written pages. Trim the wallpaper to be slightly larger than the sheets of writing. Then it's a simple matter to staple the spine two or three times and cover the end with cloth tape. It can be messy, but it's worth it. Create your own book first so you can show them the steps.

The bound books are attractive. A lot of schools keep them in their library where students can check them out. Talk to your media specialist.

Illustrations and calligraphy of student-made books are limited only by student imaginations. Clip art and the variety of fonts available on the computer provide inspiration to your less artistic students. We're always impressed with the creativity and artistic savvy of our students.

What do you do if it's spring quarter and the principal informs you that the paper allotment for the school year is used up? What do you do about publishing then?

CLASS WEBSITES Publishing students' writing on a class website that students maintain and that you oversee and supervise requires no paper or photocopy machine toner. It's also a great opportunity to team teach with your business or instructional technology (IT) colleagues in how to set up, maintain, and update a website. As we have mentioned earlier, we send home permission slips to parents so they know that students will be posting some of their writing on the class website. We also use only first names or just initials to identify each writer. Some families link their personal websites to our class websites in order to celebrate with family and friends the fact that Daria or Austin's work was published. We also contact our colleagues across the country and set up long-distance email response groups among our classes so that students in California can read what students in Colorado and Georgia have written, respond to it, encourage each other as writers, and celebrate pieces of writing that work.

ROOM DISPLAYS You probably already have a place in your room to display student writing, and you have probably found that a display of finished products attracts attention and stimulates talk and thinking about writing. But as we pointed out in Chapter 3, room displays have other possibilities. A Works in Progress section of the bulletin board—or wall or reserved corner table—is an easy way to encourage growing writers. And it helps to dispel notions that writing is quickly done in two drafts for the teacher and that what's important in writing is always the final product.

With the cooperation of the principal, there's also the possibility of displaying student writing in the halls of the school. We like to create such hall displays with short writings such as name poems and cinquains, which are easy for students to put up on butcher paper. (*Never insist that students display their writing.*) Hang the writings high to keep them out of the reach of the curious. Displays are a fluid medium and should change often. Your writing can also appear on display with that of the students.

PROJECTION PUBLISHING Dan likes to make transparencies of outstanding student papers (or papers with particularly well-written sections), and he regularly uses an overhead projector to share these with the class. If you're lucky, you have an LCD projector for your computer or a document camera set up in your classroom so you can project writing for the whole class that way. Whatever the technology, publishing writing in a format for all to see works well for talking about good student writing and for helping writers gain confidence and skill.

Caution: Please notice that we're not suggesting that you slap a kid's paper on the LCD projector and begin criticizing its faults before the entire class. Use the whole-class viewing of writing as a way to publish and share the good stuff your students are writing.

Ways to Publish Outside the Classroom

Publishing outside the classroom can be the most significant writing experience you and your students share. It should be approached carefully and should not be attempted unless the students are ready to move from the relatively safe class environment, where publishing is part of a common and shared experience, to the cold world of print read and judged by strangers. It's a scary transition but an important one—and your support and encouragement (and example) help your students to mature as writers.

THE LITERARY MAGAZINE If your school already has a flourishing literary magazine, then count yourself lucky and enjoy its benefits. Encourage students to participate in it as fully as their inclinations and activities permit. Help them select, edit, and polish their best pieces to submit to the literary magazine. Rejoice loudly with them when their stuff appears in it. Mourn with them when they don't make the cut. Use the literary magazine for its full effect with those students in your classes who are ready for a larger audience.

Because you're a teacher who encourages and supports writing, chances are that you'll be approached sooner or later to sponsor the school literary magazine. Or the bug to start a miniversion of the literary magazine just for your own classes may someday bite you. So what we offer here is a brief primer in doing the school (or class) literary magazine.

First, the basics of creating a literary magazine, from our experiences and prejudices, are as follows:

1. Everyone is creative and potentially has a place in the literary magazine. It's not just for the precious few.
2. The literary magazine begins in the classroom with the journal and the pieces that students write there. (The pieces may stay there.)
3. An effective literary magazine is not a miniature copy of *The Kenyon Review* or *Poetry*.
4. Most students are shy about their writing and about having it appear in print. Encourage them.
5. The literary magazine belongs to the students.
6. The literary magazine can be expensive, but it doesn't have to be.
7. If you do the literary magazine for money, you'll lose money.
8. Administrators sometimes don't like literary magazines.
9. The literary magazine is vulnerable to censorship.
10. The literary magazine is a lot of work.

How to Produce a Literary Magazine

There are four practical methods of producing a literary magazine. Each requires a great deal of time and work, each requires the willing help of students, and each requires the cooperation and support of the principal.

Method 1: The Computer as Desktop Publisher

Computers have profoundly affected the quality of publishing that is accessible and available to students and teachers in school settings. Special software programs exist that are dedicated to desktop publishing, and we find many of them to be quite user-friendly and effective. See what's available in your school and in your budget. Even without a special desktop-publishing program, pieces produced and published with just a standard word-processing program can look quite professional, complete with color, various font styles and sizes, columns, clip art or inserted pictures, and other features associated with published works.

Even if the pieces are produced with computers, there must be many copies of the final products.

Method 2: The Photocopied Literary Magazine

The cheapest kind of literary magazine is simply photocopied, stapled together, and passed around the school. It's spontaneous, easily produced by students, and given away. It's Tom's favorite.

If you want to be fancy, get the class artist to do a silk-screen design on heavy stock paper for a cover. It will be an attractive product and cheap.

Method 3: Offset Printing

The offset press is relatively inexpensive, and the result looks professional. The cost depends on where the printing is done and whether you include fancy extras like photographs and art work. It's often possible to get a local printer to give you a considerable price break. Many schools have their own graphics department with an offset press. Your school or one in your area may be able to print the literary magazine quite reasonably.

With offset printing, of course, your copy has to be camera ready. So proofreading and careful word processing are essential. Again, the computer is invaluable in readying your product for offset printing.

Method 4: The Full-Blown Technicolor Special

Color photographs and slick, clay-based paper and typeset printing—when you add these special touches, the literary magazine can become very expensive. It may cost literally thousands of dollars to produce.

That's out of the reach of most of us, but we have a fantasy that some day there'll be a public high school somewhere in America with a creative arts budget equal to that of a successful athletic program.

When to Begin a Literary Magazine

Begin a literary magazine when a group of kids says, "Hey, why don't we put all this good stuff in a magazine of some kind?" In short, you begin it when the students want it and are willing to work together to produce it.

It's not an easy job, and students need to know that fact when they begin. Help them, advise them, encourage them—*but don't do the work for them*. It's their magazine and will be effective only as long as the students know it's theirs and take responsibility for it. It ends when students are bored with it, are tired of working on it, or want you to do the work of producing it.

When Not to Do a Literary Magazine

Never make the literary magazine a crusade. Suggest it as a possibility to students when you see that they're ready for a larger audience than the classroom, but don't insist on it if they seem uninterested. They may not be ready to move out of the audience of their peers with their writing yet. Or it simply may not be as important to them as it is to you.

If your principal—perhaps still worried about the most recent censorship case in the neighboring district—is opposed to the idea of a school literary magazine, then look for and suggest alternatives, such as those in the following section. It's not going to help the cause of writing in the school if you lose your job.

Sometimes there's simply no way to find the money to produce a literary magazine. Literary magazines rarely pay for themselves, and you shouldn't go into debt assuming you'll sell enough copies to pay for it. You'll need some kind of financial support. Advertising, patrons, a deal with the school library or English department or school board or even the football coach—there are possibilities for paying the costs, and we've seen all of them (and some other bizarre schemes) work in one school or another. But if there simply is no money, look for other possibilities for publishing student writing.

ALTERNATIVES TO A LITERARY MAGAZINE Many schools have literary editions of a school newspaper that feature student writing. A better alternative is a regular *Literary Column* in the paper. Suggest this possibility to the editor or sponsor. Your classes may even volunteer to edit the column and, cooperating with the newspaper staff, provide a regular place for student writing to appear.

A similar alternative is a literary section of the school yearbook. And, of course, the school or class website is a fine alternative to printed publications.

Publishing Outside the School

Your local newspaper may sponsor writing contests for students, or it may even regularly feature student writing in its pages. If it doesn't offer opportunities like these for young writers, don't hesitate to approach the editor with ideas for regularly printing student writing. It's good PR, for one thing. If you live in a larger community, chances are that your local paper has an educational editor (or consultant) whose job is to work with the schools. You'll usually find this person receptive to these types of suggestions.

If your community has a local access or local television station, approach the manager with the idea for a program of students' reading their writings on the air. You may get a positive response. Locally owned radio stations may also be receptive to such a weekly or monthly show.

If you have a shopping mall or a local library in your town, they often are willing to display students' writings. Work with the art teacher in your school to create visually appealing displays that do more than merely pin pieces of writing to the wall. Sometimes, the local grocery store or all-purpose store (think Wal-Mart here) may even be willing to display students' writings, to sponsor writing contests with a donation in exchange for having their name mentioned as the sponsor, or otherwise support students' efforts to publish their writing.

In most towns and cities there's at least one literary group or group of professional or semiprofessional writers. They probably sponsor contests for young writers. Find out about them. These writers' groups are usually happy to offer assistance to student writers and teachers of writing.

Check with the professional organization in your state for writing contests and opportunities for publishing that they may sponsor—many such organizations do. The National Council of Teachers of English (NCTE) also sponsors annual writing contests for students. Additionally, ask the language arts coordinator in your school district to send you any flyers on writing contests that come through the central office. There are many of these each year, but *examine the ones unfamiliar to you carefully and critically*. Be especially wary of any contest requiring some sort of fee for entering. Have a regular place in your classroom where you post notices of writing contests.

A CAUTION Even those of us who've been writing for years grind our teeth in frustrated rage and hurt when we get one of these letters:

Poetry

1228 North Dearborn Parkway • Chicago, Illinois 60610

We regret that we cannot use the enclosed. Although we should like to send an individual answer to everyone, particularly those who request special criticism, our staff and time are insufficient for detailed correspondence.

All contributions must be accompanied by a *stamped and self-addressed envelope*. Otherwise we cannot return them or make any other form of reply, and they will be destroyed. Stamps alone are not sufficient. Contributors living abroad should enclose a return envelope and international coupons.

—*The Editors*

Consider carefully before you expose any young writer to the writer's ultimate rejection—the rejection slip. For those very few, very sophisticated young writers whom you feel are ready to venture into the impersonal world of the adult writer, your role is to give them as much support, help, and encouragement as you can.

One point that needs to be reemphasized here is that *you* share the experience of submitting writing for publication with your students. Whenever possible, send something somewhere yourself when your students do. Most of the time, writing is rejected—in fact, almost all the time. Sharing the disappointments—and sometimes the triumphs—makes the experience easier and more meaningful.

The so-called *little magazines* offer student writers the best opportunity to appear in print. Editors of the *littles* are usually individualistic and idiosyncratic, but most of them do take the time to respond *personally* to writers who submit work to them. Many of these editors are writers themselves and encourage the beginner. Besides, you can get the strangest letters from editors of little magazines (see Figure 15–2).

The *International Directory of Little Magazines and Small Presses*, published annually, is the bible for noncommercial and avant-garde writers. It lists hundreds of addresses and descriptions of magazines and small presses. It's a supermarket of places to send manuscripts.

One warning about little magazines, however. Supervise your students carefully and be frank with them about the kinds of magazines that often print experimental—and sometimes antisocial—writing.

Finally, there are the commercial magazines. A few, such as *Seventeen*, offer some opportunities to young writers. All are highly competitive, impersonal in responding, and very difficult—sometimes impossible—to break into.

Writer's Market is the best source for addresses and descriptions of commercial markets. It's published annually by Writer's Digest Books, who also publish *Writer's Digest* magazine. Get your school librarian to order a copy. It's expensive.

The same cautions apply to having students submit their work for publication in e-zines (online magazines) and/or Web publications sponsored by those outside of your school. Not all Web publications are above board, so careful screening and parental permissions are essential.

Cautions About Publishing Student Writing

Whether you're involved in publishing student writing in your classroom, in the school literary magazine, in the community, in the national press, or on a website, remember that the printed word can be cold and terribly final. Keep these cautions in mind.

1. It's *the student*, and not the piece of writing *by* the student, that's important in this process.
2. Never publish a piece of writing without the student's expressed permission.
3. Don't try to move too fast with your students. Give them time and practice to get ready, especially before publishing for strangers.
4. Always prepare students carefully for what they can expect in a particular kind of publishing venture.

Rusty Dog Press
Joseph P. Pentglass, Editor

Dear Joe:

Is your press accepting submissions of poetry
and/or fiction? If so, what are your requirements regarding form and length?

Thank you for your trouble.

Sincerely,

Tom Liner

Tom Liner

Tom —
Sorry for the delay.
Your letter fell behind my
desk and then a burglar
broke into my house and
subsequently I broke up with
the broad I was living with.
We just came out with 2 books
and are now broke — not accepting
anything. Don't give up!!!
Joe

Figure 15–2. *Rejection Letter*

5. Watch out for harsh judgments, hurt feelings, and embarrassing situations. Guard the young writer from scorn, ridicule, and sniggering remarks.
6. Protect the confidentiality of the student's journal, and the confidence and privacy of the student. For website publications, protect the student's identity.
7. Be frank, honest, and realistic about censorship, not prudish.

8. Even when publishing, remember that you are still probably the most important audience for your students.
9. Write, edit, and publish *with* your students.
10. Never forget the "naked, blazing power of print."

Work Cited

WOLFE, THOMAS. 1936. *The Story of a Novel.* New York: Scribner's.

16

Resources*

Today's teachers of writing have a distinct advantage over those of us who began teaching years ago. There are many more excellent books on designing writing instruction available to support teachers than ever before. As I work with my own high-school students, the English Department at Thornton High School, and teachers around the state as director of the Colorado Writing Project, I find many texts to inform my teaching. I have used *Inside Out* extensively as a teacher of writing and as a teacher of writing teachers. When Dan and Dawn asked if I would write a resource chapter for this new edition, I decided to organize it around the questions about the teaching of writing that I hear from not only preservice teachers, but also from experienced teachers. Here are helpful resources to use, along with *Inside Out*, as you do your best to bring writing alive to the students in your classrooms.

Should I Set Up a Writing Workshop and How Do I Do It?

Katie Wood Ray says it best when she writes, "Teaching writing in a workshop setting is highly theoretical teaching. That's why we do it—because it's theoretical. Every aspect of the workshop is set up to support children learning to do what writers really do" (2001, xii). Wood Ray's book, *The Writing Workshop: Working Through the Hard Parts (And They're All Hard Parts)*, is one of the best texts I've read to show both new and experienced teachers just how to set up a writing workshop in their classrooms. Although she discusses elementary classrooms, her text will help teachers at any level to understand the importance of the writing workshop within a school day and the essential characteristics she feels are important to the writing workshop as she envisions it. Her book includes chapters on tone and time in the workshop, managing predictable distractions, designing focus lessons, conferring with students, and assessing and evaluating student work.

---

*This chapter was researched and written by Karen Hartman of Arvada, Colorado. Karen has been an English teacher and department head at Thornton High School near Denver and is currently Director of the Colorado Writing Project. She is an outstanding teacher, a caring mentor of novice teachers, and a passionate spokeswoman for sound practice in the teaching of writing.

Nancie Atwell's second edition of *In the Middle* (1998) is an invaluable source for setting up both a reading and a writing workshop. As Atwell is quick to point out, her book does not offer a recipe for teaching writing. She says, "*In the Middle* represents what I've come to understand about writing, teaching writing, and organizing a writing workshop at this point in my evolution" (26). She goes on to say that she knows her thinking about the teaching of writing is always evolving. Her goal is "to be less caught up in adhering to a program or curriculum and more concerned with responding to my kids, leading them, and helping them grow" (26). Her book is filled with strategies she has found to be successful in her own middle-school classroom, strategies that she encourages teachers to adapt for their classrooms. Teachers will find many ideas for getting kids started, for minilessons, for responding, for evaluating, for conferring, and for publishing.

A Community of Writers by Steven Zemelman and Harvey Daniels will also give you ideas for setting up a workshop. They believe, "We are all teachers of students first, before we are teachers of any subject. And writing, real writing, requires that teachers create a special kind of group climate in their classrooms" (1998, 47). Their chapters entitled Climate in the Classroom and Planning for a Writing Centered Class help us think about our own expectations for our students. Similarly, in Jim Burke's book, *The English Teacher's Companion*, his chapter on Teaching Writing from Practice to Performance also discusses the components of an effective writing program. His "brief survey of the research on writing" (1999, 73) is a list to which teachers will want to refer when planning writing workshops.

Power and Portfolios: Best Practices for High School Classrooms, written by Jim Mahoney, takes us into the thinking of an English teacher who voluntarily relinquished power to his students as he set up a writing workshop. Mahoney writes, "I saw how enthusiastic and productive students became when they were empowered, and I remembered how limiting my classroom was when I controlled everything" (2002, 168). He frames his book within the context of a portfolio system. Readers will discover how he sets up his portfolio system, how he gets students "in a constant writing state of mind" with Writers' Notebooks, and how he organizes his workshop. There are also ideas for writing poetry, along with ideas for reading classes and ideas for figuring out evaluation.

Regie Routman's *Invitations: Changing as Teachers and Learners K–12* and her *Conversations* are both texts with rich information about teaching. *Invitations* (1991) discusses how to become a whole language teacher and the components of a whole language classroom. She looks at teaching strategies and at authentic contexts for writing, along with evaluation and classroom management. *Conversations* (2000) tackles both reading and writing in the classroom. In the writing sections, she considers the principles, problems, and goals of quality writing. There are chapters on journal writing, organizing a workshop, writing in multiple genres, and assessment, among others. Routman says her text "reflects her current thinking as a daily observer of and participant in the literacy landscape. It is not a book about whole language or phonics or a particular methodology. It is about effective teaching and what it means to be a professional" (2000, xxxix).

Carol Booth Olson's *Reading/Writing Connection: The Strategies for Teaching and Learning in the Secondary Classroom* (2003) gives teachers strategies, activities, and mini-lessons for teaching reading and writing. She shows us how to scaffold these strategies within the context of classroom lessons into activities we can adapt for our own students. Her text includes a wide variety of topics, including a community of learners, multiple intelligences, alternatives to the research paper, assessment, and motivation. Her text will also help teachers as they think about setting up a writing workshop.

How Do I Encourage Kids to Begin Writing?

The Writer's Notebook

Many teachers have asked me how I encourage my students to begin writing. How do I help them find topics? Why can't I just give them prompts? Teachers of writing know there are times when we give our students specific *genre* in which to write or specific prompts about which to write or even certain audiences to consider. What we have to remember is that in the best of situations, students will need to make these decisions for themselves as they write. We must help them discover how to dig deep within themselves to find ideas for writing, no matter how much choice we give them. Lucy Calkins, in *The Art of Teaching Writing,* says, "By supplying a topic from my own experience and giving it to my students, I indirectly taught them that their lives aren't worth writing about, that they don't have their own cherished bits of life, their own memories . . ." (1995, 12). What we must do as teachers is help our students remember important events or places in their lives about which they might want to write, and we need to help them learn to observe the world around them, always thinking as a writer.

In *Breathing In, Breathing Out*, Ralph Fletcher tells us, "Keeping a notebook is the single best way I know to survive as a writer. It encourages you to pay attention to your world, inside and out" (1996a, 1). His book is a valuable resource for teachers who are starting to use writers' notebooks with their students. He also wrote *A Writer's Notebook: Unlocking the Writer Within You* (1996b) for elementary students, but the ideas work for all ages. In both books, Fletcher encourages writers to write about what really moves them. He tells writers to write small, to write about those important little details that "make writing come alive," and to begin collecting seeds for writing, those ideas we see in the paper, on the news, on the street, or in a classroom that just might be worth writing about some day.

Lucy Calkins, in *The Art of Teaching Writing,* refers to the Writer's Notebook as a tool for rehearsal. Although Calkins' book is focused on elementary writers, it has been a resource for me as I teach not only high-school students, but also teachers of writing at all grade levels. Calkins defines *rehearsal* not as getting ready to write one piece of writing, but as "a state of readiness out of which one writes" (1995, 24).

258

A writer's notebook is a place for that rehearsal. Her book gives teachers examples of what students put in notebooks and how we can get our students to begin using their notebooks to live a "writerly life."

In *A Time for Meaning*, Randy Bomer refers to his notebook as his workbench. He says he began using writers' notebooks with his high-school students "to help my students collect data about their lives and to begin to reach for meaning in advance of writing a draft" (1995, 47). His book gives teachers ideas on how to get students started in Writers' Notebooks, how to help students extend notebook writings, and how to encourage students to begin to use the notebook outside of class to save those moments in their lives that might become written pieces. He also discusses evaluating Writers' Notebooks.

Other Ways of Helping Our Students Find Topics

Nancie Atwell, in her book *In the Middle*, discusses how she introduces her students to her writing territories. These territories include subjects about which she has written or about which she might want to write, *genre* in which she has written or would like to try, and audiences for whom she has written or for whom she might write at a future date. She asks her students to begin their own lists, adding to them as the year continues. In her *Lessons That Change Writers* (2002), she has specific lessons just for getting kids started with their writing. Besides her writing territories, she shares a lesson called Heart Mapping that she discovered at a poetry workshop given by Georgia Heard. This lesson alone can give students countless numbers of writing topics.

I love what Georgia Heard says about finding topics in *Awakening the Heart: Exploring Poetry in Elementary and Middle School*. "I've never heard a poet describe the origin of a poem by saying it came from an assignment about pretending to be a grass blade blowing in the wind, or from a poetry contest on health safety" (1999, 47). Heard tells of the ways she helps students discover where poetry can be found in all of us. She includes strategies for getting students to write about their "inner life." In *Writing Toward Home* (1995), Heard gives writers lots of valuable ideas to engage them in personal writing. She writes of bits and pieces of her own life and then gives readers strategies to begin writing.

Donald Murray, in *Crafting a Life in Essay, Story, Poem*, has excellent advice for those who have a difficult time getting started. Just discussing his list of reasons why he writes helps students think about their own purposes for writing. Teachers will want to read what he has to say about cultivating a writing habit; these are the bits of information that can help our students begin thinking like writers.

How Do I Help My Students Think and Write About Important Topics?

Last summer in one of the writing projects I was directing, a few teachers were writing about topics that meant very little to them. It was obvious from the writing and from our discussions in conferences that they weren't ready to write from their hearts about issues or people or events important to them. At the beginning of the second week, I asked them how they could possibly ask their students to write about what was near and dear to them if they themselves couldn't take that risk.

I also struggled with this issue with my high-school students. A few years ago, I taught some of the same students in my Advanced Composition class whom my son taught in his Sociology and Law classes. These students chose topics for research that they had read and discussed in their Sociology and Law classes. These topics were provocative and had grabbed their attentions and their passions. Their voices came alive on paper. My son, Andrew, teaches his classes from a social justice stance, and he began to give me articles and books to read. At the NCTE conference in Baltimore, I attended sessions given by National Writing Project presenters who teach from a social justice stance, too. I also began reading Randy Bomer and Katherine Bomer's book, *For A Better World: Reading and Writing for Social Action*. They write, "Language is the medium of democracy. Unless everyone's ways with words are accepted into the great conversation, any conception of public dialogue and mutual decision making is, at best, partial and, at worst, illegitimate and unstable. . . . If voices of the vulnerable are silent, there is no hope of renewal and justice" (2001, 2). Their book will help teachers encourage students to consider and write about those issues that affect them and the world around them. It will also help teachers show students the power of the written word.

Beverly Busching and Betty Ann Slesinger (2001) also look at social justice issues in *"It's Our World Too": Socially Responsive Learners in Middle School Language Arts*. This is a resource for high-school teachers as well as middle-school teachers who are interested in social issues—particularly those of race, class, and poverty—to engage their students in inquiry and collaboration. The authors believe that students can learn about the world and begin to see how they can act in responsible ways to help others.

Rethinking Schools has several publications that I have used to get my students writing and thinking about issues of social justice. In the introduction to her *Reading, Writing, and Rising Up: Teaching About Social Justice and the Power of the Written Word*, Linda Christensen says she wants "to get at the social roots of alienation and despair—to help students use words as a passage into interrogating society" (2000, viii). She goes on to say, "I use the term 'rising up' because reading and writing should be emancipatory acts" (viii). Her book gives us many essays and lesson plans, plus students' writings to use as models with our own students. All are focused on language arts and teaching for justice. Other publications from Rethinking Schools that I found helpful in engaging students in writing while considering values of community, justice, and equality are the two volumes of *Rethinking Our Classrooms: Teaching for Equity and Justice* (Bigelow et al. 1994, 2001).

How Do I Help My Students Sustain Their Writing?

So many teachers say to me, "Okay, Karen, my kids have a topic, they've written a first draft, but how do I help them to revise, to keep working on their pieces?"

Although we don't know what kinds of help our students will need in order to be able to revise until after we read their drafts, there are titles that have been helpful to me as I prepare focus lessons that will ask students to rethink what they have written. I might ask them about audience or purpose or if they feel there is somewhere they can show instead of tell. Barry Lane's *After the End* has been an invaluable resource for me in the teaching of revision. Lane writes, "Writing itself is revision, and if we can teach this concept to children and give them tools to develop it, they will experience the joy of discovery that keeps professional writers at their desks" (1993, 5). Lane gives us those tools to teach our students. His work with Snapshots and Thoughtshots helps students show instead of tell. His book is full of ideas for revision. If you use them to help students revise their own writing rather than as simple exercises, his strategies can give students a wealth of ideas for rethinking their first drafts. His *Reviser's Toolbox* (1999) also gives teachers ideas for lessons on revision, for writing leads, for using verbs and nouns, for working more with snapshots and thoughtshots, and for playing with time.

In her *The Revision Toolbox*, Georgia Heard uses elementary-school examples, but her ideas will work with writers of all ages. She discusses the fact that many students see the revision process as punitive. She shows teachers ways to get students to "understand that revision doesn't necessarily take place after they've finished a piece of writing, but instead revision will most likely occur throughout the writing process" (2002, 1). Her book will show you how to work with students in three main toolboxes—words, structure, and voice.

Bill Strong's book *Coaching Writing* is an exceptional resource for teaching revision in areas such as syntax, usage, style, and voice. Strong offers both experienced and novice teachers much more than ideas for revision; he writes,

> I speak for methods that might support active learning environments, including those for whole-class and small-group teaching. I argue for judicious and deliberate use of language exercises of many kinds but especially those with research-proven track records or strong rationales in theories of language development. (2001, 7)

Many of the members of the Thornton High School English Department read *Coaching Writing* together and tried Strong's ideas in our classrooms, getting together each week and discussing what worked and why. We found many of his ideas both challenging and rewarding for our students.

Ralph Fletcher and Joann Portalupi's two books, *Craft Lessons* (1998) and *Nonfiction Craft Lessons* (2001), are both intended for grades K–8. Their craft lessons give teachers a list of resources for each lesson plus a discussion section, focusing on why we should teach a specific element. The books also include a how-to-teach-it section, which helps us find ways to teach specific elements of craft to the whole class, to small groups, and even to one student during writing conferences. I found that I could use even the primary lessons with my high-school students by changing the literature I used to model specific strategies. Teachers will find lessons to help students with the revision process and lessons to help students revise for many specific elements of craft,

261

including crafting a title, using flashback, adding supporting details, and using a chart to summarize information. Fletcher's book, *What a Writer Needs* (1993), will also help teachers plan lessons for revision. His chapters on beginnings, endings, voice, and the art of specificity are especially helpful.

I mentioned Nancie Atwell's *Lessons That Change Writers* earlier in this chapter. This text shares Atwell's minilessons from her own classroom, lessons her students say helped them become better writers. The text is divided into four sections: Lessons about Topics, Lessons About Principles, Lessons About Genres, and Lessons About Conventions. In the notebook accompanying the text are reproducible handouts for students as well as overhead transparencies. Atwell tells teachers that the notebook gives us 95 percent of the materials used in teaching her lessons. She has narrated each lesson as scripts: "straightforward invitations to teachers to listen to, try on, then adapt my voice and experience" (2002, xvi). Many of these lessons will help teachers as they encourage their students to revise their writing.

How Do I Confer with Individual Writers?

Fletcher discusses the role of mentors in his book *What a Writer Needs*. I think we are much more likely to have a successful writing conference with a student when we understand what it means to be a mentor to young writers. Fletcher says that a mentor has high standards, builds on strengths, values originality and diversity, encourages students to take risks, is passionate, and looks at the big picture.

I was recently in the classroom of a young, passionate teacher who participated in the Colorado Writing Project the previous summer and was in his third month of developing a writing workshop. He told me that he was struggling with conferences and asked me to confer with his student writers so he could listen and learn. What I discovered as I talked with his students and looked at their work was that he was trying to "fix" their papers for them through the conference. He changed their wording, he crossed out whole passages and rewrote them, he corrected editing errors, and he added new ideas. Although I will continue coaching this teacher on more effective methods of conferring with writers, I also recommended several books for him to read, texts that will help him confer with student writers.

Probably the best text on holding conferences that I have used is Carl Anderson's *How's It Going?* Anderson makes it very clear that "if we take control over a student's writing and make sure that the draft has our perfect lead or our brilliant dialogue, all we've done is given a demonstration of our expertise as writers" (2000, 9). Anderson says, "we can help students become better writers by teaching them strategies and techniques more experienced writers use to write well . . . by teaching them to teach themselves, . . . and teaching them to be reflective about their writing" (9). His book shows teachers how a conference is a conversation and then discusses the difference between the teacher's role and the student's role in the conversation. He includes chapters on how we can help students learn from authors and how our minilessons lay the groundwork for conferences. He also considers the question so many teachers ask, "How do I manage the rest of the class while I am having a conference with one student?"

When I first began a writing workshop, the book that helped me the most as I conferred with my writing students was Tom Romano's *Clearing the Way*. His chapter, The Crucial Role of Conferencing, points out, "How it [a conference] proceeds depends upon many things: where the student is in the writing process, what her attitude is toward the work, what problem is foremost in her mind at the moment, how far she has moved or been nudged in previous conferences" (1987, 87). Romano goes on to describe what can happen in a writing conference, giving us examples of conferences he has held with his own high-school students. He also warns us of what not to do in a conference.

Lane's book, *After the End*, has a chapter entitled, Don't Fix My Story, Just Listen to Me. His focus in the chapter is to "show you ways to create a relationship with your students that puts them in charge" (1993, 105). The chapter offers ideas for individual student conferences, group conferences, and peer conferences, as well as helping students learn how to listen to their own internal critics.

Atwell's *In the Middle* also has a chapter on conferring with student writers. She has a section on conferences about content and craft and another section on conferences about conventions. She makes a point of saying the purpose of her conferences is not to help her students to revise. Her purpose is "to confer with kids about ideas, information, purpose, audience, language, and format so they can consider what's working, what needs more work, and what they can do next to make the writing work better" (1998, 221).

In *The Writing Workshop*, Wood Ray's chapter entitled Conferring: The Essential Teaching Act discusses the difficulties of conferring with our student writers and how we must be ready for anything because we just don't know what students will say in response to our questions. She stresses that conferring is teaching, not troubleshooting, and we must keep the conferences short because we have so many students to teach. Her ideas of the four parts of a writing conference—research, decide, teach, and make a record—will help teachers think about conferences in a logical and helpful manner.

How Can I Help My Students Write with Clarity?

Carol Jago in *Cohesive Writing* says, "Though full of promise, student writing generally lacks cohesion" (2002, 7). Her book gives teachers a method, "not a lockstep lesson plan or a simple recipe," for teaching their students how to write cohesively. She offers sections on getting kids started, writing question papers, and moving from freewriting to drafting. There are also chapters giving guidelines for teaching persuasive writing, teaching narrative writing, and teaching students to write about literature. She asserts that "the following set of beliefs keep me focused. 1) In order to learn to write, one must write. 2) Authentic tasks and topics generate the most cohesive student writing. 3) Students need both supportive and critical feedback. 4) There is no cohesive writing without revision" (85).

What Is Memoir?

A question I hear fairly often is, "How do I teach my students to write memoir and what is the difference between memoir and a personal narrative?" Nancie Atwell, in *In the Middle*, writes that teaching personal narrative in the early days of conducting workshops with her students was a safe technique for her. Kids could write about a single experience in their lives, and she could teach to that genre. "Bringing fiction and nonfiction literature into the writing workshop—reading it aloud, reading it to-gether with my kids, reacting to it with them, and naming what we noticed—changed me, changed us, and changed the workshop. We pushed off—genre by genre" (1998, 371). When she and her students began reading and writing memoir, personal narra-tive almost disappeared from her workshop. She makes a good case about why we should move our students beyond the personal narratives they wrote when they were younger. This chapter features memoirs written by Atwell's students, lists of mem-oirs to read, and a discussion of the qualities of memoirs that work as well as those qualities that don't work.

William Zinsser's book, *Inventing the Truth: The Art and Craft of Memoir*, is the absolute best resource to use as you develop plans for teaching memoir. Zinsser says, "Memoir was defined as some portion of a life; it's a window into a life" (1998, 14). The book engages the likes of Russell Baker, Toni Morrison, Annie Dillard, Henry Louis Gates, Jr., and Jill Kerr Conway in talking about their own writing of memoir.

Randy Bomer in *A Time for Meaning* in his chapter, Making Something of Our Lives, Reading and Writing Memoir, says that

> too often, the memoir is thought to consist of the reminiscences of old people and ex-presidents. But what we were seeing in the best literature we could find were neither "all about everything that happened to me" nor the "this happened" personal experience stories we too often saw in our classrooms. Often the best memoirs ex-plored a number of small, simple moments, linked by a common theme. (1995, 160)

Bomer discusses his work with his own students as they read and wrote memoir. He also lists resources for memoir.

One other book worth having as you work with memoir is Patricia Hampl's *I Could Tell You Stories* (1999). Patricia Hampl is the queen of memoir. She has been writing them and researching them and commenting on them for a number of years. *Stories* is a collection of her best essays about memoir and the process and dangers of writ-ing them.

How Can I Get My Students to Write Research with Voice and Passion?

Multigenre Writing

Megan, one of my high-school seniors, wrote in a letter to me at the beginning of her multigenre research paper on Frederick Douglass, "I enjoyed this project more than any other writing project I've ever done. I enjoyed it so much that I couldn't stop writing." Another student asked me, "This is so much fun; why haven't I done this in school before my senior year?" I first began to experiment with multigenre writing in my high-school classes when I read Tom Romano's book *Writing with Passion*. His chapter, The Multigenre Research Paper, discusses his encounter with author Michael Ondaatje's *The Collected Works of Billy the Kid*. He wondered why his own students couldn't write about interesting people in the same way. He wondered "if the students and their audience would perceive and feel more deeply through the multiple ways of seeing and knowing that various genres offered" (1995, 112). This chapter shows us the beginnings of his work and his students' work with the multigenre form. In another chapter he discusses the problems, issues, and dilemmas of the multigenre research paper. He also includes chapters on using Grammar B, writing dialogue, the evolving voice through alternate style, as well as many examples of his students' writings.

Romano's second book on multigenre research, *Blending Genre, Altering Style* (2000), offers many more examples of this approach. This text includes examples of multigenre papers from grade 7 through graduate students. I found all of the examples helpful as I worked with my students to understand the concept of multigenre and when working with specific genres. Romano shares tips on timing, the workshop routine, how to open a multigenre paper, genre possibilities, dialogue, poetry, evaluation, and much more. This text is a must read if you are going to ask your students to write a multigenre paper.

The Multigenre Research Paper: Voice, Passion, and Discovery in Grades 4–6 by Camille A. Allen is helpful for teaching younger students. Allen writes, "I've seen multigenre research papers change students' negative perceptions of research, writing, and oral presentations. When given the chance to select their own topics to research, decide which genres to write in, and determine how they want to present their findings to an audience, students change. They become empowered" (2001, 1). Her text provides the "nuts and bolts" of getting started, finding ways into a topic, helping kids writing poetry, looking at voice in nonfiction, and ways to put it all together. She also includes lots of student writing.

The I-Search Paper

When I read Ken Macrorie's book, *The I-Search Paper*, in the 1980s, it just made sense to ask my students to "allow something to choose you that you want intensely to know or possess" (1988, 62). I followed Macrorie's advice and asked them to write an

I-Search paper, searching their topics and then explaining what they already knew about the topic, why they were writing the paper, the story of their hunt, and what they learned. Juan wanted to buy new speakers for his car; Amber couldn't decide between Colorado State University and the University of Colorado-Boulder. Angela wanted to take a trip to Mexico after graduation; Brian wanted to learn how to be a better kicker for the football team.

All of these students entered into their research with enthusiasm because they wanted answers to their questions. They conducted traditional library research, but they also went into the community and asked lots of questions. Juan and his father talked to five different dealers and read the literature, trying to decide on the best car speakers for the money Juan had budgeted. Amber contacted both universities, talked to admissions' directors, and interviewed students from both institutions. Angela talked to travel agents while Brian interviewed a kicker from a local university, talked to college and high-school coaches, and read everything he could on the art of kicking a football.

Macrorie writes, "School term papers that are written from the directions in English composition books or study aids are the most unoriginal writings the world has ever seen" (1988, 54). I have to agree with him because I've read too many research papers without voice, without passion, and without the enthusiasm that I see in the I-Search papers my students write.

A Resource for Voice Lessons in Persuasive Writing

Why We Must Run with Scissors: Voice Lessons in Persuasive Writing, 3–12 by Barry Lane and Gretchen Bernabei is a collection of lessons you can use in your classrooms to help your students find their persuasive voice. Lane and Bernabei write,

> Our goal is to create classes where students are free to explore the multiplicity of voices that swarm with them and craft those voices into passionate, funny, scathing, heartwarming, ridiculous, sad, cogent, critical, ribald, eloquent pieces of writing: writing that jumps off the page, stomps on your chest, tickles your chin, rubs your belly, fills your heart with meaning and purpose; writing that pushes its way out of the box and into the real world, heart and soul and feeling. (2001, iii)

This is an ideal resource for teachers who work with developing writers—though teachers need to make sure they don't turn the ideas into lots of isolated activities that go nowhere. These activities should be used within the context of students' writings.

How Do I Teach Grammar in the Writing Classroom?

Constance Weaver, in her text *Teaching Grammar in Context*, discusses the research that shows us that teaching grammar in isolation does not improve our students' writing. A few of the suggestions she develops in her book are helpful to us as we consider ways to include grammar instruction in our writing classrooms. One suggestion she gives is, "when explaining various aspects of grammar, usage, and punctuation to help students with their writing, minimize the use of grammatical terminology and maximize the use of examples" (1996, 26). She also suggests that teachers "emphasize the production of effective sentences rather than their analysis and teach not only 'correct' punctuation, according to the handbooks, but effective punctuation" (26–27). Her book discusses ways to help kids edit while they are writing and how to deal with errors on final drafts, giving us good ideas for "Alternatives to the Error Hunt." She also gives us guidelines for the teaching of grammar that are empowering to those of us who have struggled with the question of grammar instruction. Her chapter on Learning Theory and the Teaching of Grammar is helpful in thinking about teaching grammar using minilessons.

A couple of years after *Teaching Grammar in Context* was published, Weaver edited a second book, *Lessons to Share on Teaching Grammar in Context*. This book offers articles on teaching grammar written by both experienced and novice teachers. Some of the articles are helpful to secondary teachers. The chapter Using Minilessons to Promote Student Revision (1998, 100) tells the story of Sue Rowe's work with her students as she used their writing to build minilessons in which she taught sentence combining and the elimination of verbs of being. In the chapter Learning to Use Grammar with Precision Through Effective Editing Conferences, Ellen Brinkley says, "By sitting side by side with student writers and conferring with them about their own texts we can teach editing as a skill, not as content, through individually taught minilessons. Within the conference context the writer and teacher can focus with precision on such issues as how to use a specific grammatical concept or how to correct a particular surface feature error—all based entirely on what a particular student needs to know and is ready to learn for a real purpose" (1998, 125). Other chapters include Lois Matz Rosen's Developing Correctness in Student Writing, Alternatives to the Error Hunt, Harry Noden's Image Grammar, and Tom Romano's Breaking the Rules in Style.

Harry Noden went on to write his own text, *Image Grammar: Using Grammatical Structure to Teach Writing*. Noden compares the writer to an artist, "painting images of life with specific and identifiable brush strokes" (1999, 1). He says that writing is constructed from fundamental artistic elements of grammar as well as from experiences, information, characters, or plot. Noden explains those elements and gives examples of how writers have used image grammar, plus he gives us strategies to teach our students how to use grammar most effectively in their writing. The publisher offers an accompanying CD, which contains lessons and examples.

How Do I Respond to and Evaluate Student Writing?

Many of the texts that have helped me think about responding to and evaluating student writing have already been mentioned in this chapter. Burke's *The English Teacher's Companion* is helpful in that he gives us a list of the components of effective response to student writing and a checklist to think about as we consider how to respond to too many papers for too many students.

In *A Community of Writers*, Zemelman and Daniels begin a section of evaluating writing with a discussion of the obsession with the red pen. They say, "Our obsession with perfection in mechanics actually undermines our teaching of, and students' attention to, the more fundamental aspects of composing—content and clarity" (1998, 207). They go on to discuss the importance of focus in giving students feedback about their writing. They then list and explain the teacher's roles in responding to writing: as listener and learner, as adult/protector, as encourager and guide, as coach, as expert, as copyeditor, and as judge.

Romano's chapter, Making the Grade in Evaluation: Keep Students Writing, in *Clearing the Way* doesn't give teachers a step-by-step method of responding and evaluating, but Romano does share his thoughts on grading students' writings so that he doesn't discourage his students from continuing to write. He asserts that "the grade distribution in my writing classes does not conform to the bell-shaped curve I learned about in Ed. Psych 101. I rarely grade pieces below a C–. . . . Writing is creating. It is skill, craft, art. Practice, process, and passion are crucial to the development of a quality product" (1987, 208).

"Teacher evaluation in the workshop must focus on the big picture: who a student is becoming—and who he or she might become as a writer and reader. . . . Our responsibilities as evaluators involve collecting and sifting through the evidence that reveals what a student can do and can't do, understand and doesn't understand, has accomplished and needs to accomplish" (1998, 314), says Nancie Atwell in *In the Middle*. She indicates how she goes about evaluating her students at the end of the first trimester, offers a description of evaluation in her school, and includes student self-assessment and goalsetting combined with teacher description, analysis, and goalsetting. She does not assign grades at her school. Although many of us are required to give grades to our students, her ideas can help shape our thinking about evaluating the student writers in our classrooms.

I don't think we can discuss evaluating writing without considering the use of portfolios. Some of the texts I have found helpful are listed. Fran Claggett's text, *A Measure of Success* (1996), discusses the importance of aligning assessment with curriculum. Claggett believes in teaching students how to value and assess their own achievement and growth. She shows how this alignment can be accomplished by using classroom portfolios. Teachers will find ideas for structuring reading and writing and strategies for assessment that are linked to teaching.

In the foreword to *The Portfolio Standard: How Students Can Show Us What They Know and Are Able to Do*, edited by Bonnie Sunstein and Jonathan Lovell, Donald Graves writes, "We've never needed portfolios more than we do now. In a high-speed culture with more and more quick and easy assessments that govern instruction, this book comes as a refreshing reminder of what constitutes real literacy based on a partnership with the student. Most assessments do not engage the student in significant, self-evaluative, long-term thinking" (2000, viii). Sunstein and Lovell have collected a series of articles on portfolios that are organized in three sections. The first section looks at what's inside portfolios—what artifacts students are encouraged to collect, the role of media in student portfolios, and the role of reflection. Section Two looks at the pressures and expectations outside the portfolio. Additional chapters consider how schools and districts are evaluating portfolios, how portfolios reflect our understanding of teaching and assumptions of students, and who decides the value of a student's work. Section Three considers how to use portfolios in the classroom so that the amount of writing isn't overwhelming to teachers.

Teachers should look at *Alternatives to Grading Student Writing*, edited by Stephen Tchudi, if they are interested in looking at innovative ways of evaluating writing. Tchudi says that the research in grading writing "shows quite clearly that grading writing doesn't contribute much to learning to write and is in conflict with the new paradigms for writing instruction" (1997, xii). The first section in the book looks at the research in grading and what it means for the teacher and the student of writing. Other sections look at responding to student writing, classroom strategies and alternatives to grading students' writings, and faculty workshops in alternatives to grading student writing.

What About Theory?

One of my professors in a graduate program once told me I'd never make it if I didn't move out of the practical world into the theoretical world. That's hard to do when you are teaching 150 teenagers five days a week and taking one graduate class a semester. Another professor told me that I did a pretty good job of straddling the fence between practice and theory. It is one thing to be able to teach "best practices," but we also need to know *why* they are best practices. Our practice must be grounded in theory.

So, what should we read to understand the theories related to the teaching of writing? I know it is difficult for teachers to find time to read research, and some research isn't always easy to read. Many of the books I have mentioned in this chapter are written by teacher/researchers; they are books that tell stories of teaching and students and learning. Those are the books I love to read. But, there are others that are important to our profession.

Dan, Dawn, and Tom give credit to a group of educators who helped shape their thinking about the teaching of writing, including Anne Berthoff, James Britton, Peter Elbow, Janet Emig, Donald Graves, Ken Macrorie, Nancy Martin, James Miller, James Moffett, Donald Murray, and Stephen Tchudi. Anything you can read by them will help you understand the evolution of the writing process movement. Some of these researchers follow.

Peter Elbow, in *Writing Without Teachers*, says he "tries for two things: 1) to help you actually generate words better—more freely, lucidly, and powerfully: not to make judgments about words but generate them better; 2) to help you improve your ability to make your own judgment about which parts of your own writing to keep and which parts to throw away" (1998, vii–viii). Elbow says writers must get their words down on paper first, and then they can begin to make sense of them.

Another book by Elbow definitely worth having is the impressive collection of many of his essays over the past thirty years entitled *Everyone Can Write, Essays Toward a Hopeful Theory of Writing and Teaching Writing* (2000). That's a long title for a very thick book, but it contains his most important works on freewriting, audience, voice, expressive writing, and teaching strategies.

Using case studies, Janet Emig, in *The Composing Processes of Twelfth Graders* (1971), looked at eight twelfth graders and their methods of composing, finding that many students were unengaged in school writing assignments, though highly engaged in the writing they did outside of school.

Donald Graves has been involved in writing research since the 1960s. His work has helped change the course of writing instruction in American schools. Though much of his work is done in elementary-school classrooms, his ideas are invaluable to all teachers of writing. *Writing: Teachers and Children at Work*, first published in 1983, shows teachers how to begin teaching writing in a classroom, how to confer with student writers, how children learn the skills they need to be writers, how students develop as writers, and how to document writing development. His work continues to inform the work of teachers across the country.

Donald Murray's premise in *Write to Learn* is that students must write if they are to learn how to write. "Few students can listen to a lecture on writing or read a textbook on writing in advance of writing and understand the lessons they may need to learn" (1987, xi). His text gives teachers and students strategies for discovering and exploring subjects. Students will learn ideas for collecting information, focusing their writing, organizing a piece of writing, developing their piece, and clarifying.

An interesting book, *Taking Stock: The Writing Process Movement in the 90's*, edited by Lad Tobin and Thomas Newkirk, is a collection of articles taken from the University of New Hampshire's "historic" 1992 conference on the writing process movement. Teachers will find sections entitled Reading the Writing Process Movement, Teaching the Writing Process, Institutionalizing the Writing Process, Deconstructing the Writing Process, and Narrating the Writing Process.

George Hillocks' report on studies in the research of the teaching of writing from 1963 to 1982, *Research on Written Composition: New Directions for Teaching*, points to several findings. One is the idea that grammar study, as well as the study of mechanics and correctness, has little or no effect on the improvement of writing. He also discusses the effectiveness of sentence-combining activities in improving student writing. He writes of the importance of inquiry, activities that "help students internalize criteria for guiding and/or revising their own texts" (1986, 266). His book is online at the National Conference on Research in Language and Literacy (NCRLL) website if teachers wish to look at his study in depth. Teachers can also read the chapter entitled Grammars and Literacy Learning by Hillocks and Michael W. Smith in the second edition of *Handbook of Research on Teaching the*

English Language Arts (in Flood et al. 2003). Their article looks at research in grammar and the teaching of writing.

In a more recent study entitled *Effective Literacy Instruction: Building Successful Reading and Writing Programs*, Judith A. Langer discusses her five-year study of classes in twenty-five schools that were trying to improve student learning. The book is divided into two sections. Section One discusses the characteristics of an effective English program, and Section Two tells the stories of effective teachers and programs. Her studies of more effective and typical schools show the following "distinguishing features of effective instruction":

1. Skills and knowledge are taught in a variety of ways using separated, simulated, and integrated instruction.
2. Tests are analyzed to understand the underlying skills and knowledge that go beyond test prep to the literacies needed for school and life. These are then integrated into the ongoing curriculum the students experience.
3. Coherence is achieved because connections in content and structure are made overt within and across activities and units throughout the year and across the grades.
4. Strategies for thinking and doing are emphasized to ensure that students learn procedures for approaching, thinking about, completing, and monitoring the literacy tasks at hand.
5. Generative thinking is encouraged to help students use new ideas and learning to go beyond the lesson or activity and to further their critical and creative thinking and conceptual growth.
6. Classrooms are organized to foster collaboration and cogitation, helping students hear ideas and perspectives, become inquisitive and reflective, and learn with and from each other. (2002)

Langer's work with Arthur Applebee, *How Writing Shapes Thinking: A Study of Teaching and Learning*, is also a text teachers should read. Langer and Applebee write, "There is clear evidence that activities involving writing lead to better learning than activities involving reading and studying only. Writing assists learning" (1987, 135). They discuss the importance of scaffolding instruction, student ownership, building on literacy and thinking skills students already have, support for student learning, and collaboration between teacher and student.

Teachers will find a few specific articles helpful in their thinking about the research in the teaching of writing in the *Handbook of Research on Teaching the English Language Arts* (Flood et al. 2003) other than just the Hillocks/Smith article. Anne Dyson and Sarah Freedman in "Writing" discuss important research in sections entitled: The Uses of Writing, The Evaluation of Written Language, The Processes of Writing, and The Development of Writing.

Additionally, Richard Hodges' "The Conventions of Writing" discusses the research concerning teaching the conventions of writing, which includes spelling, handwriting, and typographical elements such as capitalization, segmentation, and punctuation (Flood et al. 2003). We should also look at Mina Shaughnessy's *Errors and Expectations: A Guide for the Teacher of Basic Writing* (1977). Shaughnessy discusses the logic in student errors in her research.

There is obviously much more research in the teaching of writing, but these resources will provide beginning points as you make decisions about teaching and learning.

Which Books Should I Buy First?

"I can't afford to buy too many books on a beginning teacher's salary, Karen, so tell me which ones I should buy first." This is a statement I hear over and over from new teachers and sometimes from veteran teachers. I am sure my teaching friends would agree with some of my choices and argue for their favorite texts, but here are my top choices in no specific order:

1. *Inside Out* by Dan Kirby, Dawn Latta Kirby, and Tom Liner
2. *In the Middle* by Nancie Atwell
3. *After the End* by Barry Lane
4. *What a Writer Needs* by Ralph Fletcher
5. *The Writing Workshop: Working Through the Hard Parts (And They're All Hard Parts)* by Katie Wood Ray.
6. *Writing with Passion* by Tom Romano or anything else by Romano
7. *How's It Going?* by Carl Anderson

* * *

We encourage you to check out the resources that Karen has listed here and to add favorite titles of your own to this list as you discover them.

Works Cited

ALLEN, CAMILLE A. 2001. *The Multigenre Research Paper: Voices, Passion, and Discovery in Grades 4–6*. Portsmouth, NH: Heinemann.

ANDERSON, CARL. 2000. *How's It Going? A Practical Guide to Conferring with Student Writers*. Portsmouth, NH: Heinemann.

ATWELL, NANCIE. 1998. *In the Middle*. 2d ed. Portsmouth, NH: Heinemann.

———. 2002. *Lessons That Change Writers*. Portsmouth, NH: Heinemann.

BIGELOW, BILL, ET AL. EDS. 1994. *Rethinking Our Classrooms: Teaching for Equity and Justice*. Milwaukee, WI: Rethinking Schools.

———. 2001. *Rethinking Our Classrooms: Teaching for Equity and Justice, Vol. 2*. Milwaukee. WI: Rethinking Schools.

BOMER, RANDY. 1995. *A Time for Meaning*. Portsmouth, NH: Heinemann.

BOMER, RANDY, AND KATHERINE BOMER. 2001. *For a Better World: Reading and Writing for Social Action*. Portsmouth, NH: Heinemann.

BOOTH OLSON, CAROL. 2003. *Reading/Writing Connection: Strategies for Teaching and Learning in the Secondary Classroom*. Boston: Allyn and Bacon.

BURKE, JIM. 1999. *The English Teacher's Companion*. Portsmouth, NH: Heinemann.

BUSCHING, BEVERLY, AND BETTY ANN SLESINGER. 2001. *"It's Our World Too": Socially Responsive Learners in Middle School Language Arts*. Urbana, IL: NCTE.

CALKINS, LUCY. 1995. *The Art of Teaching Writing*. Portsmouth, NH: Heinemann.

CHRISTENSEN, LINDA. 2000. *Reading, Writing, and Rising Up: Teaching About Social Justice and the Power of the Written Word*. Milwaukee, WI: Rethinking Schools.

CLAGGETT, FRAN. 1996. *A Measure of Success: From Assignment to Assessment in Language Arts*. Portsmouth, NH: Boynton/Cook.

ELBOW, PETER. 1998. *Writing Without Teachers*. New York: Oxford University Press.

———. 2000. *Everyone Can Write, Essays Toward a Hopeful Theory of Writing and Teaching Writing*. New York: Oxford University Press.

EMIG, JANET. 1971. *The Composing Processes of Twelfth Graders*. Urbana, IL: NCTE.

FLETCHER, RALPH. 1993. *What a Writer Needs*. Portsmouth, NH: Heinemann.

———. 1996a. *Breathing In, Breathing Out*. Portsmouth, NH: Heinemann.

———. 1996b. *A Writer's Notebook: Unlocking the Writer Within You*. Portsmouth, NH: Heinemann.

FLETCHER, RALPH, AND JOANN PORTALUPI. 1998. *Craft Lessons*. Portland, ME: Stenhouse Publishers.

———. 2001. *Nonfiction Craft Lessons*. Portland, ME: Stenhouse Publishers.

FLOOD, JAMES, ET AL. EDS. 2003. *Handbook of the Research on Teaching the English Language Arts*. Mahwah, NJ: Lawrence Erlbaum, Associates.

GRAVES, DONALD. 1983. *Writing: Teachers and Children at Work*. Portsmouth, NH: Heinemann.

HAMPL, PATRICIA. 1999. *I Could Tell You Stories: Sojourns in the Land of Memory*. New York: W.W. Norton and Company.

HEARD, GEORGIA. 1995. *Writing Toward Home*. Portsmouth, NH: Heinemann.

———. 1999. *Awakening the Heart: Exploring Poetry in Elementary and Middle School*. Portsmouth, NH: Heinemann.

———. 2002. *The Revision Toolbox*. Portsmouth, NH: Heinemann.

HILLOCKS, GEORGE, JR. 1986. *Research on Written Composition: New Directions for Teaching*. Urbana, IL: Eric Clearinghouse on Reading and Communication Skills, and National Conference on Research in English.

JAGO, CAROL. 2002. *Cohesive Writing*. Portsmouth, NH: Heinemann.

LANE, BARRY. 1993. *After the End*. Portsmouth, NH: Heinemann.

———. 1999. *Reviser's Toolbox*. Shoreham, VT: Discover Writing Press.

LANE, BARRY, AND GRETCHEN BERNABEI. 2001. *Why We Must Run with Scissors: Voice Lessons in Persuasive Writing 3–12*. Shoreham, VT: Discover Writing Press.

LANGER, JUDITH A. 2002. *Effective Literacy Instruction: Building Successful Reading and Writing Programs.* Urbana, IL: NCTE.

LANGER, JUDITH, AND ARTHUR APPLEBEE. 1987. *How Writing Shapes Thinking: A Study of Teaching and Learning.* Urbana, IL: NCTE.

MACRORIE, KEN. 1988. *The I-Search Paper.* Portsmouth, NH: Boynton/Cook.

MAHONEY, JIM. 2002. *Power and Portfolios: Best Practices for High School Classrooms.* Portsmouth, NH: Heinemann.

MURRAY, DONALD M. 1987. *Write to Learn.* New York: Holt, Rinehart and Winston.

———. 1996. *Crafting a Life in Essay, Story, Poem.* Portsmouth, NH: Heinemann.

NODIN, HARRY R. 1999. *Image Grammar: Using Grammatical Structure to Teach Writing.* Portsmouth, NH: Heinemann.

RAY, KATIE WOOD. 2001. *The Writing Workshop: Working through the Hard Parts (And They're All Hard Parts).* Urbana, IL: NCTE.

ROMANO, TOM. 1987. *Clearing the Way.* Portsmouth, NH: Heinemann.

———. 1995. *Writing with Passion.* Portsmouth, NH: Heinemann.

———. 2000. *Blending Genre, Altering Style.* Portsmouth, NH: Heinemann.

ROUTMAN, REGIE. 1991. *Invitations: Changing as Teachers and Learners K–12.* Portsmouth, NH: Heinemann.

———. 2000. *Conversations: Strategies for Teaching, Learning, and Evaluating.* Portsmouth, NH: Heinemann.

SHAUGHNESSY, MINA P. 1977. *Errors and Expectations: A Guide for the Teacher of Basic Writing.* New York: Oxford University Press.

STRONG, WILLIAM. 2001. *Coaching Writing.* Portsmouth, NH: Heinemann.

SUNSTEIN, BONNIE S., AND JONATHAN H. LOVELL, EDS. 2000. *The Portfolio Standard: How Students Can Show Us What They Know and Are Able to Do.* Portsmouth, NH: Heinemann.

TCHUDI, STEPHEN. 1997. *Alternatives to Grading Student Writing.* Urbana, IL: NCTE.

TOBIN, LAD, AND THOMAS NEWKIRK. 1994. *Taking Stock: The Writing Process Movement in the 90s.* Portsmouth, NH: Boynton/Cook.

WEAVER, CONSTANCE. 1996. *Teaching Grammar in Context.* Portsmouth, NH: Heinemann.

——— ED. 1998. *Lessons to Share on Teaching Grammar in Context.* Portsmouth, NH: Heinemann.

ZEMELMAN, STEVEN, AND HARVEY DANIELS. 1998. *A Community of Writers.* Portsmouth, NH: Heinemann.

ZINSSER, WILLIAM. 1998. *Inventing the Truth: The Art and Craft of Memoir.* New York: Mariner Books.